Beyond Liberty Alone

A Progressive Vision of Freedom

and Capitalism in America

Howard I. Schwartz, PhD

Other Ideas Press
San Francisco, CA
© 2014 by Howard I. Schwartz, PhD

ISBN: 1505647002
ISBN-13: 9781505647006

Beyond Liberty Alone

A Progressive Vision of Freedom

and Capitalism in America

Howard I. Schwartz, PhD

Other Ideas Press

To my wife, Carroll,
who brings out the best in me.

Contents

Preface

Over the last forty years, a deeply disturbing and pernicious understanding of liberty has become popular among many Americans, one that has reshaped how many Americans understand our government and its politics and our place in the world. At the core of this understanding is the contention that our liberty primarily means protection of our individual rights and properties, which are themselves thought to be self-evident and natural and to exist prior to government. Through the frame of this understanding, those who hold this view protest the size of our government and the interference of government in our lives, and they dismiss the moral claims that they and their government have duties to others, including the less fortunate both within and beyond the confines of their own United States.

This understanding of liberty is not really new at all, but it is one that has gained in popularity and achieved a kind of mythological status and religious dogma among its adherents in the last part of the twentieth century and the beginning of the twenty-first, though not all those who espouse this view have thought deeply about its history, its philosophical foundations, or its moral consequences. The view of liberty I am talking about has come to dominate the politics of the Right and libertarians in the post-Vietnam period, as America has found itself in a more complex world in which globalization and economic changes have undermined the certainty of America's dominance and moral leadership and challenged some of the basic assumptions by which Americans frame their self-understanding. I call the view of liberty that they espouse the "liberty-first" position, since it puts the weight on liberty before all other competing human values.

This book critiques that view of liberty and offers a progressive alternative. Liberty, defined as "life, liberty, and property" or "the pursuit of happiness" in the American idiom, is a concept that is key to both modernity and American identity. But what liberty means and who gets to define it are questions that are up for grabs in a liberal state.

This book argues that the understanding of liberty that currently dominates is wrong in many ways: in its oversimplification of liberty's history, in its failure to understand liberty's philosophical foundations, and ultimately, in its impoverished view of human beings and the moral responsibilities they have as members of the species and as members of society. What matters most, and what inspired me to write this book, are the destructive consequences this one-sided view of liberty has for our nation, the environment and planet, our moral self-worth, our children, and what religious or spiritually oriented people would call our souls.

I will not try to rehearse my argument in detail here; it is spelled out carefully in the many pages that follow. But the thrust of my argument is that the other human values that have been expunged from the concept of liberty must be taken into account when we consider what it means to live in liberal societies. These other values include but are not limited to responsibility, debt, sacrifice, compassion, and care, and are in my view part and parcel of what liberty was always intended to mean, even if it was not always so understood. What is put forward here amounts to a progressive or liberal account of liberty that sacrifices neither liberty nor compassion in the quest to understand our duties and responsibilities as human beings and as modern selves.

In offering a progressive theory of liberty, I am also trying to counter what seems to have been the liberal abandonment of the liberty concept to those on the political Right and to libertarians. Since the nineteen seventies, there has been an increasingly strong inclination in conservative politics to grab hold of and monopolize the concept of liberty and use that concept as a banner or flag under which to marshal many other arguments about the nature of rights and government, the correct approach to taxes and the economy, health care, war, marriage, abortion, and a host of other topics. Liberty and protection of rights have often been the master concepts, if you will, under which the positions of the Right and libertarians were justified. In giving away the liberty concept and not fighting back, liberals have weakened their own position because they seemingly lost an anchor for their own positions in the assumptions about liberty in the American founding and in the rich modern tradition of liberty itself. Instead, they have allowed the Right to back them into a corner with the label "socialist" and to argue that the Right is the true inheritor of the American founders Jefferson, Adams, Washington, and Monroe, as well as the great English political philosopher John Locke, who likely inspired Jefferson and the other founders.

This view of liberty and history, however, is distorted, and progressives should not acquiesce to the Right's monopoly on the concept of liberty. What follows, therefore, is both a sustained attack on the understanding of liberty among both the Right and libertarians and an articulation of an alternative progressive understanding of liberty. What emerges in the liberal view of liberty put forward here is a view of the human being who is an individual whose labor is not entirely his or her own. Instead, as individuals we stand on the shoulders of those who preceded us and thus have obligations and debts to them, our ancestors, and to our contemporaries, who are their heirs. From that debt arises obligations to others and to the societies we are born to and create. This is the centerpiece and fulcrum for the rethinking of key concepts in the liberty tradition: the idea of what liberty means and implies as well as its central concept of property. From here we reason to an alternative vision of government that sees its role as more than simply protecting our rights and property and that has responsibilities beyond its own constituents to the species as a whole.

In developing this progressive position, I go back to and engage with the classic expositors of liberty and rights in the modern period, as well as those philosophers who arguably created the very language that our American founders Jefferson, Adams, James Wilson, and others inherited in thinking about liberty. My interlocutor is the philosophical thinking that emerged in a different time and place. It was a century that began in the English-speaking world with an absolute monarch in place but ended with a revolution that redefined the relationship of government and the people. In between, this same century produced civil war and regicide, followed by a failed commonwealth and then a restored monarchy. It was the same century that early on produced the thinking of Thomas Hobbes and at the end provided fertile ground for the thinking of John Locke.

The century I am speaking about is the seventeenth century, one that for Americans seems impossibly far away, both in time and in relevance, though it was the one that produced the language and historical frame of reference by which America's founders came to understand themselves. There is a deep irony in all this. Americans today think of themselves through the defining events of the American Revolution and our own Civil War. But for the definition of liberty among the American founders, the key defining references were in fact the historical events and philosophical reflections produced in the seventeenth century. Americans learn little about these events in understanding themselves, but these events were key in defining the thinking that emerged from the period and ultimately that entered into America's founding.

Among the key English thinkers in this century were English philosopher Thomas Hobbes, who witnessed the English Civil War, and John Locke, whose work justified and explained the Revolution of 1688, which ousted King James II of England, led to the Bill of Rights of 1689, and marked the end of absolute rule of the monarch in England. The great English philosophers who witnessed these events and reflected on them were influenced as well by continental philosophers Hugo Grotius in the Netherlands, who set the terms of the discussion about rights for the seventeenth century, and Samuel von Pufendorf in Germany, who synthesized the work of his Dutch and English predecessors, and whose work both Locke and Jefferson read.

The ideas of these thinkers transformed how moderns thought about liberty, government, and property, though these ideas also had their roots in classical Greek philosophy and the Renaissance. The idiom and language they developed for thinking about liberty, rights, and government still frames how we speak about these topics today. These ideas, moreover, were at the core of the American Revolution and the conceptions of government that were being developed in the American founding. The American founders were engaged with the thinking and writing of these seventeenth-century political philosophers, and the American colonies not only lived through and witnessed the English Civil Wars and Revolution, but understood those events as part of their own history, for they saw themselves for the most part as British colonists until shortly before they declared their own independence. George Washington had a copy of Grotius's book in his library, as one example.[1] And Jefferson read Locke, Pufendorf, and Hume, among many others. The list could go on. These seventeenth-century English events were mythic events through which the American founders filtered their own experiences and came to their own conclusions about what America should be.

There are many ways that one can approach the rethinking of liberty that is at the heart of this book. My approach is only one possible way. There are others. I was and am troubled by the superficial platitudes that one often finds under the banner of liberty in the popular discourse that continues to dominate American political language. I am trying to chart a difficult course between the popular discussion of liberty and the deep and rich academic tradition in political philosophy. As an academic by training, I find the academic research in history and political philosophy to be important and insightful. And though I am fascinated by academic discussions and some of the complicated academic debates on critical philosophical and historical problems, I am also aware of how arcane those discussions can become to the average person, with the result that deep insights from both history and political philosophy often get lost in academic discourse and never find a way to touch more popular opinion.

My goal has been to chart a course between these extremes and to try to bring some of the rich academic insight into engagement with more popular discourses. Whether I succeeded in doing so my readers can themselves judge. This, then, has been my method: Where I have found fascinating and important discussions in the academic secondary literature, I have tried to allude to these in notes but not burden the reader with all the ins and outs of academic discussions. At the same time, the discussions of liberty in popular political discussions often seem to gloss over and ignore incredibly important questions and perspectives in both history and political philosophy. This popular discourse at times is so devoid of any interesting insights that it has become sheer platitude and dogma. With such important questions about how we should run our lives, what obligations we have to one another, and what we should expect from our government, it seems incumbent upon us, as individuals, as a country, and simply as human beings, to reflect more deeply on these critical questions that may ultimately determine our fate as a nation and perhaps also as a species.

Like many writers and artists, I felt called to write this book. My journey to its creation began over ten years ago when personal circumstances led me to leave an academic career as a professor of religious studies at Stanford University and begin afresh working in a software company in Silicon Valley during the beginning of the Internet transformation. The two contexts were worlds apart, and moving from one to the other had a profound effect on me. Though I ultimately thrived in many ways in the high-tech Internet boom that has redefined all our lives, the nagging concerns with morality and justice led me to wonder whether business and the economy had to be the way they were. My own experiences in leading marketing and sales, and in helping to run the business of a public company, coupled with a much broader political debate going on in our society over the proper and respective roles of government and business, crystalized this question for me and ultimately set me off on a decade-long journey that culminated in two books and a number of essays.[2]

I believe and hope I have said something important in the chapters that follow. In putting forward a progressive view of liberty, I am going against the grain of contemporary trends in several ways. First, I am doing so by arguing that progressives do have an intelligible view of liberty that fits meaningfully into a legitimate understanding of modernity and of America's founding. Progressives don't have to be embarrassed in speaking about liberty anymore. Second, my writing attempts to chart a course between the banalities of popular discourse and the interesting but obscure minutiae and language that often define academic discourse.

Third, I believe that my way of putting together some of these discussions is unique, though I have leaned on and read hundreds of other philosophical and historical works on my way to my own perspective.[3] I acknowledge a debt to others before me but hope and believe that I have added to and enriched what has been said before.

Whether what I say is unique or not, however, is not ultimately what is important for me. I was reminded in writing this book that even Thomas Jefferson thought he had said nothing new in writing the Declaration of Independence.[4] And he was correct, for the ideas there contained nothing new that had not been said before a hundred times, as some of his most articulate interpreters and critics have said. But sometimes the same ideas have to be said multiple times for their meaning to be heard. I think of books and literature as being a lot like music in this regard, in the sense that multiple different approaches to the same theme can be interesting, illuminating, and moving, even if the ideas are not totally unique. There is no single musical rendition or work of art that exhausts the truth. Many artists and musicians contribute to our insight. So too with knowledge. It is my hope that this book says something useful to those who are concerned about the dominant language of liberty and the way our nation has taken a stance on what are our responsibilities toward our own citizens and human beings in general.

Acknowledgments

There have been many friends and colleagues who encouraged me to keep this book alive and to get my ideas out in print. Many business colleagues, Denise Kiser, Dawna Turner, Catherine Lyman, Helen Slattery, Bridget Burke, Steve Fogel, Tony Morales, Tom Goering, Elizabeth Gschwind, Minette Norman, Neville Fleet, Helen Cavender, Dan Claessens, Beth Fryder, Seth Katz, Barbara Scott, and Serphim Larsen, among many others, always reminded me that there is much more humanity in the business world than we often realize. The themes of this book resonated with many of them, and they encouraged my writing. To Chip Gettinger and Frank Closset for being comrades in arms through thick and thin. New friends such as Richard and Linda Peltzman, Tom Borromeo, Rob Lyman, and longtime friends Ric Louchard, Scott Shenker, MaryRuth Quinn, Ray Pestrong, and Mike and Bilha Bender all encouraged my intellectual inquiry and passion to find another way of thinking about liberty. To Mark Lancaster, for enabling an amazing business adventure for the last ten years. Finally, to my daughter, Penina, for conversations that always remind me of who I really am, and to my wife, Carroll, for loving this side of me and reminding me just how much more there is to life.

Introduction

Once upon a time, America was a great country with a moral vision that could have been, and perhaps at one time was, a light to other nations. But times have changed. America in the first decades of the twenty-first century is off course and adrift. Those of us who were born in America in the twentieth century were taught that our nation is an inspiring country, one with a moral vision that could and should be emulated by the nations of the world. We brought to the world a new nation, one founded on liberty, and showed the world how a great country and great democratic institutions could be made. This was a land of opportunity. We welcomed immigrants and provided means for people who worked hard to make a meaningful, successful life for themselves. We believed that there was always enough to go around, and those who would make an effort could make a good life for themselves. We prided ourselves on being the leading economy and offering what seemed like limitless opportunities to people. We believed implicitly that our economic leadership was tied to our moral leadership. What made America great was its vision of liberty at its founding and the democratic institutions by which that vision was implemented.

But in the last half of the twentieth century, we collectively lost our way. The world's economic situation has been seriously troubling off and on for over a decade. Our optimism that America could produce endless wealth and opportunity is faltering. We see jobs moving overseas to emerging economies. We know that there are other great nations afoot, particularly China and India, whose resources and talents are threatening to compete with those of America. We are worried too by the resources on the planet and by the ability of the world to support the population, which has just reached seven billion people.

In this new era, with a new set of difficult and troubling challenges in front of us, we need a new vision of America's purpose. The one that has been guiding us at the end of the second millennium and beginning of the third will continue to lead us and those who follow us deeper into the problems that currently face us. Indeed, it is partly responsible for the deepening mess we have around us. America has lost its moral compass and our collective purpose. And we threaten to lead the world to the brink of disaster as well.

How did we lose our way and what can we do about it? This book suggests an answer. In the last part of the twentieth century and at the start of the third millennium, America has been increasingly dominated by a particular ideology that is destroying our moral center and ultimately leading the United States and the world toward calamity. The irony is that this ideology portrays itself as patriotic and having "our" best interests at heart. And it does so using America's favorite language of "liberty and rights." Like all ideologies, this one tells us that it is true (not simply one world view or ideology) and that it has the best perspective on the way we should run our lives and our society. To back up these claims, this ideology grounds itself in moral argument, history, economics, philosophy, and sometimes God and religion. It claims to be true by giving us all the reasons why we should believe and embrace it and why doing so will make our lives and the lives of countless others better. But each one of the reasons offered by this ideology is flawed. Its moral arguments are fallacious, its history is distorted and one-sided, its economics is too narrow, its philosophy is mistaken, and its interpretation of religion idolatrous.

What is this ideology that has sent us off course? It is one that I shall label the "liberty-first" philosophy or the "liberty-first" platform. Those who espouse this ideology, whom I call the "liberty-first advocates" or the "liberty-first coalition" (or, when I'm not trying to be nice, the "liberty-first extremists"), are present in large numbers in the Republican and Libertarian parties and in the new Tea Party.

Those in the "liberty-first" camp are by no means all the same. They come in different varieties and flavors, making it confusing sometimes, because they do not always agree among themselves on a number of key matters. But what unites them is a key philosophical contention and assumption: that by maximizing the liberty of individuals, we maximize everything that is good in life. In the view of those in this camp, liberty leads to more productive people, to progress that brings social and economic well-being, and ultimately to a better world for everyone. Liberty is the engine that drives this growth in well-being. The output of liberty lifts everyone higher on the rising tide of social well-being. This rising tide is like a broad ocean that reaches from those of us in the developed world even to those in the Third World. Even though those in poorer countries do not have as much material well-being as do we, the engine of liberty lifts all boats, no matter where they are. We should not feel badly about the discrepancy of wealth and material well-being inside our society or between our society and others. That disparity is necessary and part of what makes the engine hum. Individuals motivated to better themselves, and surplus capital that can be invested in new innovations, are all key components of this liberty engine. If we try to "level" the material wealth and make everyone the same, we shall experience less overall growth in well-being, and fewer people will benefit. We all benefit the most by limiting individuals the least.

I call this the "liberty-first" philosophy or "liberty-first" platform because the ideology makes individual rights and liberty the primary value that matters most and that should guide us. When push comes to shove, and public policy decisions need to be made, liberty trumps other values. In other words, "liberty-first" advocates want to give the value of liberty a prerogative in public decision making when it comes into conflict with other values, such as responsibility, common good, obligation, care, compassion, and equality, among others. They think that moral concerns and justice should be matters handled by every individual in his or her own conscience, not a matter of public policy. I shall spend a good deal of time on this question of liberty's relative importance to other values later, because it is a core part of my argument about how we have gotten off course and adrift. In giving this view of liberty such a prominent place in America's consciousness, we have perverted what were otherwise quite positive impulses of the modern period. The near-obsessive focus on liberty to the exclusion of other important values and concepts is part of what is causing the world's problems and undermining America's leadership and respect. This of course is ironic, since America earned its reputation precisely because it expanded the notion of liberty in important and key ways. But America has lost much of that respect, precisely because it has taken liberty to extremes. Bringing liberty back into balance with other values is a core goal of my writing and one that ultimately dovetails with what I believe is right and just.

• • •

Before we talk about what is wrong with this liberty-first philosophy or platform, let us listen to how liberty-first advocates tend to speak: "Do not touch what is mine. It is my property and my money. I earned it. I worked hard for it. How dare government take away what is rightfully mine. How dare government use my money for someone who did not work as hard as I. Government has become too big. By becoming too large, government oversteps its bounds and infringes on my rights. When government becomes too big and too bureaucratic, it curtails my freedom, and takes my hard-earned money.

"This country was founded with a vision of liberty, and we have abandoned that vision. Those who favor bigger government or more government spending have socialist leanings or are socialists. There is a slippery slope to socialism that begins with letting government curtail individual rights. Those who do so are denying the vision of America's founders and the spirit of liberty. They are also denying what God wants. God created individuals free and equal and with 'natural rights.' 'Natural rights' are those that are God-given or 'self-evident' to reason. These rights include life, liberty, property, and the pursuit of happiness, values that are enshrined in the Declaration of Independence and protected by the

Constitution of the United States. By infringing these rights, we deny God's purposes, go against nature, and undermine the founding vision of America.

"By protecting what is yours and mine, we create a just society and a better world for everyone. Liberty is the foundation of the free market system. Economists since the time of Adam Smith, the father of modern economics, have realized that markets work best when left to themselves and when governments do not intervene. Free markets help motivate people to labor and invent. The incentives in the market encourage people to dream, to innovate, and to work hard. The market makes human character better and makes the world a better place. Through the invisible hand that is created by the thousands of transactions in the market, the market mechanisms determine how much of a product should be produced and what the price should be. Supply and demand and the mechanisms of the market are finely tuned to send signals to farmers and factories about how much of a product should be produced. When governments intervene in markets with taxes or subsidies or government-run programs, the mechanisms of the market are distorted. People suffer through that intervention, because products are not produced as cheaply as they could be. Government intervention in markets is not only harmful, it is wrong. As Milton Friedman once put it, 'Underlying most arguments against the free market is a lack of belief in freedom itself,' and 'freedom in economic arrangements is itself a component of freedom broadly understood, so economic freedom is an end in itself.'"[1]

The preceding several paragraphs provide a nice, concise summary of the key position of liberty-first proponents. We see a mixture of different types of arguments, all of which are used at one time or another by people who espouse the liberty-first position. The arguments are economic, historical, moral, philosophical, and religious. Not all of these arguments are necessarily used by the same individual, and some of the arguments are actually incompatible with each other. Not all individuals who broadly fall under this liberty-first umbrella in fact agree with each other. Those who believe the economic arguments that "free markets make for a better world" may not believe that "natural rights are God-given," and they may not even believe in God. Those who think that "our rights are self-evident" may not think God gave them to us in any traditional sense. But many of these ideas can be woven together: God gave us liberty; the founders had liberty at the heart of their vision of America; liberty is at the foundation of free markets; and free markets are best for the world in general. What unites all of these variations, despite their sometimes profound differences, is a core conviction that liberty of individuals is the key value that must be protected, no matter what. The "no matter what" is important, as it underscores the priority that the value of liberty has in public policy decision making. And it is that value that unites individuals who otherwise think very differently on some matters.

In this introduction, I shall tease these arguments apart and set the groundwork so that later I can challenge them, each in turn, one at a time. The ultimate goal is to show the power of an alternative vision for America that questions this broad, sweeping ideology that places such a narrow understanding of liberty above everything else that matters.

•   •   •

What I am calling the "liberty-first" philosophy or stream of thought has grown its number of adherents and captured imaginations in the last several decades of the twentieth century and continues to be a prominent voice in the early twenty-first century. The philosophy has been articulated in both academic and popular writing by political leaders, radio talk show hosts, and news organizations. In academic writing, among its most articulate spokespersons have been Frederick Hayek, Ludwig von Mises, Ayn Rand, Milton Friedman, Richard Epstein, among others. Politically, the ideas have been articulated by Republican presidents, most notably Ronald Reagan and, to some extent, both presidents Bush, though critics believe the second George Bush failed to live up to his own rhetoric. In England, the ideas were at the center of Margaret Thatcher's political program. Institutionally, the philosophy of "liberty-first" is supported by think tanks such as the Cato Institute, the Heritage Foundation, and

FreedomWorks, among dozens of others that have supported research and publications on the subject. On the American Supreme Court, the philosophy is reflected in varying degrees in opinions of conservative justices such as Chief Justice William Rehnquist, Chief Justice John Roberts, Justices Clarence Thomas and Antonin Scalia, among others. In the popular media, the liberty-first ideology is promoted fiercely by the radio talk shows of Rush Limbaugh, Glenn Beck, and Sean Hannity and the writings of libertarian political figures such as Ron Paul and is implicitly endorsed by media outlets such as Fox News.

One might be tempted to name this philosophy "conservative," and indeed the "liberty-first" platform is embraced by a majority of Republicans and animates the new Tea Party. Naming it "conservative," however, does not do justice to the philosophy itself, which is why many of its philosophic espousers, such as Hayek, think of themselves as "the true liberals" and why some end up calling themselves "libertarians."[2] By focusing on freedom and rights, they believe they are the true inheritors of the modern liberal tradition. While all of these individuals have important differences from one another, and some articulate the philosophy more intellectually than others, they share a common core set of values that are articulated around the liberty principle. In this sense, liberty is the key concept that traverses and holds together diverse parties of what perhaps could loosely be called a movement or stream of thought. They come together for political reasons and the practical goals that they share. Even though they have different underlying assumptions, they rally together under the banner of "liberty."

This introduction is part of a larger argument against the "liberty-first" philosophy and the development and reinvigoration of an alternative philosophy I call the "responsibility-first" philosophy. This alternative view contrasts the "philosophy of rights" that is embraced by the liberty-first party with a "philosophy of what's right," a philosophy that does not put all the weight on notions of individual rights. This other view contrasts "natural rights," which many (though not all) of the liberty-first advocates emphasize, with the concept of "natural responsibility," which shifts attention to the obligations we have naturally as a member of the human species. It is only by shifting our obsessive focus from "liberty" as the only or primary core value to others such as responsibility, care, justice, equality, humanity, and compassion, among others, that we articulate a political position and philosophy that can provide us with a moral center, restore our prestige and meaning as a country, and provide a vision in a world that is off course and adrift.[3]

In arguing we need a new "philosophy" to orient us, I am using the term "philosophy" loosely as the equivalent to "world view" or "ethos," in other words, to refer to a broad set of cultural, political, religious assumptions about what is important and why. All such world views contain and imply a tacit philosophy, though the articulation of that philosophy may be more or less explicitly intellectual.

For reasons that I will continue to explain in later chapters, I have come to the conclusion that the liberty-first philosophy is and will continue to be destructive to human flourishing. The limitations of the liberty-first orientation are many:

First, the fact that the value of liberty consistently and methodically trumps other human values is a core problem in the liberty-first agenda. Liberty is one important value, *but it is not the only important human value.* And when the relative weight of liberty in human decision making is shifted and balanced with other important human values, a more just, humane, and compassionate human flourishing is made possible. Indeed, I will argue that part of what animates the modern liberty tradition itself is precisely the question of how to balance rights and responsibilities. If we take away the right in society to adjudicate this balance, we paradoxically destroy what liberty is.

Second, many liberty-first advocates appeal to liberty when it is convenient for them, but not when it is inconvenient for them, thus demonstrating that they are not really consistent with their own overt position. If we look at their use of liberty, we can see that many (though not all) are really endorsing liberty first when it suits their purposes. They invoke liberty when they want to rail against government being too large or to promote the right to own guns, but they run from liberty when they talk about marriage between gay people, the right to abortion, the choice to die, or even the right not to say the Pledge of Allegiance.[4] In other words, they pick and choose when to invoke liberty, because liberty is a smoke screen or cover for a specific philosophical, religious, moral program. This inconsistent use of liberty by many liberty-first advocates shows that what is at stake is not really liberty per se. And it also shows that liberty is a concept that gets filtered by a set of values. When understood this way, the question is always how liberty should be implemented in a liberal society. By what values should it be understood and concretized?[5] There is no absolute answer in a liberal society that must balance the values and perspectives of many different peoples who may not all agree with each other.

Third, liberty-first advocates distort the meaning and history of liberty as a modern and American concept. Advocates of the liberty-first position equate one understanding of liberty with "the only" understanding of liberty. They project an overly simplistic understanding of liberty back onto the American founders and onto God and traditional religious concepts, and they tend to ignore and oversimplify the history of the modern tradition of liberty in general. We shall see that it is possible to embrace the concept of liberty without ending up in a position like that of the liberty-first advocates.

Fourth, liberty-first advocates often justify their view on liberty in terms of an overarching economic philosophy about free markets. They often argue that "liberty" and "free markets" mean the same thing and collapse the distinction between the two concepts. Milton Friedman, for example, argued that economic liberty is part and parcel of liberty. But I shall argue that liberty and free markets are very different concepts. The justification for free markets is not the same as the justification of individual rights. Indeed, the justification of free markets is usually pragmatic and economic. Economists favoring free markets say they are more efficient than other kinds of markets and will maximize human flourishing. This is the typical foundation of the free market argument, using the consequences and the outcomes to justify the position. This pragmatic argument differs from the claim that "we have natural rights to liberty that should not be infringed." When we distinguish the two positions (as some proponents of free markets do), we disentangle a pernicious and dangerous combination of ideas that are spontaneously combustible. By challenging each of these ideas on its own terms, it is possible to show that the two arguments cannot and should not be conflated. The protection of liberty does not necessarily mean we should have no rules governing the economy. And the value of free markets has no implications for rights. They are separate arguments. The theoretical positions of economists should not be taken as gospel any more than those of the priests of the Middle Ages. Economics is just a "social science," and even the "natural" sciences have evolving and changing understandings of the world. Economics is no different. The quest to create a science of the human ultimately failed, and economics is no different from other human or social sciences in this regard, as we shall discuss later. What reigns as truth for our economics professors should not necessarily dictate our moral positions on social justice, responsibility, and other obligations of the human species. *It is time to stop treating economists as the priests of modernity.* I have more to say about this topic in one of the subsequent chapters.

The limitations of the liberty-first position alluded to above are academic and intellectual. Yet the consequences are broad and serious. The notion of liberty espoused by the liberty-first advocates does just the opposite of what it purports. It undermines human flourishing; it ravishes our planet; and it vitiates the notion of equality that is implied by and ultimately is the foundation of the concept of liberty. Ultimately, the liberty-first ideas must be rejected if we have any hope to bequeath to future generations a planet that allows liberty to flourish. For if we do not fight back against what is a limited and myopic view of liberty, the inequality of the present world will increase, the environmental destruction will reach a point of no return, if it hasn't already, and liberty will disappear under much stricter government regulation and, what may be far worse, a massive policy of controlled distribution. The sad irony is that the views of the liberty-first advocates are more likely to lead to socialism or totalitarianism than those of the people they criticize for being socialists.

Simply put, the question before us is this: What political philosophy should carry us forward and guide us for the next century and at the beginning of this new millennium? If we act now, we do not have to abandon the concept of liberty altogether to address the concerns in front of us. But to avoid dire consequences for the planet and ultimately for human liberty, we must return to more of a classic notion of liberty that understands freedom as one value among other important human values, and as a right to embrace and live by along with other values. By interpreting liberty in light of other important human commitments, we not only build a moral-political philosophy for the future but renew and restore some of the most important dimensions of human thinking in the past, including the best of the great religious traditions and critical insights of modernity.

I refer to this philosophy of the future as a philosophy of "natural responsibility." It is contrasted to a philosophy of "natural rights" and balances concepts such as free markets and individual rights with a rich set of other key human concepts, such as responsibility, debt to history, public good, compassion, equality, love of one's neighbor, and a host of other rich moral and religious concepts that have slipped away from us. Such a philosophy is both a move forward and a return to what was great in the past, but without some of the past's limitations. I shall have more to say at another time about the word "natural" in the term "natural responsibility." In contrast to those who argue for "natural rights," a philosophy of "natural responsibility" shifts the perspective or center of gravity in our thinking beyond liberty to a broader circle of key human concepts and ideas. This philosophy takes seriously that liberty was always defined in terms of other conceptions, including human nature, science, God, morality, responsibility, equality, among others. Concepts such as justice, compassion, responsibility, obligation, care, love, equality, all have their appropriate place in the mix alongside liberty as valuable and important moral ideas. Liberty is one important concept. It gets a vote but not a veto. This is why I title this book *Beyond Liberty Alone*. One does not live by liberty alone, just as one does not live by bread alone. The point is not to abandon liberty but to balance it with other important values and see the meaning of liberty in light of those values. Just as a single musical instrument does not make for an orchestra, so too a single value to measure human good does not make for a good political philosophy. The difference between the philosophy of natural responsibility and the philosophy of natural rights appears on a whole range of issues: they differ on the notion of what a human being is and what truth is about, on the question of how we should think about God, religion, the meaning of modernity, history, and the purpose of America, and on the place of economics in our political life. On these and other key topics, this philosophy of natural responsibility differs from the tendencies of the liberty-first advocates. What differentiates this conception of liberty is in the entire underlying set of assumptions that make liberty intelligible.[6]

Core to the concept of natural responsibility is the conviction that we are more interdependent as a human species than we typically grant. This idea seems so self-evident that it hardly seems worth mentioning. Unfortunately, the notion of human interdependence has disappeared almost completely from the rhetoric of the liberty-first advocates. They hold positions as if human interdependence doesn't matter or as if human flourishing in general will occur by completely unfettered individuals pursuing their own self-interests. I disagree with both of those propositions. I believe that we must take seriously, both morally and philosophically, the ways in which humans are interdependent with one another across generations and across geographic, national, social, and religious boundaries. This has always been true, but in our current day, when the interconnected nature of our economies is more evident than ever and when environmental destruction is possible in our lifetime, the ways we are intertwined are more self-evident and more consequential than ever before.

In countering the liberty-first philosophy with a philosophy of natural responsibility, the goal is to shift the focus of people's thinking beyond themselves to the ways in which they are ultimately interconnected and mutually entangled. In some ways, there is nothing radically new in this shift in perspective. It is arguable that the notion of "humanity," in counterpoint to the notion of myself, "my nation," "my people," or "my God," framed some of the great insights of the modern Enlightenment as well as particular strands at various moments of many religions. But the notion of humanity has seemingly lost much of its power in the now-current variation of the liberty-first philosophy. Humanity, or the human species, is a way of thinking about ourselves that transcends both our limits as individuals and as America, the nation. I believe that if we shift our gaze to include the unit of humanity more prominently in our thinking, we will come to understand liberty in a different way, as requiring and containing within it other values that are also important and indeed sacred in their own right. By doing so, we align with some of the insights of the great religious traditions in ways that restore other lost insights of modernity and return to a view of liberty that is more at home with how liberty has at times been understood. What is at issue is both the definition of liberty itself and the relative balance of liberty and other values. The philosophy of "responsibility first" or "natural responsibility" that I talk about here reinvigorates the importance of the concept of humanity and the idea of the human species in order to recapture the very essence of what liberty means. From that rethinking comes a broader and more nuanced understanding of liberty.

In reframing how we think about liberty and the responsibilities that spring from our freedom, I ultimately point to a new vision of America with both heart and soul. I use the metaphors of heart and soul to talk about these broader values that comprise our humanity. To some, these are matters of the heart: compassion, caring, love, solidarity, empathy, and sympathy. To others they are also matters of the soul: what people believe God wants of us and what our most spiritual natures are seeking, whether we believe in a traditional understanding of God or not. In embracing these other values, I believe we also return to lost insights about liberty that reach back to the American founders and the modern philosophers of liberty. In my estimation, when the founders wrote about liberty, they meant something deeper and more profound than do our liberty-first proponents today.[7]

I realize that "liberty-first" adherents can and will shift their arguments and positions in response to mine. They will argue that they too are concerned about humanity. They will say that I misread history, modernity, America, and economics. But the larger goal here is not really to change the mind of the liberty-first adherents. That ship has sailed, and it is, in my mind, a sinking one. This reflection is written to those in the younger generation who have not yet made up their minds. As they look at the liberty-first stream of thought, some are being convinced that it is right. But there are other young people who feel in their gut that it is wrong, though they do not always have the right language to combat the hypnotic effect of oversimplification that is implicit in the liberty-first positions. My writing is written for them, to try to give them some additional language and ways of thinking beyond the limitations and perversions of the liberty-first philosophy. Those of us who feel that the liberty-first philosophy is not right and represents an oversimplification have the hope and aspiration of getting the next generation to think more deeply, to open their minds and hearts more broadly to a wider set of commitments, and ultimately to come to a new understanding of American history and modernity. That battle over minds and hearts is one that we must wage on all fronts: philosophy, economics, history, morality, religion, and the way we do business and regulate markets.

Chapter 1
The Paradox of Liberty

We Americans are particularly concerned with our liberties because we see liberty as core to what it means to be American. After all, the United States was founded with a vision of liberty as articulated in the Declaration of Independence and institutionalized in the Constitution of the United States. To embrace liberty is to embrace what it means to be American.

But what does liberty mean, and from where does this commitment to liberty come? Over the last several decades we have been given one particular perspective on these questions. Liberty, we have been told, is synonymous with the rigorous protection of our individual or natural rights. Any constraints on those rights are compromises of our cherished liberties, an abandonment of the original American way and vision, and ultimately destructive to our country.

Those who promote this view of liberty point in particular to the size and bureaucracy of the American government as the source of the most threatening compromises and dangers to our liberties. In their view, liberty by definition means that government should be small and stay out of our lives. The bigger government becomes, the more invasive it is, and the less liberty we have. Why is this so?

Big government by its very nature oversteps its boundaries in countless ways: it meddles in our lives and tries to make rules, about gun control and smoking, as examples, that curtail our individual liberties and violate our God-given or natural rights to be free. Big bureaucratic government also invariably creates programs that require higher taxes and that thereby rob us of our hard-earned dollars, which are siphoned to programs that we have never endorsed, such as abortion clinics, or to people who are lazy and do not deserve the benefits. Big government also invariably steps into policy areas where it doesn't belong, such as trying to mandate health insurance or the type of health insurance we choose. In addition, big government also inappropriately intervenes in economic markets with laws and taxes that try to shape economic behavior. Over and over again, big government oversteps its bounds and infringes our liberties or takes our property. For those who hold this view of liberty and the corresponding view of government, the crusade to make American government smaller is analogous to the vision of the founders and the original Boston Tea Party, which wished to end Great Britain's control over the American colonies and American economic trade.

In what follows, I insist there is another tradition of viewing liberty that does not understand the role of liberty or the role of government this way. Instead of thinking of liberty as a set of natural or individual rights that must be protected no matter what, this other tradition also sees liberty as including a set of obligations, duties, sacrifices, and responsibilities that come into being as members of social communities and as human beings. Liberty in this view means living justly as part of and within a social community and as a responsible member of the human species.[1]

With this understanding of liberty comes a corresponding shift in the understanding of government. Rather than seeing government as a threat to our liberties, government emerges as one of the mechanisms through which we try to implement and live out our mutual responsibilities to one another and to the generations who have come before and to those who will come after us. This alternative perspective sees government as a positive force and an instrument in helping us achieve our liberty, rather than an evil empire stealing it away.

I will argue that this shift in thinking about liberty is authentic in various ways. It is rooted in the great insights of modernity; it is consistent with the views of the American founders; and it is a logical conclusion from both traditional and modern religious understandings of God. Moreover, this view of liberty can also resonate for atheists, who do not root their understanding of liberty in a religious tradition that posits God.

It is my contention too that this alternative vision of liberty allows us to restore America's heart and soul. Liberty ceases to be a selfish egocentric concept that it has become. Instead, we can see our liberties as ways in which we promote the benefits and well-being of other human beings, not just protecting what is rightfully ours. What we think of as "rightfully ours" changes and emerges out of engagement with other human beings, who also share our society and the planet that we inhabit. Liberty is about how we manage to live justly as human beings.

To understand and uncover this other tradition of liberty, we must go on an intellectual journey, teasing out the underlying assumptions that inform the now dominant and distorted myth of liberty. We shall learn that much of what we have come to think about liberty—and by extension what we call "America" and even "modernity"—is either mistaken, lacking nuance, or simply wrongheaded. And what we uncover is something far more ennobling, enriching, and ultimately better for us all on this collective journey we make.

Most people think that the meaning of liberty is self-evident. They will tell you that liberty refers to a set of natural or individual rights that must be protected. Yet, if we probe deeper and ask what the concept "rights" means, people often stumble and have a hard time explaining what rights are, though they are often certain they are "natural," "self-evident," or "God-given."

People who are more articulate may explain that rights are protections of that which legitimately belongs to them (such as their lives and properties), as well as the actions or activities they are entitled to perform without interference (such as free speech or freedom of conscience). Rights, then, are entitlements or legitimate protections of what we own and what we may do. We have rights in the same sense that we have things. There is a close and interesting analogy between rights and property, which is itself said to be a right. Liberty is the collection of these legitimate rights.[2]

There are a number of limitations with this popular understanding. Most important, it misses the fact that liberty does not refer only to protections of what is mine. Liberty paradoxically also implies limitations on what I can do. Liberty is not just my protection but other people's protections too. Just as I am protected from them, they are protected from me. The popular understanding of liberty that emphasizes my rights and privileges misses the fact that liberty implies restrictions and limitations, by its very definition. When we emphasize what protections liberty gives me, we are thinking from an egocentric view of liberty. When we see liberty in a broader context and understand how your liberties mean my restrictions and vice versa, we are a taking a bird's-eye or social view of liberty. When seen only from an individual's vantage point, liberty looks like protections of what belongs to me. When seen from the vantage point of multiple people at once, liberty emerges as a set of trade-offs and compromises between many individuals.

This point about liberty is so basic and important that it bears repeating: My liberty implies your restriction. My right to my property means you can't touch it. My right to life means you have no right to take it from me. Every one of my rights implies your corresponding limitation. This double-sided nature of liberty can be thought of as the paradox of liberty. My liberty implies your lack of liberty, and your liberty implies limitations on mine. The bigger my liberty is, the larger the set of restrictions on you. My rights are carved out only by setting limitations on yours.

There is something incredibly profound about this insight that liberty implies limitation and not just protection or privilege. This restrictive side of liberty is often overlooked, because the word "liberty" itself tends to be associated with the word "freedom." Yet "liberty," as is now evident, implies something more complex. It refers to both freedom and restriction, or, to put it another way, liberty refers to the *freedoms that are made possible by living together* under restrictions.[3]

The freedom of living in society and human community is of a different sort of freedom than that which could theoretically exist were we to live alone on a desert island or in an uninhabited area, though fewer and fewer of such places exist anymore. Were we to live alone without law in what early modern theorists conceptualized as a "state of nature," we would be totally free to pursue all our desires, because we would not have constraints placed on us that arise from living with other people. The constraints we would face would come from limitations of our environment and our bodies as living human creatures. We still couldn't fly like birds, as an example, because this is a limitation in our bodies (until we built planes). But within the boundaries of being a human being, we would be totally free to do as we wished. Our freedom, however, would still be within a constraint of having no other humans around and therefore would be limited by a lack of what other people might produce. We would never invent an airplane by ourselves. Our liberty would be constrained by what we could never produce or imagine. Our desires would be limited by our own capacity for invention. But we would be totally free to act as we pleased within those limitations.

We thus both gain and lose something when we live in human communities. We gain the benefits of human companionship, and we reap the many rewards of life in society. We can socialize, we can have friends and families, and we benefit from what other people have produced and invented. Living with other human beings enlarges our liberty in the sense that we now have an opportunity to take advantage of new experiences, opportunities, and products that did not exist before. Our liberties are enlarged in the sense that our environment has been expanded with new ideas and products that we would not have thought of or developed on our own.

Yet these benefits of living in a human community come with a theoretical cost and sacrifice. To live together, we have to curtail some of our desires. We can't do whatever we want, because we don't want the other guy or gal to do whatever he or she wants either. We give up something or limit ourselves to get something in return. We make compromises so that others will make concessions as well. Liberty in society is thus different from a theoretical liberty that would exist were we alone on an island or in nature.

This "social liberty" is really the only kind of liberty we as human beings have ever had. Very few people have ever lived completely alone, and those who have began their lives originally in families, learning language and culture, before they isolated themselves. "Natural liberty," or the liberty alone outside of all social life, is thus a theoretical construct that really does not exist. Most of the time "liberty" is just a shorthand for "social liberty," which means the kinds of liberty that are possible in certain types of societies and communities.

When we see liberty from the vantage point of the other person, we realize that liberty is not just about protecting what's mine but protecting what's yours, and his and hers and theirs. Liberty is a state of balance between people who are agreeing to limit what they do in exchange for others limiting what they do. Liberty in this sense is an agreement to live together within a set of rules. It is a kind of trade-off or compromise and, if we are lucky, a win-win. Philosophically we have shifted the meaning of liberty from "protecting my rights" to "living in balance together" or "living peaceably or with justice together." The former understanding is contained within but superseded by the latter. My rights emerge out of an agreement that we have to live together and to draw boundaries. Rights from this vantage point are the places where we respect each other's boundaries.

In the last several decades, we have tended to hear a lot about the benefits and protections liberty gives us. Yet we have rarely heard or read about this other side of liberty, in which we give up freedom in order to make social life possible. The rhetoric has all been on the side of our rights, and very little on the side of our sacrifices, compromises, and responsibilities.

Limiting Desires, Making Compromises

To step back for a moment, I have reframed the question of liberty from a discussion of "my rights" to a discussion of what it means to be social beings and the compromises we make because we are human. I am saying that the two questions are really two sides of the same coin.

What our rights should be has to be answered in terms of what it means to be human and to be social animals. This is a very different way to approach the discussion about our liberties and our rights. Instead of asking "What's mine?" we ask "How can we live together?" and "What is the nature of being human?" The way we ask our questions defines how we think about our answers. Instead of talking only about rights, we talk about compromises and sacrifices we make. Sacrifice is at the heart of what it means to be human. We implicitly make a deal. We limit our desires in exchange for benefits that we receive from a human community.

This limitation of desires is one of the first things we are taught as children: that we can't act on all our desires and must abide by rules in the family. Our desires must be channeled into socially productive behaviors and shaped by our cultures. That is at the heart of what the family does as it raises children. And even the natural rights philosophers recognized that children do not have total freedom until they reach the age of maturity, however that is arbitrarily defined in each society.[4]

The limitation and shaping of desires is core to what it means developmentally to grow up and ultimately become an adult. We are taught to share and to channel our desires into productive types of activities. We are given the status of adult when we have matured enough to know what is expected of us in a particular society. Each society defines that passage to adulthood differently. The difference between a newborn and a two-year-old and between a two-year-old and a five-year-old is a leap in both cognitive functioning and how we handle our desires. This restriction of our desires is somehow core to what it means to become an adult and be a human being. This dimension of being human is rarely talked about in political discussions these days in favor of "our rights." Indeed, discussion these days hardly even asks at all about whether we have obligations and responsibilities as human beings.

There is something core to the human experience of learning to limit desires that has been recognized by both religious traditions and modern political philosophy. Why is it we have to sacrifice desires in order to be social? Why can't everyone have everything that he or she wants?[5] The answer is that there is limited supply. And our desires grow and expand in the context of our cultures and economic settings. Human beings are not innately desirous of cars or jewelry or computers. Those are desires that develop around core natural or basic needs, such as desire for food, shelter, health, and companionship. Desires expand because we live in societies that produce goods and opportunities. The problem of rights, therefore, is the same as the problem addressed by economics. How do and should we manage scarcity?[6] What do we do with the fact that there is not enough to go around? The question, of course, ultimately is, who gets to decide what limits our desires? Who sets the rules of the compromise? That will be a key question as we move forward with our critique and one that will take us back to the question of the role of government.

To summarize the first criticism of the liberty-first position, it is this: Liberty contains a paradox. To be social and therefore human is to put certain limits on our desires and our liberty. Why has this language of limitation and sacrifice disappeared from our political discussions? Discovering the absence of such language is the first chink we will put in the liberty-first armor. For when we recognize that social life means limitation and that we benefit only because we sacrifice and compromise for it, we have to end up with a different notion of rights. At issue is not only our protections or rights, but what kinds of sacrifices we should be making to live in communities. Who should make those sacrifices, and how are those sacrifices justly shared? These two questions are at the heart of the liberty concept and tradition. I will take up these issues in a subsequent discussion. Let me now turn to the second limitation in the liberty-first argument: the way in which the language of rights simply misses the larger question of natural responsibilities.

On Natural Responsibilities

It would seem so self-evident that human beings have responsibilities to each other that it is both ironic and sad to have to even bother defending the idea. Yet such, apparently, is the world we live in. Indeed, the focus on "self-evident" and "natural" rights has so dominated political debate over the last three to four decades that we have all but forgotten that there are other human values that should enter into political discussion and shape political practice.[7] It is time to remember that being human comes with a set of obligations and responsibilities in addition to something called rights. I say "remember" rather than "discover" because in some sense this idea is returning to an understanding that we have had at many times in earlier religious and philosophical traditions but subsequently deemphasized and even lost.

In arguing that we have responsibilities and not just rights, I am extending my argument from the previous section. There I argued that the very notion of rights contained a paradox because liberty requires sacrifice and limitation in order to achieve protections and privileges. I now wish to deepen this argument by showing that the very notion of rights is itself too narrow to serve as the only concept by which to organize and regulate political life. My argument here has several dimensions to it.

First, I am pointing out that the concept of responsibility and everything that responsibility entails is core to what it means to be human. There is, in other words, something about being a human being that creates moral responsibilities. This seemingly self-evident insight fundamentally changes how we think about our rights and duties in society and the role of government itself. Rights should never be talked about in isolation from responsibilities and duties. Responsibilities and duties devolve upon us as both citizens and as members of the human species.[8] Those who hold the liberty-first position acknowledge that people have responsibilities. Yet they think responsibilities are a private matter carried out via charity and have nothing to do with how societies should operate.[9] They are so wrong.

Second, the realization that we have responsibilities, and not just rights, is as self-evident and natural as any notion of rights. If we believe *rights* are self-evident and natural, we should believe *responsibilities* are self-evident and natural too. I will consider later whether, and in what sense, rights are indeed self-evident because, like others before me, I have some doubts that rights are as transparent to reason or self-evident as some people think. Before tackling that discussion, however, I want to show that responsibilities are at least as self-evident and as natural as rights. That puts responsibilities and rights on the same playing field, so to speak.

Any claim that our rights should be protected because they are natural or self-evident would carry along with it a corresponding claim that we have responsibilities and duties that are natural and self-evident. This is what I mean by a political philosophy of "natural responsibility." A philosophy of natural responsibility is an antidote or balance to the obsessive focus on natural rights. In other words, responsibilities are as natural and self-evident as rights.

Third, from the conclusion that responsibilities are as self-evident and natural as rights, it follows that they should have an impact on how we govern ourselves politically and morally. This is exactly the claim of those who argue from the self-evidence and naturalness of rights. They claim that the purpose of governments is to protect our rights, because those rights flow from the nature of how things are or how things are meant to be. It is noteworthy to see how the rhetoric of some liberty-first advocates insists that rights are more natural and more basic than governments. That is a dubious assumption that I will probe later. Let's start by arguing with them on their own terms first.

If governments should protect rights because they are natural, then they should protect responsibilities because they are natural too. I have already discussed how the very notion of rights implies sacrifices and limitations. When we enter society, we must sacrifice and limit ourselves. We give up some liberties as we gain protection of rights and the benefits of living together. That is the trade-off of social life. I am extending that insight here and insisting that being human comes with responsibilities too. To live in communities, we have to have responsibilities. Government is not just the "umpire" for rights that exist prior to government but also has a role in supporting human responsibilities, which are part of what it means to be human. In this line of thinking, government has obligations beyond a minimalist protection of rights. Government has also an obligation and purpose to support, enable and, in some cases, enforce human responsibilities that people bear, both as members of the specific society in which they live and as part of the more general human community.[10]

This focus on responsibilities represents an important shift away from the narrow way in which liberty-first advocates think about the role of government. Yet it is in line with how a number of the important early modern-rights philosophers envisioned government's role. They believed that government included the protection of the public and common good and not simply individual rights. In some cases, they also thought of responsibility to the human species to form part of what natural rights included. The very idea of the public good has all but disappeared from the language of the liberty-first position today. The focus is on personal wealth rather than the commonwealth. Indeed, liberty-first advocates make a mockery of the very idea of the public good, claiming that anything that tries to take account of the public or human good is socialism and contrary to natural rights. Nothing is further from the truth. It is they who pervert the modern liberty tradition.

Finally, there is an argument to be made that rights are neither self-evident nor natural, a position that I and many others endorse, including even some thoughtful individuals in the liberty-first camp. I will postpone that discussion temporarily, because I want to first take on and dispose of the very problematic assumption that only rights are natural, and not also responsibilities.[11]

Chapter 2
The Natural Source of
Rights Debated

Why is it people believe rights are self-evident and natural? In fact, many people don't bother to think about the basis of those claims and simply repeat a truth they assert to be self-evident. Americans know that the Declaration of Independence, the US Constitution, and the Bill of Rights all protect our self-evident rights. But they don't think deeply about what provides the foundation of those claims. For many people, rights are self-evident simply because they are part of our American tradition. So where did the idea of natural rights come from, anyway?

The claim that rights are self-evident or natural is an idea that took shape in its modern form in the seventeenth century in the writings of political philosophers such as Hugo Grotius, Thomas Hobbes, Samuel von Pufendorf, Algernon Sidney, John Locke, and a host of other lesser-known writers.[1] The idea had predecessors in the classical Greek philosophical tradition and in the Christian synthesis of Greek and Christian thought in thinkers such as Aquinas. Our modern ideas of rights were developed in a particular historical context to address a particular set of pressing problems. If today some of these seventeenth-century thinkers seem obscure and irrelevant except in university political philosophy classes, then we should recall the fact that America's conception of natural rights goes back to the late eighteenth century. Jefferson himself penned the Declaration of Independence in June 1776, and he and other founders were familiar with and were influenced by the writings of seventeenth-century philosophers on rights. Jefferson, for example, quoted John Locke, Samuel von Pufendorf, and David Hume in his early legal writings, and many think Locke in particular was of critical importance to Jefferson when writing the Declaration.[2] To put things in perspective a bit, it is important to realize that Jefferson was twice as close in time to John Locke as we are in time to Jefferson; yet Jefferson still obviously holds enormous symbolic influence over us two hundred years later. The ideas of Jefferson, and the other founders, of course, did not emerge out of their heads. They stand in a tradition reaching back into the early modern thinking about rights. The ideas that we have today about rights, governments, God, religion, and morality were in many ways shaped by discussions that emerged in that century. Contrary to how Americans sometimes think, history did not start with the Declaration of Independence.

The proposition that certain human rights are natural and self-evident emerged out of a European intellectual tradition that was focused on proving that there was a "law of nature" or "natural law" by which human beings should live. This was an idea that reached back to Greek philosophical ideas in antiquity and had been taken up into Judaism and Christianity as well, which originally did not have the same notion of a "natural law."[3] This law of nature was understood to be the common moral foundation for how human beings should live with one another. Natural law was thought to be discoverable by human reason and thus accessible to all people who had reached the age of maturity, regardless of their nationality, religion, geographic location, or historical period. Knowledge of the natural law thus did not depend on access in time or place to God's revelation, which was thought in the West to have been dispensed first to only the Jews via Moses (Old Testament) before it was published more broadly through Paul's mission to the gentiles (Gospel, New Testament). In the modern view, even those peoples who lived before God's revelation or geographically distant from the land of Israel, the place of God's revelation, were capable of discerning the foundations for the moral law.

It is significant that today most people who speak about their natural rights do so without referring to the concept of natural law at all. They talk only about what they are "empowered and entitled to do," but not about their limits, duties, and responsibilities. In the century that shaped that idea of rights as we now know it today, the concept of rights was inextricably entwined with the idea of natural law and limitation as well. One could not speak about one without the other. How so?

The relationship of the two concepts depended on how the particular philosopher construed the relationship of natural law and natural rights. Some thought that rights were "entitlements" whereas "laws were obligations to do or not to do" certain things.[4] For others, natural rights preceded and gave birth to natural law, which came later. For still others, natural law was the foundation of natural rights and preceded them.[5] And for others still, natural rights and natural law were different names for the same idea.[6] The very fact that there was no agreement on the source and meaning of natural rights is an interesting point to which we return later, for it tells us something important about the variability and constructed nature of our subject.

Despite their differences, there were a number of commonalities in how the seventeenth-century philosophers approached the discussion of natural rights and natural law. All of these philosophers were ultimately interested in revealing the moral foundation of human life, which they called the "law of nature." The very fact that they had to "discover" the source of moral life illustrated how fundamental shifts in European thought had put the very foundation of morality in question. More specifically, the traditional Christian religious appeals to God's revelation and scripture ceased to be the only compelling source of morality's foundation.[7] The birth of the modern natural rights tradition was ironically an answer to a growing doubt about the ability of revelation, as interpreted by the Roman Catholic Church, to provide a compelling foundation for human morality. The idea of natural rights represented an attempt to explain how we could have a common morality amid so much moral and religious diversity of human opinion and practice. This point is worthy of more discussion as we try to come to some understanding of what role natural rights should play today, because the question of how much certitude we can achieve in knowing how we should live good and moral lives should play a role in how we think about our rights and duties.

There were a number of reasons for the loss of confidence in traditional Christian religious explanations for the source of morality. The Protestant Reformation, followed by Europe's religious wars and the Counter-Reformation, made it clear to many Europeans that even Christians could not come to a single understanding of God's will as expressed in scripture (the Old and New Testaments). Catholics and varieties of Protestants warred over fundamentally different understandings of Jesus's teaching and the role of the church, as well as who had secular power.[8] European wars that were in part about the interpretation of God's Christian revelation showed that only power and the sword could solve the question of what revelation meant, even among Christians. As Grotius put it in the early seventeenth century, one of his motivations for writing his great work was that "I observed throughout the Christian World a Licentiousness in regard to War, which even barbarous Nations ought to be ashamed of: a Running to Arms upon very frivolous or rather no Occasions; which being once taken up, there remained no longer any Reverence for Right, either Divine or Human, just as if from that Time Men were authorized and firmly resolved to commit all manner of Crimes without Restraint."[9]

To add to the complexity, the European age of discovery and exploration and the encounter with non-European and non-Christian peoples astounded Europeans with tales of cultures that had fundamentally differing practices and moralities and some that, from a myopic European Christian world view, seemed to have no morality at all.[10] How were these varieties of cultures and religions to be explained? Did the lack of access to God's revelation mean that all peoples were sinners and damned? Were some less human than others? These intellectual changes, coupled with a growing respect for the rigors of the scientific method, a growing influence of skepticism, and new rationalist philosophies under the influence of Galileo (1564–1642), René Descartes (1596–1650), Sir Isaac Newton (1642–1727), among others, helped bring into question earlier ways of thinking about the foundation of truth and human morality and started a shift toward human reason as the foundation of science and as the premiere way for many of discovering human truth.[11]

In responding to these fundamental changes, the philosophers of natural right pondered a series of questions: How do we have certitude that there is right and wrong? Where does human morality come from? Can we say anything about the core principles of that right and wrong? What are the limits of our knowledge? Given the limits of our knowledge, what is the right and best way for human beings to live together?

These were very big philosophical questions they were asking, questions that today seem to have been sidelined completely in our political discussions. We have stopped asking such deep philosophical questions; we argue as if they are already settled. The early modern thinkers, by contrast, were exploring the frontiers of human knowledge, trying to understand how we know what we know, and the limits to our knowledge. They had doubts that scripture and revelation alone could answer all the key pressing questions of the day. Some of them also had doubts about a traditional understanding of God. And they thought that reason, as a distinctive faculty of human thought, could provide the foundation for human moral behavior. In asking these questions, and in the answers they offered, these thinkers began to reshape how we, their descendants and intellectual heirs, thought about morality, truth, religion, rights, politics, and God. Their language entered into and partially shaped the founding of America. And we still live with and use much of their language today.

What is most relevant for our present discussion is how the notions of rights, law, morality, and responsibility were all intertwined and presupposed one another. The early modern thinkers were not just pondering what rights humans possessed, but also what obligations they had as rational, social beings and, for those more religiously inclined, as creatures of God. Some emphasized the social nature of the human creature, and others the divine source of law. Most emphasized the identity of what reason discerned and what God wanted. They did not all agree on whether belief in God was necessary as a source of human morality. As the daring early-seventeenth-century philosopher Hugo Grotius put it, "And indeed, all we have now said [about discerning the law of nature and human morality] would take place, though we should even grant, what without the greatest Wickedness cannot be granted, that there is no God, or that he takes no Care of human Affairs."[12] Among those who thought a belief in God was necessary for a moral law, some had a conception of a divine Creator and rational God, a conception that had moved a great distance away from more traditional ideas of God as a source of revelation who was subject to no laws.[13]

All of these thinkers saw rights as embedded in a much larger story about the foundation of human morality. Natural law or the law of nature were the concepts they used to speak about the responsibilities that come with being human. So how specifically did they construe the source of natural law and its relationship to natural rights? There were two broad streams of thinking.

One stream of thought argued that the law of nature could be discerned by reason from the nature of the human being and the instinct toward self-preservation.[14] The other stream of thought discovered the basis of natural law from human observations of the world's order and wonder, and the ability of reason to infer a supreme Creator. In both cases, rights were balanced and constrained by a fundamental natural law and morality. Indeed, in some thinkers it was the very containment of rights with natural law that enabled societies to form and human beings to achieve their natures as social beings.

Let us look a bit more deeply at each of these positions. Our goal in doing so is twofold. First, I wish to show that responsibilities and sacrifices were thought to go together with rights. Second, I want to show that the very notion of rights rests on some story and conception about what humans are or should be. These points set the stage later for telling a better story about what rights and responsibilities we should recognize and embrace today alongside our notion of rights.

Rights from Human Nature Itself

One stream of natural rights thinking concluded that human reason can deduce the foundation of morality from the social nature of the human creature. Everything in the world has its nature. The essence of human nature is to be social and live in communities, a point that could be discerned by human reason. For some thinkers, the social nature of the human being is simply part of our human character.[15] For others, the social nature of human beings developed or emerged in response to the experience of life on one's own and the instinct toward self-preservation.[16] For those who thought humans were social by nature, natural rights and natural laws emerged together as two sides of the same coin. To be social, humans needed both protections (rights) and laws by which to regulate their interactions. Both natural rights and natural law were discerned by human reason in the quest to make social life feasible.

Those who thought that human beings *became* social and were not inherently social by nature understood the relationship of rights and natural law differently. Prior to the socialization of the human species, individuals had "unlimited natural rights" in the sense that they were like animals of prey, who act out of their own instincts of self-preservation. In this state, there was no "right" and "wrong" and no "law," until humans reasoned and learned that social life was a better way to achieve protection for themselves and their property, and to participate in the material benefits of society.[17] In this sense rights were understood to be amoral or nonmoral, much like animal instincts. Saying humans had unlimited rights to each other's lives, bodies, and property was like saying that animals had a right to prey on one another, because they act according to their nature for self-preservation.[18] Rights in this sense were "right," because they described the sheer way humans were before they became social creatures. If one is religious or more theological, one could say this was the nature of human beings by design.

Some understood the drive toward social life as a mechanism to relieve individuals of the fear and dangers of living without protections, while others understood the drive to sociability as deriving from the benefits that society confers. Either way, these thinkers thought the character of social life presupposes and requires humans to live within constraints and predictability. There can be no total liberty in a state of society. Total liberty without law would lead to a breakdown of social life, to insecurity and, in the view of some, ultimately to a spiraling of fear and violence.

This is so because humans are driven by passions, ego, and desires for power, money, and fame, and thus compete for the same resources. Without the predictability of law, there could be only limited commerce, no inventions, and really no civilized human life. The very benefits of social life emerge from the predictability of law and from a power that can enforce that law.[19] From the social nature of the human creature, therefore, reason can deduce the need for a set of laws that can structure and control human interaction. It was reason that helped humans realize the need for law and thus lay the foundation for social life.[20] In this sense, the law of nature set restrictions on the unlimited rights that humans otherwise had and made human beings into social animals. Or, to put it another way, humans ceased to be the wild animals they were and became human beings when they discovered the basic rules ending violence, which was the same as the law of nature.

It is important to remember these seventeenth-century thinkers did not yet know Darwin's theory of evolution, though some of them seemed to assume that humans differentiated themselves from a wild animal state through the use of their reason. This view of human beings, incidentally, was not self-evidently compatible with the scriptural creation story, in which Adam and Eve were created as full-fledged human creatures with speech and reason. The meaning of Genesis and the creation story played an important part in the debate over rights, since scripture was commonly accepted as the true description of the human creation. The meaning of the Genesis creation story, however, was itself hotly contested, and the same story could serve as the foundation for an argument against individual rights and for the royalist tradition ascribing all power to a political sovereign, as we shall see. In any case, all of these philosophers saw social life as part and parcel of what it means to be human. Becoming human and differentiating from the other creatures involved a kind of trade-off and sacrifice in which rights in nature and outside of social life are abandoned and hemmed in by laws of nature. In this sense, what is distinctively human is not liberty, which all animals have, but discovering and living with a moral law that restricts liberty and differentiates humans from animals.[21] Humans, in other words, are animals with reason and laws. Humans are animals that have curtailed their natural liberty and rights.[22]

As is now evident, the emphasis of these social-oriented thinkers was as much on the laws of nature that constituted and limited human experience as on the natural rights or entitlements that humans have. For example, one of the earliest and most important modern philosophers of natural rights, Thomas Hobbes, reasoned that the first law of nature is "seek peace and follow it."[23] In his view, the need to seek peace is a broad realization that leads humans to pursue ways in which they can live together well with other people. It leads to the second law of nature: that people should lay down their rights in nature and be content "with so much liberty against other men, as he would allow other men against himself." This second law of nature is considered identical with the Golden Rule in the Gospel that "whatever you require that others should do to you, do ye to them."[24] The Gospel and revelation thus included truths that were also discernible independently by reason.

The foundation of social life, Hobbes argued, depends on a "need to lay down one's right and divest oneself of liberty." At the heart of social life is a renunciation of rights (i.e., instincts) that otherwise would belong to us. From this second law of nature arises others. The third law is that people must fulfill their contracts, which is the foundation of and paradigm for social life itself.[25] A contract involves my transferring to you my rights to my things and the willingness to curtail what are otherwise my rights for your benefit.[26] More surprising is the more expansive view of natural law and positive duties articulated by Hobbes. Indeed, there are seventeen other laws of nature that specify how people should treat each other to make social life possible. Among others listed, people should (4) have gratitude, (5) be willing to accommodate others, (6) pardon offenses for which others have repented, (7) not take revenge for revenge's sake, but only for corrective purposes, and (8) not declare hatred or contempt of another.

The point here is that in this stream of thinking, reason—reflecting on the social desires and character of human beings, and the benefits which social life endows—concludes that we go beyond simple protections of property and treat each other with respect, gratitude, accommodation, and so forth. The protection of rights was not the only moral issue that mattered.

The argument that natural law was derived from the social nature of human beings was compatible with but not dependent on the idea of a Creator God who intended human beings to be social creatures. As John Locke, one of the other most important thinkers in the modern tradition, put it, God did not intend for human beings "to be alone," alluding to the first chapter of Genesis, as proof that humans' social nature was a God-given characteristic.[27] The same claim was repeated in the early American founding as well to link this argument with a religious foundation.[28] Nonetheless, the argument for the natural sociability of the human species was not necessarily dependent on the idea of God as a foundation for human morality, since one could infer a natural law from human sociability even if God did not exist or did not care about human beings.[29] For this reason, one thinker concluded that the laws of nature should not even be properly called "laws" because they were conclusions or theorems of reason, whereas the word "law" is properly reserved for the word "of him, that by right hath command over others."[30] Since the notion of law implied a lawgiver, the conclusions of reason should not be called laws. For obvious reasons, some of these thinkers were thought to have been atheists, though the climate of the day required that they deny and hide such a claim, and a number of them had to flee their home countries at one point or another to avoid imprisonment or death by political authorities for what they had written.[31]

The Creator as a Source of Law and Rights

A second major stream of thought deduces natural law and natural rights from the inference that God exists. Though appealing to a conception of God and thus more religious in flavor than the argument from sociability, this view differed from and represented a threat to the more traditional religious view that God had given humans morality through a specific revelation (the Old and New Testaments) or by inscribing natural law on the human heart or conscience.[32] In this second stream of thought, human reason, reflecting on both the beauty and order of the natural world, infers that there must be a powerful and wise Creator of all things, a proof of God still very popular today.[33] In addition, reason infers that human beings cannot have created themselves, for otherwise they would have given themselves immortality. Reason can thus deduce that there must be a Creator who is more perfect than a human being. From this reasonable conclusion it follows "that above ourselves there exists another more powerful and wise agent who at his will can bring us into the world, maintain us, and take us away."[34] Humans are thus led to the knowledge of a superior being, and thus to a Lawgiver, to whom we are subject.

Furthermore, we can also reason that this superior power has an intended purpose for us, "for it would be contrary to wisdom" to assume this Being created us for no purpose at all and that "all this wonderful equipment of the person is not bestowed on us so we can be idle." What, then, is that purpose of our creation? We were created in part "to render praise, honour, and glory" to God.[35] Beyond duties to God, we also have restrictions on ourselves and responsibilities to our neighbors and ourselves.[36] We can deduce that the law of nature not only requires a prohibition on theft and murder, but also enjoins us to cultivate certain sentiments, including "tender affection for parents" and "love of one's neighbor." One is also obligated to perform certain actions, such as "outward worship of the Deity, the consoling of a distressed neighbour, the relief of one in trouble, the feeding of the hungry."[37] This focus on others is very much a part of the law of nature. Indeed, the law of nature insists on the peace and preservation of all mankind, and "when his own preservation comes not in competition, ought he, as much as he can, to preserve the rest of mankind."[38] Indeed, love of one's neighbor is a summary of the law of nature.[39]

In this stream of thinking, the law of nature and natural rights exist independent of any human impulse to social life or to self-preservation. It is not the social character of the human being that provides the foundation for rights and laws. Rather, the rights and laws are rational conclusions when we understand that there must be a Creator. Contrary to what some other natural rights thinkers insisted, rights did not exist first and law emerged later. Rather, humans were in essence always reasonable creatures and therefore could always discern a Lawgiver who had expectations of human behavior. We were rational from our very inception.

Though this argument from God is "religious" in tone, it is important to understand that this foundation of rights was thought to be broader than the more traditional religious understanding that derived morality from revelation. Since all humans had reason, the implication was that one did not have to be Christian or Jewish to perceive the moral law. Anyone, anywhere, at any time, in theory had access to the law of nature through reason's discernment of a Creator God. This was a significant deviation from the more traditional religious view that one must have had an experience of Christ, or be exposed to revelation, or live a Christian way of life, to be a moral being and live right in God's eyes. The discernment of a Lawgiver and Creator was the foundation for both natural law and our natural rights.

So what rights can we infer from our discernment of a Creator? Our rights to life and liberty, for example, emerge from our inference that we were created by God. Since humans are God's "workmanship," and we are thus all "equal and independent," none of us has a right to harm the life or liberty of another person.[40] This argument differs from the assumption we take for granted today that "we own our bodies and selves." On the contrary, here each person is in essence God's property and therefore has no right to harm or take the life of another. For the same reason, we cannot take our own lives, which belong to God. As John Locke would summarize this view in his classic statement,

> The *State of Nature* has a Law of Nature to govern it, which obliges every one: and Reason, which is that Law, teaches all Mankind, who will but consult it, that being all equal and independent, no one ought to harm another in his Life, Health, Liberty or Possessions: For Men being all the Workmanship of one Omnipotent, and infinitely wise Maker: All the Servants of one Sovereign Master, sent into the World by his order, and about his business they

are his Property whose Workmanship they are, made to last during his, not one anothers Pleasure: and being furnished with like Faculties, sharing all in one Community of Nature, there cannot be supposed any such *Subordination* among us, that may Authorize us to destroy one another, as if we were made for one anothers use, as the inferior ranks of creatures are for ours.[41]

Restating this view in more contemporary language, we were not made for one another's instrumental use and cannot treat each other like inanimate objects or property. Our rights to life and to liberty, which here means the right not to be enslaved, arise from the fact that we belong to God and are God's "workmanship." Since we belong to God, we cannot belong to one another. The same logic applies not only to our lives and liberty but to "health," which should not be injured for the same reason. It is interesting that "health" is included in this list of rights here, suggesting an opening for a much broader notion of rights than "life, liberty, and property" often seem to imply. Later we shall consider how difficult it is to determine what is included in our natural rights and what is not.

What about the basis for the right to property? How do we infer from the insight that there is a Creator that we should have rights in property? According to this stream of thought, reason and revelation both tell us that people, once created, have a right to self-preservation and thus to natural resources that makes sustenance possible.[42] In addition, humans have a right to make use of natural resources for "the support and comfort of their being." It is through their labor or work that people take possession of what is a shared natural resource. Humans own their own labor and will.[43] When they carry out their work in gathering acorns or growing crops, they in effect invest their labor in it, and it thereby becomes theirs. Just as we are the property of God because God created us, our labor to produce, improve, or remove something from its natural state creates property for us. I shall come back to this all-important right of property again later, because it is so central to the argument about liberty, economics, and markets and is worthy of a much longer discussion.

In addition to life, liberty, health, and property, there are also two rights considered to be surprising or strange.[44] The first is the individual's "executive" right to judge and punish a person who violates the law of nature, and the second is the right not only to receive but to forcibly take reparations for harm or damage to oneself. The right to judge and punish one who offends the law of nature was thought to exist prior to the existence of social life, because there could be no law without the power of enforcement. Prior to social life, it was the natural right of every person to execute judgment and punishment of natural law. Ultimately, of course, this state of affairs was not very satisfactory, since biases would invariably arise when judging matters related to oneself or one's loved ones. Feuds and violence could easily escalate. Dissatisfaction with the biased means of resolving conflicts was one of the key motivators for individuals to join together in societies and create civil governments. In doing so, individuals relinquished their natural rights to judge and punish offenders, turning that power over to a society's executive and judicial systems. They gave up these individual and natural rights in order to secure what would be a more fair, impartial, and secure state of affairs.

I wish to step back now from this highly abbreviated survey of the early modern natural rights tradition to draw some general observations about rights and responsibilities. First, we have seen that the natural rights thinkers argued that there were limitations placed on rights, and they called those limitations the "law of nature" and the "dictates of reason." Theoretically, the only time there was total liberty was in nature, and even there, some thought it was limited by a natural law from God. They all thought, in some form, that the essence of either becoming human or being human was not our natural liberty per se but, on the contrary, the discernment through reason that we have to curb our desires, transform ourselves into social creatures, and take responsibility for our species as a whole. They agreed that this realization was always available to human reason, though some thought reason first discerned God and then the natural law, while others thought the discovery by reason of natural law emerged from a prior experience where humans had a social inclination or were more like animals of prey and suffered in the violence of the state of nature. In either case, it was not rights and liberties that defined human beings but limitations on rights, and the fact that humans stepped out of or were separated from animal nature.[45] By ceasing to act like animals of prey, by giving up the rights or instincts of nature, we became the human beings that we are. In this view, the renunciation or transformation of rights, rather than the granting of rights, is what makes us quintessentially human. This is a rich insight that is similar in some ways to my own claim that responsibility is as natural as rights. Until quite recently in our Western traditions, rights were never understood in isolation from duties and sacrifice. If we are to continue using rights language, and it appears that it will not be easy to find a new language anytime soon, then we should at least bring back the notion of natural responsibility and sacrifice as well.[46] One of the peculiarities of the current language of the liberty-first advocates is that rights are often thought of independent of any kind of responsibilities. Responsibilities are thought to be a private matter. I shall return to this question of responsibility below.

Chapter 3
Life, Liberty, and
the Pursuit of Responsibility

I have argued thus far that the idea of natural rights is itself dependent on some prior framework of ideas about human nature, reason, God, among other values. If this is so, then the values and ideas we have about ourselves and our place in the world naturally contribute to how we think of and define our rights. Liberty-first advocates, however, pretend as if rights are self-evident, independent of one's other convictions. But this is not the case. Instead, rights are crystallizations and summaries of people's beliefs and moral convictions. People who differ from one another in moral convictions also have different notions of rights and what they should include. For this reason, rights don't mean the same thing to every person and every generation. Even the very core natural rights, such as "life, liberty, and property" or "life, liberty, and the pursuit of happiness" are rights that people understand in different ways, not to mention the controversies over whether we have a natural right to bear arms, to have an abortion, to commit suicide, to marry whomever one pleases, to take one's own life, and so forth.

What I am saying is that rights may seem self-evident and natural, but that is so only within some framework of convictions about what we are and wish to be. The question that emerges, therefore, is, what set of convictions do we want to provide the framework or foundation for our notion of rights? When liberty-first advocates argue something is a right, they are doing so within their own very distinctive framework of convictions. But there are other frameworks that render an alternative view of rights compelling. In what follows, I want to illustrate this point by returning to the insights that responsibilities and sacrifices are as "natural" as any notion of right. From this point of departure, we shall arrive at a conception of rights that differs from the one that has become dominant today.

It would be a mistake to think that what differentiates the two views I am discussing boils down to simply a difference between a religious and nonreligious view. The idea of natural responsibility can flow from either a religious or a secular world view, and one can embrace notions of natural responsibility whether or not one is religious or believes in God. This is a position that can join together people across religious and nonreligious lines. Clearly, the notion that we have natural responsibilities would in fact seem to naturally align with Western Christian and Jewish religious views much more than the alternative view espoused by liberty-first advocates, many of whom adamantly claim God is on their side and focus only on rights, and less so on our responsibilities. In addition, one can embrace a notion of natural responsibility without a belief in God by understanding the ways in which we stand on the contributions of those who came before us. So the debate between liberty-first and natural responsibility advocates need not be about whether God exists or has expectations of us. They hold one construction of rights, God, and human beings; I and others, another. It is to this other view that we now turn.

• • •

If we still choose to use the concepts of natural and self-evident rights, then we should also insist on the concept of natural responsibilities. The notion of "natural responsibilities" is similar in some ways to the notion of natural law discussed above, though we will be more modest about words such as "natural" and "law." What is natural is by no means self-evident, since notions of what is natural in human beings are themselves up for grabs and interpretation. And the notion of law (in natural law) implies either a power that can make and enforce the law or a rule that is embedded in nature itself. My notion of natural responsibilities is more modest, implying a set of moral obligations that have the force of right on their side from within a particular but compelling way of understanding ourselves and our place in the world.

The notion of natural responsibility insists that there is something about what it means to be human that places responsibilities and obligations on us and that limits what we can rightfully do. I wish now to develop this idea in language that is more contemporary but that builds on both seventeenth-century insights that made rights so important to us, and on notions of responsibility that were also available in traditional Judeo-Christian religious traditions.[1]

The notion of natural responsibility emerges from an understanding of our human character as a dependent and interdependent creature that benefits from the lives and contributions of thousands of people who have lived before. To restate this in language that can resonate for religious people, God created us to be dependent and interdependent and to be social creatures. This dependence and interdependence provides the conceptual foundation for realizing we have obligations and responsibilities to the species as a whole first and to each other as individuals second. This interdependence we have is part of what it means to be human, and it precedes the creation of individual political societies and provides the framework within which individual political societies should operate. We are not born isolated as individuals, like the biblical Adam and Eve, but as members of a species with a long and rich history, and as dependent creatures who can't survive without the care of a parent or other adult. The dependence and interdependence I am speaking about is both historical and personal.

Historically, the human creature that we are today is the result of countless other efforts, activities, risks, and choices of human individuals who preceded us. From an evolutionary perspective, we in fact became human through countless smaller changes brought on by alterations that reshaped our very nature and made possible our upright posture, our opposable thumb and forefinger, our higher symbolic cortical functioning, and the various other characteristics that make us human creatures. These capabilities provided the foundation on which our human ancestors discovered fire, learned to hunt and cook, and realized they could domesticate animals, practice agriculture, count numbers, and create abstract symbols, among other great achievements. Even if one prefers to see these evolutionary developments as under the guidance of God, one can embrace the idea that humans have become what we are through countless contributions of thousands before us. We did not do this alone. Everything that we presuppose today was bequeathed to us by others. Engines, electricity, light bulbs, penicillin, automobiles, airplanes, computers, lasers; the list goes on. While there are great scientists and inventors such as Leonardo da Vinci, Benjamin Franklin, Thomas Edison, Marie Curie, Alexander Graham Bell, to name only some of those who broke through to new insights and inventions, they stood on the shoulders of countless earlier inventions and insights. They could not have done their work without the prior contributions of those who created fire and invented language, symbols, math, telescopes, wire, lenses, plastic, the microscope, electricity, and countless other inventions that made their work possible. So even the greatest inventors of the human species relied on work done by countless unnamed individuals who came before.

We should stand in awe of this fact that we are the recipients of the work and insights of millions of people that have come before us. We are not born on a clean slate. The work they did transcends the boundaries of nations, religions, genders, race, and time. The contributions diffused across the human species and advanced the species, though some of the inventions may have harmed us as well. Paper invented here, alphabets there, fire in one place, symbols someplace else. Silk came from there, gunpowder from someplace else. Every people and religion contributed something important to the collective results. The species as a whole grasped hold of these incremental changes and reshaped who we literally are. Whether or not the individual inventors aimed at benefiting themselves and their families or bequeathing something to posterity, they did in fact give us thousands of gifts for which we contributed nothing, just as they inherited a wealth of knowledge and inventions from those who came before them, all the way back in time. The point is that nearly everything we accept as part of our human landscape is given to us by others who came before. We often tend to focus, however, on the inventors who had the breakthrough final discoveries. Yet they would be nothing without the generations before, including even our very selves, our very bodies and brain, developed through the activities of earlier ancestors. There is nothing about us that was not contributed by a collective effort of generations.

So what do we make of the fact that we take our place on an edifice that has been built by others? The insight should reshape how we think about ourselves, our rights, and our responsibilities. To begin with, we should see ourselves on a collective journey as a species, not just as individuals who are disconnected and spring out of nothing. The notion that we have only rights and not responsibilities implies that we do it all ourselves, that we achieve what we achieve on our own. Nothing is further from the truth.

To begin with, our very human essences, our very human selves, came about through the collective efforts of our human ancestors. For those who accept an evolutionary perspective, our erect posture, our bipedal locomotion, our capability of language, and our extensive tool making were achievements of our species and the species from which we descended. To be sure, we can understand those transformations to be the outcome of natural selection and in some sense an accidental process, though religious folks would be right to point out the magnificence of that process and the possibility it was an expression of something larger and more purposeful. But even if the process was simply accidental, it seems that we would want to acknowledge the contributions of those who came before us. I feel grateful not just to my grandparents, who migrated to this country before I was born, but I owe some debt to the American founding generation for their vision and to the country to which my grandparents could immigrate. There were tens of thousands of others before them whose contributions large and small made my life easier.

Our very humanness as individuals is the result of this collective journey of our species. As such, these capabilities belong not to individuals themselves, but to the species as a whole. For a modern culture that cares so deeply about property, it is clear that the capabilities that make us human belong to no one in particular but to everyone together. No one owns language and speech, eyesight and upright posture, fire and boiling, or the other thousands of inventions that have entered the common wisdom of our species.

The question, of course, arises: What rights or duties do we have with these inventions of our collective species? Most of the time, no one pays any attention to them at all. They are simply taken for granted in the background of everyday life. We use them with no thought to these gifts from the past. Yet it is from here that we can and should infer a collective duty and responsibility to the species as a whole and to other human beings. Why so? Most of the efforts of those in the past were not kept private but made public and collective, and as such they belong to the human species as a whole, not to individuals. And while none of us is charged for use of fire or language, we are making use of something that belongs to the collective. They are like "national parks" of the whole species, benefits of the whole, not of individuals. Or one can think of them as books from the library that we have checked out for personal use, though they belong to the community as a whole. When they belong to the whole and not an individual, we have a responsibility to treat them differently. The fact that these inventions from the past are collective and not private is evident in the fact that there are no rules about the use of these inventions from the distant past. Had the species wanted to privatize these inventions, it theoretically could have, though in practice that might have been difficult. Just imagine if the inventor of fire or cooking kept it privatized and part of his or her own estate. Of course this idea sounds ridiculous, because it would have been impossible to do so, and these capabilities have become part of the common stock of knowledge. Most inventions passed into the collective, because they were shared and diffused across cultures, or because we have no memory of their creation. We shall look at a similar argument about the collective nature of the earth and property later and think about what our collective obligations are in that regard as well.

What duties then do we have? I argue that we have a duty to benefit the species as a whole, and not just ourselves, our families, our communities, and our nations. We take from the collective knowledge of our species, and we owe something back to the species as a whole. The duty arises like a contract with others of our species. We collectively own this knowledge and these capabilities. They belong to no one in particular but to all of us in common. Collectively we have been granted capabilities and knowledge that we take from the library of collective knowledge. We have a pass or card to use this accumulated wisdom, but only on conditions. There are responsibilities, I am arguing, that are implied in taking advantage of what was bequeathed to us and what we own in common. We shall talk much more about the notion of common ownership when we get into the topic of property and how the natural rights tradition understands the derivation of this natural right. Think for the moment of any property held by more than one person in a partnership. The use of that property is defined by the goals of the partnership as a whole. Rules for use of joint property are set by the partners, to benefit them.

If humanity owns the intellectual property that makes possible life as it is today, why would humanity not define the use so that it benefits everyone? When we see the origin and ownership of what we benefit from, we realize that the use of human knowledge has been perverted. Today, liberty-first advocates see our human capabilities and our bodies as belonging to each of us as individuals. But our very capabilities in some sense seem to belong to the species and are "granted" to us to use as individuals. In what sense did we create our own eyes or noses or vocal cords or minds? Why do we get to take personal private possession of ourselves? Our individual gifts, whether as musician, intellectual, inventor, or athlete, seem to take place on a platform that was gifted to us through our genes, which have the contributions of thousands of others before. More traditional language might say that God created us through our parents. As noted previously, for example, John Locke argued that we have rights because we are God's property. We can articulate the same idea without invoking religious or theological language. We can see that what and who we are as human beings is given to us as much as it is made by us. While individuals have an opportunity to develop what they are given, we are given a core human platform on which to build. The people who build a business start with funding from venture capitalists, to whom they owe something back. Something similar seems appropriate for all these capabilities and gifts with which we start our journey. Why do we think that all the in-born capabilities belong to us alone? If we are religious, are these not from God? And if we are not religious, are they not from our collective journey?

In the liberty-first ideology, what we are given, whether in our bodies or in our life situations, is ours exclusively. Whether we are born into wealthy nations or impoverished ones, into well-off families or poor ones, whether we have talents of music, intellect, or athleticism, makes no difference according to liberty-first ideology. Somehow the individuals who inherit these accidents of history deserve them. They assume that the gifts each of us are born with are ours alone as well. But in what sense do we or should we be the exclusive beneficiary of the accidents of history?

There are many ways in which we can ask this question, and we shall come back to it many times to differentiate our view from that of others, for our assumption is that everything that we have is built in some sense on the collective contributions of thousands who have come before us. Why then would the benefits belong only to us and our descendants alone? Why does a baby born in an advanced Western nation deserve so many more opportunities than a baby in some other country? Just because our ancestors migrated to Europe and then to America, why should our lives be so radically different in quality and opportunity? Why in the same nation should a baby born into a rich family deserve so much more in opportunities than a baby in a poor family? To what extent should I be rewarded or punished by the decisions of my ancestors and by the accidents of history?

Our opponents will call this way of thinking "socialism." But it is something else. This approach is a moral way of thinking about the gifts we are given and the accidents of history. It is a way of seeing ourselves in the world in the evolving story of the human species. This perspective has with it an understanding that we did not make ourselves completely, that thousands of others contributed to who we are. Our opponents cannot deny that this is true by calling it "socialism." This perspective is a moral way of engaging the world and is fully compatible with capitalism, though the meaning of capitalism will shift under our scrutiny as well.

This way of thinking is not socialism, because we are not advocating that the collective owns everything and that there is no private property. The notion that we owe something back to the species is a moral position, a view of our "natural state" as members of a species. I am arguing that the platform on which we live our lives is collective in origin. The notion that we owe something back for what finances our ventures is in fact a core conviction of capitalism itself. Just as no one claims it is socialism when we have to pay a bank back for a loan, or pay back a venture capitalist for his or her investment, it is not socialism when we owe back to the human bank for the capital with which we start our venture. The capital we work with and have received is our language, brains, abstract thinking, upright posture, and our collective knowledge, such as fire and inventions. The notion that we have a debt to the lender is completely compatible with the core assumptions of capitalism itself.

My argument is that at least part of the fruit of my labors should go to humanity as a whole. When I leverage common knowledge, I am implicitly making a deal. The collective gives me rights to use what is collective property for my own advantage. It makes sense that the partnership would give me such privileges only if I am willing to contribute back to the collective.

One might object that we cannot identify the owners of this collective the way we would the owners of a company. But this is a false objection, for we continue to owe the bank for our debts, even if the owners changed many times over.

The question is what to do with the contributions of the past. Assuming that the contributions were distributed, it seems only reasonable that some percentage of the benefits should be shared. Since the ancestors who built this human platform we live on were ancestors of us all

(Adam and Eve, in the language of scripture), then the human capital they gave us should be paid back to their heirs, who are everybody. Once we recognize a claim or debt of the past, on what basis could we exclude one race, geography, or group of people from the benefits? The question is, how do we pay back this debt to the heirs? If we look at capital investments today, we have a model that can help us understand how we might go about this. Venture capitalists take a share in the company in which they invest. The founders of the company take an interest as well. If all works well and the business succeeds, the founders and the venture capitalists both share the benefit. It is a shared risk. The founders often need the outside capital to get their business off the ground. The venture capitalists who provide the funding capital make a calculated risk. They know that many of their investments will fail. But they also know some, such as Cisco, Google, and Facebook, will bring huge returns that more than outweigh all the losses. Something like this model should govern the human species. Human beings in general benefited from the capital investments of the ancestors. Europe and America grew faster and had greater success in material wealth than other geographic areas. These geographies should pay back to the investors, or their heirs, which is humanity in general. This should be understood not as a redistribution of wealth, but as a payback of a debt for an investment. To some extent we recognize this obligation implicitly through foreign aid offered by countries and private donations made by individuals to other countries. But we often look at this activity as generosity instead of obligation and debt.

This idea of payback on capital investment, of course, is only a metaphor. But it is important to see that in the world of capitalism, there is an analogy to the idea of investment that I am invoking here. This idea of natural responsibility has no danger of slipping into socialism. But unlike our opponents' position, which holds that we deserve and own everything we have, including our bodies and the fullness of our labor, this position assumes that we got here, to where we are now, on the shoulders of others. It is a simple but profound insight. While it is true that different individuals end up doing more or less with what they are given, this alternative position can also account for that. We do not take away everything that one achieves. We have a win-win split. Individuals who work hard with the investment they were given get to keep more than those who do not. But they also have to return more of the profits to the prior investors.

The problem with the liberty-first position is that it treats ownership of the body and labor as belonging to the individual only and completely ignores the impact and contributions of the species (and, for religious folk, even the oversight of God) that have made us what we are. That view also treats responsibility and "giving back" as morally good but left ultimately up to the individual's heart and soul. On the contrasting account here, we cannot see everything about ourselves as our own property. Who we are and what we can do represent the contributions of a species and, in religious language, we are the creatures of God. If we build our lives on the platform and investments of others before us, then we have a duty to the heirs of those predecessors. We are not completely our own persons. Those responsibilities are natural in the sense that they take account of nature, what God intended, and how we have become who we are. We recognize, of course, that any account of nature can be contested. But I offer here at least an alternative view of nature that does not place all of the ownership of the body and self with the individual and that provides grounds for arguing we have natural responsibilities. We shall see that this alternative view has significant ramifications.

On Natural Responsibilities of Parents and Children

The notion that we have a debt for what has been given to us is already a familiar and respected idea for most of us because of how we think about familial relations. Let us start first from parents' responsibilities to children. Most people agree that parents have a kind of natural duty to their children. We bring them into the world, and we consider it natural and obligatory that we should help our children through the process of maturing and becoming adults who can function on their own. These parental duties may be instinctual, and our moral commitment to our offspring, reflected in many though not all animal species, may be part of our natural heritage, reinforced by cultural and religious conceptions. The early care includes providing sustenance and protection and teaching children language, culture, morals, and so forth. Not all parents live up to these expectations, of course. Some abandon their babies. Others raise their children poorly. Different families may disagree on what values to teach or how long that responsibility lasts, but most people would agree that these responsibilities are somehow implied by becoming a parent. We see them as "natural" to who we are as human beings, and we see something similar in the animal kingdom, though humans are peculiar in having a much longer period of dependence during childhood than most other species.

This notion that the parents have duties to children, interestingly enough, differs from the view that children are "property," a view put forward, for example, by some royalists, such as King James I and Robert Filmer in the seventeenth century.[2] They argued that there was an analogy between the sovereign in the state who had absolute power and the father in relationship to his children.[3] John Locke had to argue against both of these positions in his *Second Treatise on Government*, and he made the case that the parents did not own their children but had natural responsibilities to them.

If we shift now to the perspective of children, most would agree that children owe something back to *good* parents. Whether one likes one's parents' values or not, one realizes that good parents provide the foundation for the child and launch the child into an independent life. That child has obligations to the parent for those contributions, and most children recognize it in one way or another. The child-parent analogy helps us understand and concretize the intergenerational obligation that we have to our collective ancestors. To be sure, the relationship between us and our collective human ancestry is not tangible and immediate in the same way as that between a child and parents. But the nature of the obligation is analogous. We recognize obligations to those who contributed to who we are and our well-being. Our parents have duties to us by bringing us into the world, and we in turn have reciprocal duties if they took their responsibilities seriously. The obligation between us and prior generations is analogous but collective. We stand on the foundation that they built. We owe something to them in return. But since they are no longer living, we owe it to their heirs.

Their heirs, like our brothers and sisters, are relationships we have through shared and common "parents." The relationship of siblings is less direct than that of parent to child. Siblings may be very different from each other, and often the key connection is a shared childhood, memories, or shared parents. We typically recognize obligations to these relations as well, flowing from common experiences and shared parents. Siblings often, though not always, will help siblings in distress. This sense of duty to siblings may extend, though with less intensity, to cousins, other relations, and even close friends.

The point of this discussion is not to say that our obligations to our past and our contemporaries are precisely like those of parent-child or of siblings. They are only metaphors to help us understand how we do recognize certain kinds of obligations that arise out of the past from people who have contributed to our well-being. The relationship to previous generations is more remote and less tangible, to be sure. But the foundation of the responsibility is just as natural and just as important.

To summarize, the sense of obligation to the past and to our common human ancestry is what helps constitute us as human beings, a species that recognizes some sense of duty toward one another. We have duties that arise out of what we have been given. This common platform, the very core of what our humanness is, our knowledge that has been transmitted to us, our ability to think, to reason, to use fire, to symbolize complex thoughts, the invention of engines, computers, and penicillin, these are part of an inheritance that creates obligations in us. Were we not to take on this burden of responsibility and debt to the past, then we should be deprived of the right to use these gifts. With the right comes the responsibility.

The person who takes as much as he or she can without giving back and honoring the debt to the ancestors and their heirs is like a person who has stolen property that does not belong to him or her. We call such a person a thief. We should not give a pass anymore to those who use and do not pay back. The payback is not "charity" at the whim of the person who does well. It is an obligation that arises from standing on the platform that others had built. The payback is required, just as in a bank loan or venture capital investment. Those who think they earned it all by themselves are deceived. We shall have more to say about this notion of property and debt below.

Chapter 4
Why Rights Are
Not Self-Evident

Those who prioritize natural rights over other moral and philosophical considerations do so in part because they believe rights are self-evident and natural. In fact, the notion of natural rights is precarious. By precarious, I mean that the foundation and specificity of natural rights are up for debate and not at all self-evident, contrary to the position seemingly articulated by the Declaration of Independence and the natural rights philosophers who wrote earlier. Since natural rights are up for debate, what our rights are and mean is difficult to specify outside of some political process and some social community with a set of values, aspirations, hopes, and philosophical commitments. To put it more paradoxically, liberty is not a self-evident set of moral commitments that is clear up front, but a process through which we define what our rights are and should mean. Thus liberty is best understood as a particular moral and political philosophical theory about how to distribute power, goods, and resources fairly in a society in which there is no single notion of truth that is commonly accepted.

In turning to the precariousness of natural rights, I want to deepen the critique that has guided us so far. We have already seen that our opponents make several mistakes in how they think about human beings, rights, and liberty. In particular, they overemphasize the importance of rights to the exclusion of other values, and they miss the ways that sacrifice and responsibility should inform how we think about ourselves, our lives in society, and ourselves as part of humanity. At this point, I wish to turn back to the notion of natural rights that has such a grip on our American imagination and show just how ambiguous the notion of natural rights really is and how problematic it is to rest American decision making on rights alone. If what natural rights are and mean is indecisive, then we need to revisit the assumptions about the respective roles of government and individuals, which have been based on rights.

What emerges is a picture of liberty as a process, rather than a set of substantive and clearly defined rights, that attempts to distribute power fairly among a broad range of stakeholders, precisely because there is no agreement on substantive truth commitments. It is in part the lack of agreement on truth or reason that generates the need for a process that distributes power and resources fairly in a society that embraces liberty. Where truth is agreed upon, the problem of distributing rights and resources and power is less problematic, though the interpretation of the truth itself may still be subject to debate. This understanding of liberty turns upside down the traditional relationship of liberty and rights. Instead of liberty meaning something concrete in nature, it comes to take its meaning from within a liberal and social political process that values the fair distribution of power, resources, and access to power. Liberal societies are those that produce liberty due to their vision and self-understanding and because of their desire for some notion of human equality and fairness, which is the source of liberty.[1] It is the fact that the society is liberal and values diversity that it produces rights, rather than that rights produce liberal, diverse societies. Rights emerge through a social, political process that values not only the individual but the fact that humans have many different truth commitments. In this formulation, a particular type of society gives birth to liberty, and not the other way around. Liberty does not exist before or outside of society. Liberty emerges through specific forms of social, political processes and cultural commitments. This insight has important ramifications, since it complicates the traditional understanding of government's role with respect to individual rights.

To understand why this view of liberty and rights makes sense and is compelling, it is worth contrasting it briefly with the alternative view, put forward by many liberty-first advocates and following the mistake of some, though not all, of the early modern rights thinkers. In their view, rights are in nature or God-given, and therefore they exist outside of or before social life. For this reason, rights are "inalienable," meaning people can't sell or give them away. I don't have a right to end my life or sell myself into slavery, though some early moderns thought you could give yourself into slavery under certain conditions. Since these rights precede political societies, people enter society only on the assumption and condition that their lives will be better in society than outside society. If society stripped them of all the rights that they had in nature, they would never join society nor give up their freedom in nature. For this reason, societies and governments cannot legitimately exercise power to take away or curtail individuals' rights, since those rights exist outside of or prior to society.

There are a number of difficulties with this view of the relationship of rights to societies. To begin with, it is impossible to prove that rights exist in nature. We have already seen in fact that there are different justifications of rights (e.g., God gave them to us, reason discerns them, and the social character of human beings makes them self-evident). While debate continues about whether some notion of right and wrong is universally recognized, the fact that we can't agree on the foundation of specific rights or the substance of our rights is really a problem about which few seem willing to talk.

If we cannot agree on how we know that rights exist, how could we possibly agree that we know what our rights are? This question seems so self-evident that it is startling how few people think about it. The reason we tune out this question is because the assertion "we have self-evident rights" is an American tradition that is accepted uncritically. It is accepted like a religious dogma or revelation, without scrutiny. It is evident in the Declaration of Independence, understood to be enshrined in our Constitution and Bill of Rights, and protected by our Supreme Court and the structure of our republican government. But if modernity questioned anything, it made tradition a subject that could and should be thought about criti-cally. The questioning of tradition was at the heart of both the Protestant Reformation as well as the modern Enlightenment's doubt that revelation alone could provide the foundation of all knowledge.[2] This questioning of tradition continued in the founding of America, where the founders prided themselves on their critical thought and engaged the key think-ers and philosophers of their day. They would have been disappointed to know that Americans today accept their ideas uncritically like religious dogmas that cannot be questioned.

Neither God nor Reason as a Foundation of Natural Rights

We have already seen that there was no common agreement among natural rights thinkers about what the foundation of natural rights is or should be. Some argued natural rights flow from reason's discernment of God, the moral Lawmaker. Others argued that rights flow from the social nature of the human being that is grounded ultimately in the desire for self-preservation. All argued that rights could be discerned by reason. This disagreement should be, and in fact became, disturbing for those who wanted to find some grounding for a universal moral law.

After the failure of European Christian communities to come to agreement on what God wanted of Christians, natural rights thinkers intended to find a foundation for rights and morality in the conclusions on which reasonable people could agree. It was a noble vision. They sought to ground human moral life on a human science that would end once and for all the religious debate about the nature of truth and the essence of human character. They ultimately failed. The expectation that the new "natural philosophy" (later to be called "human" or "social" sci-ences) could be as objective as the natural sciences did not materialize. Ask most people who teach humanity and social sciences today. Over the last three centuries since the Enlightenment, sociologists, anthropolo-gists, psychologists, and even economists would all try to create a science of the human that would be as rigorous as the natural sciences and that could discover the underlying laws of human nature. But none has ever come close to the achievements of the natural sciences.[3] The aspiration to identify laws of human behavior has been elusive in the social sciences, and some believe it is even elusive in the natural sciences itself. At least it has been elusive enough to seriously doubt whether laws of morality can ever be produced to everyone's satisfaction.[4]

Even in the seventeenth century, when the modern notion of natural rights was developed, it became increasingly obvious that reason might fail to provide a universal foundation for rights. Ironically, the problem was that reason turned out to have some of the same problems as religion and revelation. Reasonable people could and did come to different conclusions. Not all reasonable people could agree on the foundation of natural rights (e.g., there is a God versus there is a social inclination) nor on the particular boundaries of those rights. They disagreed, for example, on whether reason led to the conclusion that the sovereign should have supreme power or whether property was a natural right. They disagreed also on whether one could invade and conquer another country that was not observing the laws of nature. These debates foreshadowed the similar situation in which we find ourselves. The fact that reason cannot solve the problem of contested moral ideas is still evident today when we debate continuously whether we have rights to guns, abortion, gay marriage, euthanasia, health care, free markets, and so on. Both sides of the discussion see themselves as reasonable in their conclusions. Both sides think they are defending our natural or self-evident rights. The language of rights is in fact used to defend opposing opinions. One obvious example is abortion, where the rights of the unborn entity are opposed to the rights of the mother to choose. Rights can be used to defend both positions. The same can be said for the debate over gun control. On the one side, those who want to carry firearms argue they have a right to bear arms. Those opposed can argue that the restrictions on guns are part of a right to protect life.

Even Reasonable People Disagree

The problem with the self-evidence of natural rights is everywhere around us and always has been. If we had self-evident rights, then reasonable people would agree. Unless we declare everyone who disagrees with us incompetent, intellectually lazy, or stupid, then we have to come to the conclusion that even reasonable people disagree on what's reasonable.[5]

Many of our contemporary debates about rights are in fact an attempt to define precisely what liberty means. We may agree with the abstraction that "we have rights." But our sense that rights are "self-evident" is typically achieved only when the idea of rights is stated so abstractly that the detail of what the right actually protects does not get in the way of agreement. As soon as we try to put specificity on a right, agreement often dissolves. This character of our rights language is analogous to us saying we all "love America," even though we have very different concepts of what America is. Or when people say "I believe in God," some think of God as a personal being, while others think of God as the nonpersonal laws of the universe. The concept of liberty has a similar feel to it. Agreement with an abstraction covers disagreement at a more fundamental level. This point is important as we think about how liberty should work in a liberal society.

Recent debates over whether one has a right to bear arms, a right to same-sex marriage, a right to die, a right to end one's life, a right to abortion, a right to polygamy, all point to the way in which the bucket of rights has quite a bit of elasticity that can expand or contract depending on how one views rights in general and the rights to life, liberty, and property in particular. Almost anything we cherish can be defined as a right. What constituted debated rights in the past was different from what constitutes the subject of rights debates today. And we can be assured that what constitutes the focus of rights will shift again in another fifty years. Those debates may be about who can have water and at what cost or whether we have the right to have as many children as we wish because we lack sufficient resources for the human population. We cannot foresee the circumstances in which people live, and therefore we cannot say precisely and with certitude what rights will matter. And even if we could agree on what the core natural rights are, what they mean in specificity would itself be a matter of debate.

Modern natural rights thinkers did attempt to draw a distinction between "natural rights," which were from nature or God, and "civil rights" (or the "law of nations"), which were created by specific sociopolitical institutions and were granted by particular societies for individuals. Natural rights were thought to be universally discernible, while civil rights were specific laws or protections offered by specific societies.

This distinction between natural and civil rights is all but forgotten today as people argue over their rights in general. In part, this is because it is very difficult to say what right falls into the bucket of "natural rights" and what falls into the bucket of "civil rights." Take the rights enumerated in the Bill of Rights, the first ten amendments to the Constitution of the United States. Are they natural or civil rights?

Is the right to a free press a natural right or a civil right? Could it be a natural right when the press doesn't exist in nature? Or is the right to a free press an extension of a natural right to speak one's mind in nature? And is that right of speech just an extension of the right to liberty itself? Who decides what a valid extension of a right in nature is? And is an extension of a right in nature a natural right or a civil right?

What about the right to bear arms? Could there be such a right in nature when arms had not yet been manufactured? Does the right to bear arms not already suppose the existence of arms that one can have a right to bear? And does not the manufacture of arms imply the existence of human communities that invented them? In what sense, then, can the right to bear arms be a natural right that precedes social life? Or rather, is the right to bear arms just an extension of the right to protect myself by any means, which is an extension of my core natural right to life? But again, what is a valid extension of my right to life, and who gets to decide? Is it clear that my right to life can be extended to guns that are invented by humans? And if guns, why not a right to own a tank or bear nuclear weapons?[6] Where and how do we draw the lines? Does nature tell us where those lines are, or are those civil lines we draw, and who gets to set them? If it is society that draws the line between natural and civil rights, how can anyone claim they have natural rights as if those rights do not emerge from a social decision?

Do we have a right in nature to same-sex marriage? Is there even a notion of "marriage" in nature, or is the very concept of "marriage" not already a religious and cultural conception imposed on a type of relationship that also contains sexuality? In nature, is "copulation" the same as "marriage"? Is there marriage in nature at all? When animals reproduce, are they married? And since many animals do not pair with partners for life or even for more than a mating season, in what sense can marriage be natural? What implications do we draw from animal species that exhibit homoeroticism and polymorphous sexuality? Surely marriage is a concept that carries certain religious and cultural assumptions that arise from human communities and certain understandings of men, women, God, the sacred, and so forth. In what sense, then, can marriage be a natural right? And if it is instead a "civil" institution, then the specific society has in its purview the right to define it as it pleases, including the right to eliminate the institution of marriage completely if it wishes. Marriage itself is a human institution, so how can there be a natural right to it for anyone, including heterosexuals? Isn't marriage then by definition a civil right? And thus isn't the debate over gay marriage really just a debate about what we in this society want to include in the category of marriage? Do we not have instances of cultures in which polygamy seems to be accepted as the norm, including the culture of the biblical Israelites?[7] And isn't the very concept of marriage already a human construction and symbolization of a certain kind of relationship? The answer has nothing to do with nature but has everything to do with our values: our ideas about God and privacy and what love and sexuality are.

The point that I am making is that there is little clarity about which rights are natural and which rights are derived from society. This is because all rights are in fact civil rights, for they are the rights that society picks out to affirm as most important. It is society that arrives at a notion of what's natural based on a set of convictions and propositions about what it means to be human and what it means to be a member of that society. Each society has convictions that it develops about how what it sees as core rights should be implemented and extended for its particular social setting and moral commitments. Of course, these decisions may represent compromises between competing views if the society does not impose one set of convictions on everyone.

What about the very right to life itself and the inclination to self-preservation, which is what many early moderns defined as the primary natural right? It is arguable that this right is the very foundation of all the other rights, since even the rights to liberty and to property are interpreted as extensions of the right to life itself. Isn't the right to life a clear and self-evident natural right? Natural right advocates say yes, though they arrive at that conclusion through various routes. Some see the instinct to self-preservation as inherent in nature and in human beings.[8] Others have argued that life is sacred since it is given by God. In the classic formulation by Locke, we have a right to life because we are God's workmanship. Since we are each God's property, no one has a right to hurt us. Perhaps the different ways of arriving at the right to life do not matter, and the conviction that there is a right to life is more basic than its justification. But even with the right to life, we see varying interpretations of what it means and how it should be implemented.

For example, is the right to life unqualified? If so, then there should be no capital punishment. The fact that some societies practice capital punishment shows that there is a view that certain human behaviors justify the extinguishment of an individual's right of life. Even the classic natural rights thinkers argued that one could take life under certain conditions, such as the life of a murderer—or even when a thief enters one's house at night.[9] They argued that anything that borders on a threat to one's own life can be met with the right to take the life of another. But what borders on a threat to my life and what kind of crime might be so egregious that the criminal's life should be taken are both difficult questions that depend on other values and assumptions.

A similar issue arises in discussions of war. Pacifists argue that there is no condition under which it is right to take a life. By contrast, the "just war" tradition assumes that there are conditions in which it is justified to go to war and take a life. Those who embrace this tradition argue that states and nations are in a state of nature with respect to each other and can go to war under certain just conditions.[10] However, as we might expect there are disagreements over what constitutes "just causes" too. Some viewed the violation of Christianity as a cause of just war; others the violation of the laws of nature.[11]

The debate over abortion is also at least in part a debate over the definition of life and when life begins. Since the beginning of life is itself dependent on religious conceptions of what life is and when it starts, the debate over abortion is a debate about what life itself means. And the argument over whether people should have a right to end their lives or to practice euthanasia is a debate about whether the right to life belongs to a person him- or herself or is sacred and belongs to God. Who is going to adjudicate whether life is our own or belongs to God in a society where not everyone believes in God? And who is going to be the authoritative interpreter of God's wishes anyway in a society with various religions that understand God differently? Who decides when my God says something different to me than your God says to you? If one looks beyond our own modern culture, there are societies that seem to have very different convictions about life. In some, there is evidence that cannibalism or human sacrifice may at times have been practiced. And so the conviction that life is sacred and what that means seems to a certain extent to be culturally dependent. Whether these practices or positions are morally justifiable or defensible is complicated. Each side can tell its own reasonable story about the positions it holds. And even the most seemingly savage practices of other cultures look reasonable to those societies, and a lot more reasonable to us, when ethnologists, anthropologists, and scholars of religion understand other cultures from the inside out. Indeed, the whole history of modern anthropology and ethnography since the late nineteenth century has been to debunk the sharp dichotomies we in the West have had between "savage" and "advanced" cultures.[12]

What we realize, when we dig beneath the high-level claim that "we must protect our rights," is that it is indeed murky what the source of those rights is, what is included in them, and what they specifically mean. Even if some of us are sure we know what our rights are and what they mean, not all of us agree. And therefore any attempt to say what our rights are and mean is to impose a perspective on a group who may have different conceptions. One could try to argue that it doesn't matter what people think, because a particular notion of natural rights is either authorized by God or inscribed by the founders in the Declaration of Independence or the US Constitution. But none of those arguments suffices to quell the ambiguity inherent in natural rights, for at issue is precisely the question of who gets to say what God or the founders meant. The attempt to discern a clear intention in scripture for understanding God's intent or in the Declaration of Independence and the US Constitution raises the same problem. Not everyone reads these documents the same way. The original intent in scripture or among the American founders is debated by different groups, be they religious authorities, historians, or Supreme Court justices. Even historians cannot come to a consensus on a single account of what happened or what a particular document means.[13] If that is so, then an account of liberty must take account of the divergent views not just about religion and God, but about what truth and morals are and, by extension, even what rights are.

All of this is to say that those who appeal to natural rights oversimplify an immense problem when they try to settle the question of government's limits and our rights. The matter is not so simple or clear-cut, because as human beings we have divergent views of morals. So how do we constitute a society when people differ not only in religion, but in their moral convictions and their conceptions of rights?

•   •   •

The early modern natural rights philosophers did not quite see the full implications of reason's failure to provide a self-evident foundation for morality, though glimmers of the problem had started to appear. They were already fully aware of a diverse range of religious and moral views and practices among the world's peoples. Most acknowledged a difference between inconsequential cultural variations, which some called "positive law," "the law of nations," or "civil law," and a universal moral law that they called the "law of nature."[14] It was recognized that each nation had its own tastes and ideas and that cultures differed from one another. What one group liked to eat or the accepted rules of behavior could vary across societies, and many of those differences were perceived to be insignificant cultural variations or matters of taste. But natural rights thinkers argued that the moral law was not a matter of taste, and some expected that reason would and should have led everyone to the same moral conclusions. The fact that there were variations even in what appeared to be core moral principles was a problem that had to be explained. As Locke posed the problem, "If indeed natural law were discernible by the light of reason, why is it that not all people who possess reason have knowledge of it?"[15] There was in fact no easy or compelling answer to this question, because the question itself had a flawed assumption: that all people using reason always arrive at the same conclusions.

The answer the natural rights thinkers gave was ultimately unsatisfactory. They concluded that human diversity on moral matters, religious beliefs, and practices was due to the fact that some individuals and even whole nations had not yet opened themselves up to the light of reason and thus had not embraced the laws of nature.[16] If only people could be shown reason through education (or in some cases forced to see reason), they too would come to the same conclusions about morality, God, religion, and natural rights. The encounter with native peoples with wildly different lifestyles, moralities, and religions posed a devastating and ultimately unanswerable challenge to this natural rights perspective. The divergence about what people thought was reasonable was as problematic as the earlier debates about what God wanted.

One important early modern natural rights thinker, Thomas Hobbes, concluded that reason could not be relied upon to bring people to agreement on all moral and religious matters, with the consequence that human beings are always in danger of dropping back into a state of war. To address the insecurity of reason, this thinker proposed that there must be an all-powerful body or sovereign in society that could resolve disputes and determine the religious beliefs of society.[17] Since reason could not bring people to agreement on fractious issues, there must be a single power in society that imposed an answer. One of the great ironies of the modern period is that one of the most important early modern natural rights thinkers who shaped our language and ideas about natural rights endorsed the need for some social body or person to have absolute power in society to dictate laws, values, and even religion.[18] He concluded that only by giving a sovereign power absolute control was it possible to solve the problem that *neither religion nor reason* could lead people to agreement.[19] This absolutist notion of government was ultimately rejected in the natural rights tradition of the seventeenth century. Yet the fact that such a position was held by one prominent natural rights thinker shows that the very notion of natural rights does not lead to just one particular conception of government. *The very meaning of natural rights itself is part of what we debate as part of a liberal society.*

Even John Locke, the recognized father of the liberal modern natural rights conceptions, may have harbored his own doubts about the ability of reason to lead us to a common moral law. Locke's doubts would not matter were his writings not such a strong foundation for the American view of rights. Some political philosophers today see such a strong link between Locke and the American founders that they even want to use Locke's positions as the framework by which we eliminate debate about the meaning of our own constitution.[20] For those interested in the history of ideas and the possible roots of American philosophy, stay with me in the paragraphs that follow as we take a more detailed look at possible doubts about reason that may even be visible in Locke's writings.

• • •

In Locke's famous *Second Treatise on Government*, in which he is credited with setting out his core philosophy of government and rights, and one to which liberty-first advocates often appeal, Locke assumes that the idea of natural law is universal and evident from reason's ability to discern a Creator God. As a younger man some years before, Locke had written a series of essays explaining the foundation of natural law.[21] But in his *Second Treatise*, Locke never defends the existence of natural law or God, the moral Lawmaker, which sits as a foundation for his argument for natural rights. Though Locke relies extensively on the concept of natural law in this treatise on government to derive rights and conclusions about proper political arrangements, he notes that "it would be besides my present purpose, to enter here into the particulars of the Law of Nature."[22] The existence of a natural law was an assumption seemingly taken for granted in this influential work of political philosophy but never explicitly defended. The lack of any justification of natural law in the *Second Treatise* raises an interesting question that hovers in the background for anyone attempting to understand Locke or to build a political philosophy of right that rests on both Lockean ideas and those of the American founders. Why did Locke not elaborate his ideas about natural law in his treatises on government or come back to develop them later in his life? Did Locke realize that his early arguments for natural law were problematic in some way, or did he think natural law had already been proven?

A similar question arises from the missing justification of natural law in Locke's *An Essay Concerning Human Understanding*, Locke's majestic and influential work, which is ultimately a search for the very foundation of knowledge and led both contemporaneous friends and critics of Locke to press him for an updated justification of natural law.[23] The missing argument about natural law raises an interesting and interpretive problem in understanding Locke but also for any theory of rights that tries to depend on a Lockean approach. Some interpreters assume Locke simply took for granted the views of his earlier essays on natural law, written as a younger man, and felt no need in the later discussion of government to repeat arguments about natural law and God's existence that he had made earlier and that had been developed by other writers who had published since his essays.[24]

Yet this answer may be too simple. The ambiguity in Locke's position is compounded when Locke examines the foundation of human knowledge. Locke tells the story that he wrote the *Essay* in response to a discussion with friends about the foundation for morality and possibly natural law. While Locke's *Essay* was a revolutionary perspective on the way the mind and reason construct knowledge from the senses, it is clear Locke himself felt he fell short of the goal of finding the foundation for morality. In the *Essay*, reason's capabilities appear much more tentative than they do in his earlier essays on natural law when he was a younger man, even though the later work starts with assumptions and language from the former. In the later, more mature context, Locke is more skeptical, describing the mind as an active agent that uses reason to construct the very notions of time, space, duration, weight, identity, mass, and infinity with which it engages the world. These are not innate ideas but frameworks through which the mind engages the world. The mind is thus active in producing the framework of knowledge that we humans have, down to the very bedrock of our foundational conceptions of time, space, weight, solidity, etc.

After spending six hundred pages showing how limited human knowledge is and how active the mind is in interpreting input from the senses, Locke reaffirms his claims that reason can also arrive at a notion of a God whose existence is presupposed repeatedly throughout the work. Locke demonstrates knowledge of God, however, in what is a strikingly short and unsatisfying chapter for a thinker who has thought so deeply about how we come to know what we know.[25] Perhaps Locke was simply assuming the proofs of God's existence were already demonstrated and the foundation of those conclusions didn't need to be reexamined. Whether intentionally or not, Locke's work on the constructed nature of human knowledge ultimately throws doubt on his own conclusion that God and morality could be discerned by reason.[26]

Indeed, a reader of Locke's *Essay* can't help but wonder whether Locke himself had doubts about whether God was as "unreal" or as "constructed" as space, time, and duration, other concepts needed and produced by the human mind. Even the idea of infinity, which is really required to come to the idea of God, is acknowledged by Locke to be itself constructed by the mind as an extrapolation from concepts of space and duration. Locke's reassurances to the contrary seem hollow, as when he writes the following about the impossibility of having certainty about spiritual beings such as angels: "Angels of all sorts are naturally beyond our discovery;... the knowledge of his own mind cannot suffer a man that considers to be ignorant that there is a God. But that there are degrees of spiritual beings between us and the great God, who is there, that, by his own search and ability, can come to know?"[27] It is understandable that some of his earliest critics and religious contemporaries (such as the Bishop of Worcester) thought Locke's understanding of reason and knowledge undermined traditional Christian faith and had led to a slippery slope to atheism.[28]

In any case, Locke reasserts his claim that the mind has enough knowledge to discern God. He writes that "How short soever their knowledge may come of a universal or perfect comprehension of whatsoever is, it yet secures their great concernments that they have light enough to lead them to the knowledge of their Maker, and the sight of their duties."[29] Toward the very end of his extremely long treatise, he repeats in a very short and, by the standards of the rest of his book, an unsatisfyingly shallow argument that the mind can discern a Creator God.[30]

In the context of this lengthy treatise on what the human mind can and cannot know for certain, a treatise that demolishes the notions of innate ideas, including the innate idea of God, and that reveals an active mind that constitutes what it experiences as much as it receives from the outside world, one wonders how genuine Locke is when he makes the traditional argument for the discernment of the Creator. Is it really possible that the same thinker who spends upward of six hundred printed pages discussing how the mind comes up with the ideas of space, mass, time, substance, duration, and even infinity, would feel content with only nine pages on how the mind arrives at the idea of God, the timeless and boundless Creator? Perhaps. Perhaps Locke had not taken the final step and turned his own critical thinking toward the foundational religious assumptions on which he grounded morality. And that is an understanding of Locke that many of his interpreters assume.[31] Yet Locke's reticence on the question of God and the origin of the natural law looks suspicious, and one can give many historical reasons why Locke would have been reluctant to draw out the more radical implications of his own thinking on the idea of God and be subject to the charge of "Hobbism," which was how atheism was described in his day. In fact, Locke's *Essay* never delivers on its purported purpose of finding the ground of the moral law and of ethical conduct. Locke thus fails to achieve what he set out to do. He leaves no solid foundation for the natural law, which itself provides the foundation for his view of individual rights, which are, according to Locke, the basis of government. It seems that subsequently Locke may have written his work *The Reasonableness of Christianity* in part as an attempt to sort out some of these problems left unresolved by his theory of knowledge in the *Essay*.[32]

We may never know whether Locke came to doubt his argument that reason could lead us to a moral law, though some interpreters, myself included, believe he was aware of this failure.[33] In the end, it doesn't matter. Within thirty years, others had come to have such doubts. Indeed, within his lifetime, deists such as John Toland, Anthony Collins, Matthew Tindal, among others, were already picking up on the tensions between reason and revelation and leveraging reason to call into question whether major sections of revelation were really not from God at all.[34] Whether or not Locke reached that point on his own, his work certainly accelerated the tensions between revelation and reason. Furthermore, the realization that reason alone could not solve the ambiguities about morality came to be defined as one of the failures of the Enlightenment itself. In this way, the problems that the century started with, namely, how to arrive at a moral law when revelation's meaning is disputed and when there is such human variability in thinking and practice, had been shifted in the century that followed to reason itself. Reason would crumble as an identified source of common agreement.

By the middle of the eighteenth century, the very notion of natural rights could be dismissed by philosophical thinkers as the fiction of a political party. The great philosopher David Hume, for example, argued that the notion of natural rights and "social contract" is as much a fabric of speculative principles to justify a political party as the view that God authorized divine rule and monarchy.[35] Doubts about natural rights made their way into the founding of America, caused the American founders to hesitate to initially rely on natural rights arguments in the period leading up to the Revolution, and may have influenced Jefferson himself, though these misgivings were forgotten once they were enshrined in the Declaration of Independence.[36] By the middle of the nineteenth century, the very notion of natural rights had appeared to the utilitarian philosopher Jeremy Bentham as "simple nonsense: natural and imprescriptible rights, rhetorical nonsense—nonsense upon stilts," and philosophic doubts about the validity of the concept have persisted among philosophers since that time, leading many to prefer a utilitarian approach to morality and ethics.[37]

When Reasonable People Disagree

To step back for a moment, the larger problem before us is this: How do we create a society if both reasonable and religious people cannot achieve agreements on even basic principles? Perhaps religious people are right that there is a Creator God and that God has certain expectations of us as human beings. If there is a God who actively cares about the world, then it would seem reasonable to assume that such a God had ideas about how we should live. Christians, Jews, and Muslims, among other religions, certainly think so. But the problem is that not everyone agrees with them, either on the fact that there is a God or what that God wants of us. Even those in the same religion do not agree among themselves, as was already apparent in the seventeenth century. Catholics, Protestants, Lutherans, Evangelicals, and Mormons cannot agree on what God expects of society, not to mention the disagreements among Jews, Muslims, Buddhists, and other non-Western religions. The same problem of diversity in religious beliefs and in what counts as reasonable has not gone away by the appeal to natural rights. The toleration for religious differences that began to emerge in the seventeenth century and was ultimately embraced by the American founders through the work of Adams, Jefferson, and Madison, among others, recognized that political institutions should not try to resolve the disagreements about religious truth. That should be left to the afterlife for God to resolve.

What the early modern natural rights philosophers did not see quite as clearly is that the very same problem is present in trying to found both moral law and natural rights on reason. Not all reasonable people come to the same reasonable conclusions. And while some reasonable people might be right and others wrong, who gets to define what is reasonable in the first place?[38] People who think they are right feel they should be the ones to decide. This ambiguity in what is reasonable itself turns out to be a core issue that any theory of liberty must solve. Hence, the question before us is, what are we to do when there are conflicting views of what is reasonable? Should we have a separation not only of church and state, but a "separation of reason and state" as well? If we separate reason and state, then how do we come to any decisions about what our founding principles are or imply? Are we left with mere consensus or rule by a supermajority and no other foundation? From where should we derive the moral limits on the acts of the majority if there is no law of nature to which we can appeal?

The problem for the advocate of liberty is not, then, the problem of relativism (i.e., "there is no truth"), but the problem of diversity ("people have different views of truth"). If we all agree that reasonable people can disagree, the question becomes: How can we live together given that we do not agree on whether there is a God, what that God wants, or what counts as reasonable? Human beings will not come to agreement on the nature of the human being, God, or the absolute, nor the correct moral law. Ironically, the believer in God, the advocate of reason, and the relativist all end up with the same problem on their hands when it comes to living together. They can either impose their standards on others through the use of power or persuasion or seek some other mechanism for resolving differences of opinion about what the founding principles are or should be. We could, as one natural rights thinker urged, opt for an all-powerful sovereign body in society to end the debate, or we could revert to a monarch who simply dictates what is right and wrong. Sometimes, in our current messy and broken political processes, those options look good. But we tried those approaches in the past, and the sacrifices they entailed seem too big.

So what do we do? This ultimately is the big question before us. One conclusion is clear. Our opponents have stripped the discussion of rights of all its complexity. They have oversimplified the question. They have assumed that the foundation of rights and the meaning of rights are transparent and self-evident. They are not. That was a mistake of Locke and other seventeenth-century natural rights thinkers who thought natural rights were self-evident. The American founders had already begun to realize that natural rights were not self-evident.[39] But the language of natural rights made it into the Declaration of Independence and has therefore been celebrated as the core principle of our nation. When liberty-first advocates argue that their view of rights is the only view of rights, they are wrong. There are many ways to think about rights, and by extension God, the nature of the human being, and our moral responsibilities. Which view of rights should guide us depends ultimately not on the notion of rights per se, but on the frameworks and values by which we implement rights.

The question at hand, then, is, how is it best to construct and run a society when the very fundamental assertions of what is right and wrong are contested? This question, it seems to me, takes us to the heart of the matter. This is a question that I believe the original natural rights thinkers were ultimately trying to answer. They thought reason could provide the answer, though some of them had already begun to realize that reason might not provide an adequate foundation. The disagreements that fragment democracies are between people who all believe they are rational and reasonable men and women. The hope for some rational standard on which we could all agree has proven impossible. Therefore, we have to rethink how we understand the purpose of government and individuals in societies where rights are made, not found, and where there is no agreement on truth or morals. It is to this answer that I now turn.

Chapter 5
We Hold Equality to Be Self-Evident

If the concept of natural rights provides an ambiguous foundation from which to guide society, then from what moral foundation should we begin? Is it not the case that any starting point for our moral convictions is inevitably and ultimately contestable? Isn't it true that there is no way to find a starting point for the creation of society or a political system that is not ultimately doubted by some individuals or groups? Yes. All of this is true. And that is the point.

If society can never achieve 100 percent unanimity on what its core and founding convictions are, then every society is invariably imposing some founding framework or vision on minorities who don't agree. To find this repression at the heart of any democratic institution is a startling insight when one thinks about it. It means that by nature, any society with a rule of law has an act of repression against some minorities who don't agree with the majorities on either the vision of truth or the specific laws. Of course, compared to systems that lodged absolute power in the divine royal right, a reliance on a majority or supermajority rule gives a much greater number of people much more say, at least theoretically, over the institutions in which they live. Still, it is important to realize that on every issue and law, some minority of people will not agree, though the nature of the repressed minority may vary depending on the particular issue and the law. The repressed minority may be people of a certain gender, color, religion, or class. But anyone with a divergent view from the majority is in a way a repressed minority, though many repressed minorities we don't find morally significant; for example, those who want to drive a tank or drive faster than sixty miles an hour could be a repressed minority too.[1] Thus we are always drawing lines in our laws between those minorities whose interests we ignore and those whose interests we want to protect. The key point is that any point of view that is institutionalized with power represents an act of repression on some minority who doesn't agree.

Let's face it. There is only one truth upon which we can all agree: to argue and disagree is part of the nature of the human being. To live together in societies requires that we don't all agree and that some people's views come to win over other people's views. It is this willingness in fact to "win some and lose some" that comes to characterize life in democratic societies. At stake first, then, is the question of which founding principles and vision should frame the to-and-fro of social life and how the assumptions that define our collective life should change and evolve. Second, we must consider whether there are cases in which the rule by majority or supermajority is not acceptable and situations in which certain kinds of minorities should be protected. By what criteria do we distinguish those moral situations in which majorities should not be allowed to repress minorities from those in which they may?

Even in the founding of America, which is one of the clearest examples of a country founded on a social contract, there was still fundamental debate and disagreement on many key principles. The Declaration of Independence, the document that now enshrines the American collective philosophy and vision, actually papers over differences and doubts about the source and validity of natural rights as well as the legitimate right of Americans to the lands they possessed.[2] The same is true of the US Constitution, which was drafted in secret over a period of four months in 1787 by a group of delegates sent from the various states to ponder the weaknesses of the then existing Articles of Confederation. Their discussion was fraught with debate over how government should be structured and where and how power was to be lodged and balanced, especially between the states and the national government, but also across economic lines, among states of different sizes, and between those with agricultural versus commercial interests. If rights were transparent and clear, there would have been no need for debate. In the end, nearly every delegate had compromised on some strongly held position, and not all the delegates to the convention were willing to sign and endorse the final compromise, including noteworthy individuals such as George Mason, Edmund Randolph of Virginia, and Elbridge Gerry of Massachusetts.[3] The subsequent ratification of the Constitution was itself hotly contested in the states, anticipating the emerging development of the Republican and Federalist political parties, which held fundamentally differing views of federal and state power, liberty, international relations, and a host of other substantive positions.[4] The Constitution was hardly a document that achieved unanimous assent or had a single meaning, even from the start.[5] And as soon as the Constitution was ratified, Federalist and Republican parties emerged that debated its very meaning, a debate that obviously continues today.

The claim among some that we need to revert to the "lost constitution" is thus sheer nonsense, since there was never a single understanding of what the original constitution meant.[6] So even in the formation of the United States, there were winners and losers in the formation of the founding document and in its interpretation. The notion that there was a single, clear, univocal meaning of the founding principles of American life is wrong.[7] The same is true of the Declaration, which had multiple different ways of being understood, even shortly after it was written.[8] This problem, incidentally, is the identical one that affects any literary interpretation and also the interpretation of religious scriptures. The original meaning is and always will be contested.[9] The very history of the Supreme Court shows that even the body that determines what the Constitution means can change its mind over time in response to the history of its own traditions, new situations, and new circumstances.

Since there is never unanimity on founding principles or what principles of truth mean without an authorized interpretive body, the question is how it is best for humans to organize themselves. The philosophy of natural rights is one way in which modern societies have created a foundation and framework in which to talk about roles and responsibilities when breaking free from the absolute power of monarchies and the Catholic Church and other religious authorities. However, we have seen some of the pitfalls of relying on natural rights. I have already argued that if we do insist on staying with the language of natural rights, we should at least shift our language to include natural responsibilities. There is no reason that we don't see responsibilities as being as much a part of nature as we do rights. But I wish to now go further and argue that a better language or conceptual framework than "rights" for organizing modern political societies would be the language of "equality."

It is ironic to position the concept of equality as distinct from the notion of natural rights. In many ways, the emphasis on equality has always been at the heart of the modern natural rights tradition and is arguably part, if not the core, of its very foundation. The notion of human equality was not new or exclusive to the modern natural rights tradition.[10] But the modern natural rights thinkers put natural equality front and center in their thinking about rights, and the question of equality was at the heart of the seventeenth-century debate about the power of the sovereign and the nature of rights.

In doing so, the early moderns consciously differentiated themselves from the position of Aristotle, who had assumed that people were born to certain natural roles, such as slaves and masters, leaders and followers. Aristotle's writings and philosophy had been rediscovered in Europe from the middle of the twelfth to the middle of the thirteenth century, when translations of his works from Greek and Arabic into Latin made them important to medieval philosophy. While at first they were censored by the leaders of the Catholic Church as ideas that seemed at odds with Christian thought, Thomas Aquinas was able to show an alignment and thus reconciliation of Aristotelian and Christian thought, thus providing a foundation for modern philosophy. In this way, Aristotle's views, as accommodated to Catholic teachings, become important in early modern thought. The idea of a natural hierarchy in nature had been embraced by some but not all of the defenders of royalism in the seventeenth century, leading to a debate about what nature and God had intended in human creation. Aristotle's position was still sufficiently credible in the early modern period, for example, to help justify the enslavement of the native populations of Latin and South America in the Spanish conquest of South America.[11] Aristotle's position was also credible and persuasive to many defenders of royal prerogative. Edward Hyde, 1st Earl of Clarendon, for example, chided Hobbes for rejecting Aristotle's position of natural inequality.[12] Similarly, Sir Robert Filmer, the author of *Patriarcha*, saw the claim of natural equality as a pernicious and threatening doctrine and attacked it in his defense of natural hierarchy and the divine right of kings. Even some of the natural rights thinkers, such as Samuel Pufendorf, who thought humans were created free and equal in nature, still concluded that individuals could be enslaved after a conquest or could sell themselves into slavery if they so chose. Others, such as Hobbes, thought humans were created equal, but still concluded that there was a need for an absolutist sovereign. In the early modern period there was not agreement on whether humans were by nature equal and, if they were, what the implications of that original equality were.

By 1776, when Thomas Jefferson first wrote, "We hold these truths to be self-evident that all men are created equal" in the Declaration of Independence, there was already a two-hundred-year modern tradition of thought about what equality meant and what it implied for social and political life. It was still not clear in the colonies, however, whether equality should include "negroes," who were enslaved in many of the Southern colonies and played a fundamental role in those economies. The issue was so divisive in the colonies that the subject was stricken by Congress from Jefferson's first draft of the Declaration of Independence when Jefferson tried to blame King George III for preventing the colonies from ending slave trade, a dubious claim on Jefferson's part.[13] The issue was taken up once again a decade later in the 1787 Constitutional Convention, when representatives were trying to draft a constitution for the United States. Other points of disagreement among the states included the question of slavery. Southern states were fearful that Northern states would have enough power in the federal government to take away their right to own slaves. One compromise achieved at the convention, among many others, was the agreement to leave the status quo in place and not tackle the slavery question again until 1808. Instead, slaves would count as three-fifths of a person for the purposes of reckoning proportional representation in the House of Representatives.[14] This was a compromise between the position of those in Northern states who thought slavery was an immoral institution and violated natural rights and the views of those in Southern states who thought the new national government should have no power to interfere in states' business and that slavery was key to their economy. At one point in the debate, Gouverneur Morris from Philadelphia would point to the contradiction in the compromise of the convention and say, "Upon what principle is it that the slaves shall be computed in the representation? Are they men? Then make them Citizens and let them vote. Are they property? Why then is no other property included [in calculating proportional representation]?"[15] Agreeing to take the slavery question off the table had been one of the key compromises at the Constitutional Convention, and thus the liberty of Africans was sacrificed for the sake of the union of the states. Without that compromise, the United States would likely not have come into existence, at least at that moment in time.

Indeed, from one perspective, what we have been doing in the modern period is trying to work out both the implications and complications of that founding assumption of human equality.[16] I call it a founding assumption or point of departure because the equality of human beings is not something that can be proved or is transparent in nature, contrary to what the modern natural rights theorists sometimes seemed to imply. On the contrary, various kinds of natural differences are evident between human beings. They differ in physique, intelligence, artistic talents, and so forth. The claim that humans are equal, therefore, represents a claim that many of the differences that exist in nature are trivial or insignificant *with respect to some other more important standard.* Thus, the claim that there is equality in human beings must be a way of looking at the world that depends on a value judgment about what matters. Humans are equal to each other with respect to some other value that transcends the differences that are evident among them. That equality of humans is a founding assumption or starting point for political philosophy and not a fact of nature may indeed be reflected in Jefferson's language that "We *hold* these truths to be self-evident," indicating recognition that these truths are *not* in fact self-evident, but something we *hold* to be true. Indeed there were already doubts in the American founding that rights were natural, a point that I have written about in great detail in another context.[17]

Jefferson was familiar with and standing in a tradition that had its modern articulation in the seventeenth century. To situate Jefferson and thus the American proposition on equality in the modern discussion, it is useful to look at two important but very different modern expositions of equality in the prior century and see how the concept is justified and worked out.

The two positions on equality that I want to contrast differ from each other in a number of ways. The first comes from Thomas Hobbes (1588–1679), a philosopher who lived most of his life in the first half of the seventeenth century; the second from John Locke (1632–1724), a philosopher who lived most of his life in the second half of the same century. The earlier philosopher lived through the English Civil Wars and the beheading of King Charles I. The latter philosopher was born after the restoration of King Charles II to the throne and lived to see the abdication of King James II in what some have called the "Glorious Revolution" and the signing of the English Bill of Rights, a document that is a predecessor of the American Declaration of Independence and the American Bill of Rights. These are key events in British history, of equal weight in British consciousness to the American emphasis on the Stamp Act, Boston Tea Party, and Declaration of Independence. To most Americans, however, they are relatively unknown, though they were prominent events of significance to the American founders, who still saw themselves as "British Americans." One of these philosophers locates the origin of equality in the divine creation of human beings; the other derives equality from the nature of human mortality, perceptions, and fears. One starts from human equality and ironically ends up justifying the absolutism of the sovereign; the other starts with equality and envisions a society governed by the majority. In one, human equality is the catalyst or driver for the creation of a political commonwealth and the limitation on rights. In the other, equality is the basis for rights that exist in nature. In both, equality plays a critical role in defining how power and resources should be allocated among human beings. Let us now turn to these positions.

Although his political philosophy ultimately ended in absolutism, Thomas Hobbes is often thought of as the greatest philosopher of the seventeenth century, and his philosophy fundamentally shaped the discussion throughout the century.[18] Hobbes framed a conception of human equality in nature that resonated throughout the century and ultimately culminated in the more familiar formulations of John Locke, who in turn influenced the American founders. In *Leviathan*, published in 1651, Hobbes started his discussion on rights by assuming an equality of human beings in nature.[19] He wrote that:

> NATURE hath made men so equall, in the faculties of body, and mind; as that though there bee found one man sometimes manifestly stronger in body, or of quicker mind than another; yet when all is reckoned together, the difference between man, and man, is not so considerable, as that one man can thereupon claim to himselfe any benefit, to which another may not pretend, as well as he. For as to the strength of body, the weakest has strength enough to kill the strongest, either by secret machination, or by confederacy with others, that are in the same danger with himselfe.[20]

It is ironic and surprising that the philosopher, who ultimately argued for the absolutism of the sovereign, begins his argument with human equality in nature. This use of equality by Hobbes has surprised scholars, leading to a debate over whether he really believed in human equality or was using the concept as a pragmatic idea he felt necessary for peace.[21] And yet in doing so, Hobbes made human equality the center of his political philosophy and thereby influenced the agenda for the discussion throughout the seventeenth century and ultimately into the founding of America.

It is important to realize that Hobbes is *not* arguing that people in nature are actually equal in all ways. In fact, earlier in *Leviathan* he writes, "For if all things were equal in all men, nothing would be prized."[22] Instead, Hobbes is arguing first that the observed natural differences in physique or quickness of mind are not sufficient to warrant that one person either should or would recognize another's claim to have greater benefits or rights.[23] Why so? Hobbes's answer is this: even the weakest person, or a person who is not as quick intellectually as another, can kill a person by stealth or through collaboration with others. Thus "strength of physique" or quickness of wit does not guarantee protection of one's life from another.

Why does this vulnerability to death imply everyone is equal in nature? There is some debate on precisely what Hobbes was implying here. One way to understand Hobbes is that we are all human in our basic mortality and in our ultimate desire to preserve our lives. These are core features of our common humanity in nature that are more significant than any variation in physique. Being tall or strong doesn't mean we are any different with respect to our mortality and fear of death. Nor does a slight physique mean we are any less dangerous to another person. Being more intelligent than another does not mean that that person cannot surprise and kill us. Hobbes's idea here is close to the familiar idiom that positions "death as the great leveler or equalizer."[24] Since anyone can be killed by another, neither physical strength nor quickness of wit gives a person invincibility against death. Everyone is vulnerable all the time to violence and death in nature. We are all equal in that vulnerability.

Hobbes argues that the differences of mind are trivial in the same kind of way as physical differences. "And as to the faculties of the mind...I find yet a greater equality amongst men, than that of strength. For Prudence, is but Experience; which equall time, equally bestowes on all men, in those things they equally apply themselves unto."[25] Here Hobbes is arguing that experience, effort, and learning have the power to level natural intellectual differences over time, though he overstates his case, implying that experience can level all natural differences, though that is obviously not the case.[26] Yet his basic point is that much of what we think of as maturity or skill is the result of experience and practice and not inherent in nature itself.[27]

These arguments provide the basis for Hobbes's view that "[t]he question who is the better man, has no place in the condition of meer Nature; where, (as has been shewn before,) all men are equall." In holding this position on equality, Hobbes was arguing against Aristotle's position that differences in nature should be reflected in both human roles and benefits. "The inequality that now is, has bin introduced by the Lawes civill. I know that *Aristotle* in the first booke of his Politiques, for a foundation of his doctrine, maketh men by Nature, some more worthy to Command, meaning the wiser sort (such as he thought himselfe to be for his Philosophy;) others to Serve, (meaning those that had strong bodies, but were not Philosophers as he;) as if Master and Servant were not introduced by consent of men, but by difference of Wit: which is not only against reason; but also against experience."[28]

In distancing himself from Aristotle's position, Hobbes locates the origin of inequality in civil law and society rather than in nature. While there are all sorts of natural differences he recognizes in nature, the meanings of those differences are human artifacts. That is to say, the status of master and slave, ruler and ruled, cannot be inferred from the natural differences that do exist. Neither leadership nor slavery is a natural attribute of human beings, though strength and wit may be. In locating these sorts of inequality as arising from social life, Hobbes starkly frames the terms of the discussion for the modern period. For the question becomes, how should equality figure in social life? In some sense, it is this question that we have been working out for the more than four hundred years since Hobbes framed this question.

As is clear, Hobbes never says that people are equal in all ways. And he realizes that not everyone might agree with his view that people are equal in nature in all the ways that matter and are significant. Consequently, Hobbes makes a second pragmatic argument to buttress his overall position. If people aren't really equal in nature, *they nonetheless perceive themselves to be equal in value.* This human perception of overall equality drives human behavior and experience. Here is how Hobbes puts it:

> If Nature therefore have made men equall, that equalitie is to be acknowledged: or if Nature have made men unequall; yet because men that think themselves equall, will not enter into conditions of Peace, but upon Equall Termes, such equalitie must be admitted. And therefore for the ninth law of Nature, I put this, *That every man acknowledge other for his Equall by Nature.* The breach of this Precept is *Pride.*[29]

Hobbes is arguing that even if people in nature are not equal, they nonetheless still perceive themselves to be equal, at least in the most important respects. Since people perceive themselves equal in value, they won't enter into agreement to live in peace unless it is on equal terms. Thus for social life to work, people have to feel that their basic perception of equality is recognized in the rules of the commonwealth. Even though the sovereign has absolute power, the equality of the ruled has to be in place for peace to be achieved. One won't relinquish one's rights in nature to seek peace unless peace guarantees equal treatment.

For Hobbes, equity or "fairness" thus plays a central role in the laws of nature, which are the basis for peace. As we saw already, Hobbes's ninth law of nature states, *"That every man acknowledge other for his Equall by Nature.* The breach of this Precept is *Pride* [italics in original]." The eleventh law stems from a similar principle and ensures impartiality or equality before the law and before a judge: "it is a precept of the Law of Nature, *that he* [the judge] *deale Equally between them.*" And "the observance of this law, from the equall distribution to each man of that which in reason belongeth to him, is called EQUITY, and (as I have sayd before) distributive Justice."[30]

Hobbes also argues that equality should also enter into the division or allocation of natural goods as well. His twelfth law, which concerns the "Equall Use of Things Common," states *"That such things that cannot be divided, be enjoyed in Common, if it can be; and if the quantity of the thing permit, without Stint; otherwise Proportionably to the number of them that have Right. For otherwise the distribution is Unequall, and contrary to Equite."*[31]

Hobbes is here arguing that natural resources that cannot be divided up, such as the air and the seas, be enjoyed in common unless there is not enough to share. If there is not enough, then it should be divided proportionally, so that the divvying up of natural resources is tied to the conception of equality. As he says in the thirteenth law, "For equall distribution, is of the Law of Nature; and other means of equall distribution cannot be imagined."[32] The thirteenth law extends this insight to things that cannot be divided proportionally or enjoyed in common. In this case, "Then, The Law of Nature, which prescribeth Equity, requireth, *That the Entire Right...*be determined by Lot" or by the alternative method, which is "First Possession" [italics in original]. In other words, where natural resources cannot be easily allocated evenly, another method of distribution is to be used that is fair to all, namely, the use of lots or "first possession," where the first person who takes possession of land or resources is the owner of that resource. How private property can be reconciled with the principle of equality and shared resources in nature is a key difficulty for the early moderns and a topic that we will take up in detail in the next chapter.

To summarize, Hobbes himself traveled a great distance in seeing social life as originating from and actualizing this proposition that humans are all equal in nature. He argued, first of all, that it is the basic equality of human beings that is ultimately responsible for the need and desire for social life. Because humans are equal in key ways and perceive themselves equal to each other, they want and desire the same things and think they are worthy of having what each other has. It is their equality or perception of equality, in other words, that creates desire for the same goods. "From this equality of ability, ariseth equality of hope in the attaining of our Ends. And therefore if any two men desire the same thing, which nevertheless they cannot both enjoy, they become enemies; and in the way to their End…endeavour to destroy, or subdue one another."[33] Since strength does not protect one person from another, each is ultimately vulnerable to death at the hands of another. The essential equality before mortality leads to a spiral of war in nature that has no end. Humans come to realize that the only way to end this spiral of war is to seek peace by creating a commonwealth with a political authority that ends the spiral of violence and helps protect them from the danger of each other. In this way, humans come to recognize they cannot have a stable social life without a political commonwealth. But the commonwealth is only better than life in nature if they make equality and "equity in law" core principles of political life. For this reason Hobbes puts equality and equity as key principles in the laws of nature that govern social life and to which the sovereign is ultimately beholden. Equality is the foundation of peace.

If we turn now to the latter part of the seventeenth century and look at John Locke's *Second Treatise on Government*, we find that equality plays a comparable though different role at the foundation of his political philosophy. Locke, like Hobbes, also notes the similarity in basic human faculties and capabilities. The state of nature is not just a state of perfect freedom but also

> A *State* also *of equality*, wherein all the Power and Jurisdiction is reciprocal, no one having more than another: there being nothing more evident, than that Creatures of the same species and rank, promiscuously born to all the same advantages of Nature, and the use of the same faculties, should also be equal one amongst another without Subordination or Subjection, unless the Lord and Master of them all, should by any manifest Declaration of his Will, set one above another, and confer on him, by an evident and clear appointment, an undoubted Right to Dominion and Sovereignty.[34]

Like Hobbes, Locke understands the proposition of equality to be an inference derived from the basic similarity in human faculties and capabilities. There is "nothing more evident," he claims, than that humans should be equal to each other without subordination or subjection. Ironically, of course, nothing was seemingly less evident in the seventeenth century than that very fact. Indeed, Locke was being disingenuous in claiming that human equality was self-evident. In fact, his whole *First Treatise on Government* is devoted to refuting the claims of the royalist Robert Filmer, whose popular book *Patriarcha*, written before 1642 and the outbreak of the English Civil War and published posthumously in 1680, argued that equality of human beings in nature was nonsense.[35] Though Filmer arrived at absolutist conclusions similar to Hobbes's and those of other royalists, such as John Heywood, Adam Blackwood, and John Barclay, he was troubled by their reliance on the idea of original human equality and liberty.[36] He saw the potential of human equality to undermine the power of the monarchy and instead argued that arguments for royal power should rest on natural inequality.

Writing about the idea of human equality and liberty in nature, Filmer argued that if he could "confute this first erroneous principle [of natural liberty and original equality of mankind], the main foundation of popular sedition would be taken away."[37] Filmer based his argument on a reading of scripture, which he, like most of his contemporaries, took to be both revelation and the true history of the human species. According to his popular work, God had created Adam as father and master of all human beings and as owner of the whole world.[38] This is what God meant when he instructed Adam to "be fruitful, and multiply, and replenish the earth, and subdue it: and have dominion over the fish of the sea, and over the fowl of the air, and over every living thing that moveth upon the earth."[39] From Adam's original "ownership" derived the supreme authority of kings and of fathers through principles of inheritance and primogeniture. Adam owned everything, including the whole world, and his wife and children. His sons inherited from him and passed on their inheritance to their children. From this view of creation, Filmer justified the divine right of kings, one manifestation of a patriarchal system where children were owned by the father and women were subordinate to husbands. That Locke felt compelled to write a whole book refuting Filmer's claims after he had already drafted substantial parts of his *Second Treatise on Government* shows that Locke understood that natural human equality was not yet self-evident to everyone.[40]

It is interesting, however, that though Locke devoted a full treatise to arguing that natural equality, and not patriarchal inequality, was implied in scripture, he never argued very thoroughly for the proposition that reason could discern that all humans were created equal.[41] Instead, Locke appeals to earlier authorities who had already accepted the proposition that all humans are equal. He appeals, for example, to the writing of Richard Hooker, an influential Anglican priest and theologian (1554–1600), whose rationalist religious theology shaped the Church of England, which had departed from the Catholic Church. For Locke's readers in England, an appeal to the Anglican Hooker would have been a potent reference at a time when Protestants feared the reintroduction of an absolute Catholic monarchy.[42]

In his *First Treatise on Government*, Locke reminds his readers that even writers in the absolutist tradition endorsed the equality of human beings in nature. He notes that *"Sir John Hayward, Blackwood and Barclay, the great Vindicators of the Right of Kings could not deny, but admit with one consent the Natural Liberty and Equality of Mankind, for a Truth unquestionable."*[43] If the *Second Treatise* takes natural equality as a foundation in natural law, the *First Treatise* is a sustained argument that natural equality is also assumed in the story of creation in scripture. Interestingly enough, Locke nowhere mentions Hobbes and his emphasis on equality. This silence on Hobbes is poignant, since Locke's *Second Treatise* draws conclusions vastly different from Hobbes's philosophy, though starting with many of the same assumptions as Hobbes.[44] In Locke, there is no emphasis on mortality as the great equalizer of human beings nor on the spiral of war caused by the equality of human desire. But Locke does offer a short justification of human equality that derives from reason. The equality of human beings is one of the laws of nature that humans rationally derive from the rational assumption of God, the Creator. We have looked at this passage before, but it bears repeating.

> The *State of Nature* has a Law of Nature to govern it, which obliges every one: and Reason, which is that Law, teaches all Mankind, who will but consult it, that being all equal and independent, no one ought to harm another in his Life, Health, Liberty or Possessions: For Men being all the Workmanship of one Omnipotent, and infinitely wise Maker: All the Servants of one Sovereign Master, sent into the World by his order, and about his business they are his Property whose Workmanship they are, made to last during his, not one anothers Pleasure: and being furnished with like Faculties, sharing all in one Community of Nature, there cannot be supposed any such *Subordination* among us, that may Authorize us to destroy one another, as if we were made for one anothers use, as the inferior ranks of creatures are for ours.[45]

In language that anticipates the Declaration of Independence and may have influenced Jefferson or George Mason, who influenced Jefferson, Locke argues that equality derives from humanity's creation as God's workmanship. If death was the equalizer and "value reference point" for human equality in Hobbes, God plays that role for Locke. With respect to God, all humans are equal.[46] We are all made by God and thus the property of God. Since we are God's property, one person cannot harm another, for to do so would be to harm God's property. Like Hobbes, Locke also appeals to the fact that humans have the same fundamental human nature and similar human faculties to justify human equality. Whereas human similarity for Hobbes means we are all vulnerable to death at each other's hands, Locke sees the similarity of our basic human faculties as ruling out subordination of one human to another. Subsequently, Locke clarifies that the human equality he is speaking of is the natural freedom not to be "subjected to the will or authority of any other man." This fact that no human is under the "jurisdiction or authority" of another in nature becomes the basis in Locke for the social contract and shared political authority. Locke is careful to point out that this notion of equality does not mean that humans are the same in fact or that certain human characteristics, such as age or virtue, might not give some people deserved precedence over others.

> Though I have said above, Chap. II, *That all Men by nature are equal*, I cannot be supposed to understand all sorts of *Equality*: Age or Virtue may give men a just Precedency: *Excellency* of *Parts* and Merit may place others above the Common Level: *Birth* may subject some, and *Alliance* or *Benefits* others, to pay an Observance to those to whom Nature, Gratitude, or other Respects, may have made it due; and yet all this consists with the *Equality*, which all Men are in, in respect of the Jurisdiction or Dominion one over another; which was the *Equality* I there spoke of, as proper to the Business in hand, being that *equal Right*, that every man hath, to *his Natural Freedom*, without being subjected to the Will or Authority of any other Man.[47]

For Locke, this understanding of equality in nature has far-reaching consequences, for it means that the creation of political power, which includes the right to make laws and to punish offenders, does not belong *naturally* to either kings or some other sovereign body. It also means there are no slaves in nature nor people who should naturally be ruled or be rulers. Political power belongs to each and every individual, who can transfer that power by choice and contract to the political bodies that represent the commonwealth.

To summarize, we have seen that more than one hundred years before Jefferson penned the Declaration of Independence, there were major positions staked out by early modern political philosophers arguing that equality should be the foundation and centerpiece of political philosophy and that equality was closely linked to idea of natural rights. Jefferson was saying nothing new when he put equality at the centerpiece of American political philosophy. In his first draft of the Declaration, Jefferson's language sounds a lot like Locke's, as many interpreters have noted.

Jefferson Draft as Likely Presented to Franklin	Rough Draft "Fair Copy" as It Likely Looked When Presented to Congress
We hold these truths to be ~~sacred and undeniable~~ self-evident that all men are created equal & independent; that from that equal creation they derive in rights inherent & inalienable [Adams's copy reads "unalienable"], among which are the preservation of life, & liberty, & the pursuit of happiness;	We hold these truths to be ~~sacred and undeniable~~ self-evident that all men are created equal ~~& independent; that from that equal creation they derive in rights~~ they are endowed by their creator with ~~equal rights, some of which are~~ inherent & inalienable rights [Adams's copy reads unalienable], among ~~which~~ these are ~~the preservation of~~ life, & liberty, & the pursuit of happiness;

In the first version of the Declaration of Independence, Jefferson uses language that is much closer in concept and wording to Locke's statements about equality, with which we know he was familiar.[48] Here Jefferson says that "all men are created equal and independent." We see that Jefferson was toying with calling the ideas "sacred and undeniable" instead of "self-evident." In either case, the emphasis is that equality flows from an equal creation and that the equality of the creation is the source of rights. Locke had said something in almost identical language, referring to humans as "equal and independent" as well. But gone in Jefferson's version is Locke's emphasis on the fact that we are God's *workmanship* (i.e., property of the Creator), which in Locke was the justification of equality. Jefferson's language emphasizes that equality comes from the act of creation, and it leaves open and undefined the question of what is the basis of thinking that God created humans equal.

In the next version of the Declaration, after a revision by Jefferson with input from the Committee of Five (which included John Adams and Benjamin Franklin), men are still created equal, but now the emphasis on the source of rights has shifted. We are now "endowed" by the Creator with inalienable rights. They do not flow explicitly from our equal creation or from our equal status as God's property. We simply hold equality now to be self-evident. It is beyond the scope of the present study to look in detail at Jefferson's position on natural rights and the possible influences on Jefferson, which I have done in another context.[49] Suffice it to say here that Jefferson was both familiar with and standing within the philosophical traditions of the seventeenth century, but also expressing his differences from that tradition. In fact, he may have had doubts that rights were natural and self-evident, and this may be reflected in his statement that "we hold" these truths to be self-evident.

We Hold Equality to Be True

Even this short traverse across the seventeenth century and into the founding of America in the late eighteenth century shows that there was an emerging modern contention emphasizing human equality. The full impact of that concept was not yet fully grasped or explored. But there was an emerging argument that although human differences existed in nature, those differences are to be treated as negligible with respect to another absolute and transcending value. For Hobbes, that other value was death, and for Locke it was God. Jefferson's language stands closer to Locke's position than to Hobbes's. In any case, we can see that equality is a proposition that flows from a particular system that has a point of view and a set of absolute values. Those systems of thought or political philosophies place human equality as one of the key foundational principles by which humans should be understood and by which human society should be organized.[50] This emerging tradition, moreover, sees human inequality as emerging out of social life and by human consent, not a divine decree embedded in nature. Inequality comes from human beings, not nature or God.

If we step back for a moment, we can understand the equality of human beings as a philosophical foundation or starting point for the modern period. This is one way of interpreting what the early modern philosophers meant when they claimed that humans had an original equality in what they called the "state of nature." It is true they often meant something literal by the state of nature, referring at times to the state of humanity at creation, in earlier times of human history, and in simpler societies living closer to nature like those of the American Indians. They also used the terminology state of nature to describe any group of people living in communities with no authorized political power.[51]

Today we don't resonate with the claim that we can infer from the state of nature what human beings are or were meant to be. Those of us who believe Darwin's theory do think that our evolution may tell us interesting things about how our natures are partially shaped as we became the distinctive animals we are. And clearly equality was not something that was true in evolution, though competition, desire for community, and care may have all played a role in the evolution of our species. For this reason, we don't take seriously the claim that people were equal "in a state of nature."

Nonetheless, we can take the idea of equality in a state of nature as an aspiration or regulative idea to which we aspire, and in this sense it becomes foundational for who we want to be.[52] We imagine and dream about human equality as a value, though there may never have been individuals living in a state of nature or full equality, even in simple societies. Equality, in other words, becomes the foundation and point of departure for our political commitments.

If we take equality as the foundation of what humans ideally should be, then it makes sense that equality should play a critical role in political communities as well. And indeed both Hobbes and Locke see equality as critical to life in the commonwealth and under government.

The claim is that humans are equal in their basic "humanness" and thus equal in character, value, and nature in some fundamental and critical respects. The basic claim is that the differences in nature are not differences that are morally significant, meaning that they do not warrant giving one person or group power, control, and rights over another by nature. The basic equality in humanness and value is translated into an equality of rights and protections. Thus no one is born a king (contra positions of monarchs such as King James I and royalists such as Filmer), nor is anyone born a leader, a follower, or a natural slave by natural right (contra the position of Aristotle). Nothing about our existing differences means that humans have the right to own or hurt each other or have fewer aspirations or desires. Humans are sufficiently equal in what counts that they have no right to be lord over each other, own each other, or hurt each other. They are equal enough that they are of the same value before the ultimate, whether that be God or nature or simply a foundational position.

There is nothing in nature that tells us that we are equal. On the contrary, the claim that we are equal is in fact a rejection of nature, for nature does not really make us equal or the same. The claim that humans are equal is thus one way of looking at the world, arguably one of the great assumptions of modernity in the West, and distinguishes modernity in some ways from many of the life-forms that came before it or that may lie outside the West. One might say it is one of the "moral" commitments of the modern West that transcends many other religious differences, at least for some people.

In the Middle Ages, hierarchical distinctions between peoples were acceptable in the Roman Catholic Church, in feudal social structures, and in the political institutions of the emerging nation-states. With the turn toward early modernity, the belief that God or fate had made some people superior to others in essence or in value and that those differences should matter in the distribution of roles, rights, and power, was no longer as self-evident as it had been previously. The change came about in complex ways that are the stuff of histories about the transformations spawned by the end of feudalism, the Reformation and Counter-Reformation, the Enlightenment, emerging capitalism and industrialization, and the history of England in the seventeenth century. Whereas the debate initially focused on who had absolute power, the pope (the church) or the monarch (the secular power), the debate eventually evolved more broadly into a discussion over whether the people held the rightful source of absolute power.[53]

From Rights to Equality

The shift in focus from the language of rights to the language of equality represents a different way of thinking about our political and social aspirations. In some ways, the impulse toward equality was always implicit in and the foundation for the discussion of rights. But for several reasons, it is arguably better to organize the aspirations of our political system around a vision of human equality than around a vision of natural rights.

First, a vision of equality seems to incorporate more of a notion of responsibility and fairness than does an emphasis on natural rights, which tends to obscure or hide these other critical conceptions. Natural rights seem to focus on individual protections but not on social responsibilities. Equality, by contrast, pulls us toward a vision that we are in this together and must share resources and challenges together. Equality, in other words, tends to focus us on our shared humanness and less on our unique individuality. Recent philosophers who have explored the meaning of equality recognize that it means we look at people not just under their roles or titles, but from their own perspective and from an understanding of their own self-understanding and histories. Even the seeming platitude that "we are all human," which is implied by equality, has meaning in systems in which dimensions of basic humanness are overlooked, denied, or explained away. As Bernard Williams puts it, it "does mean that each man is owed the effort of understanding, and that in achieving it, each man is to be (as it were) abstracted from certain conspicuous structures of inequality in which we find him."[54] What I am suggesting is that, of the impulses of modernity, the most noble is the quest to take seriously the equal value of human beings even more so than the equal rights of individuals, even though the two conceptions have been intimately related.

What does this vision of equal value imply? Equal value differs somewhat from "equal rights," which still slips back into the language of rights. Equal value implies that we take as a hypothesis and as a working proposition that although we may have different sources and standards of truth (e.g., religious or not), we will work with a shared assumption or conviction that all humans are of equal value, equal in their basic human-ness, and worth understanding from their own frame of reference and histories. Not all religions or philosophies will agree. Thus we stake our modern program and our American project on the proposition that we will explore the full ramifications of equality. This is our launching point and moral center that should guide our thinking and practices. What this means in practice is something we can and will continue to debate. But that debate is more fruitful and helpful for Americans and humanity than our debates over our individual rights. If we shift the discussion away from rights toward the discussion of equality, then we begin to think not just what my entitlements are, but what also are my obligations and duties. Why is this so?

In focusing on equal value, we have to look at the distribution of goods, power, and opportunities, and wonder whether the benefits that accrue from our gifts, privileges, and talents, and our place in history, belong exclusively to us and whether those that accrue to others should belong exclusively to them. Equal value forces us to think about not just ourselves and our entitlements, but ourselves in relationship to others; not just about what we have, but the distribution of power and resources in societies and among nations. The concept of equality is more "rela-tional" by its very nature than the concept of rights, which is more indi-vidually focused.

As I have said, the concept of equal value can be understood as a mod-ern hypothesis or a founding conviction. To be clear, I am not arguing that equality is natural but that, on the contrary, it is not natural. Noth-ing in nature tells us we are all equal in value. It is a position that we take above or outside nature as we aspire to be something better than what we otherwise might be by nature. For those who are religious, they can understand this in religious terms. God expects us to transcend our baser natures and turn toward angels. We aspire to overcome more base incli-nations, which are filled with passions, ego, avarice, jealousy, lust, and so on. For those who are not religious, we can see the human quest as one in which we try to uplift ourselves and aspire to be a nobler type of ani-mal than animals of prey, or, if you prefer, more like communal animals, such as ants or bees, than those that are more individually focused. We take equality as a good organizing principle, as an aspiration and ideal by which to organize our practices, our social rules, as a way to draw humans out to be better creatures than we otherwise would be.

When we organize ourselves around a quest for equal value, we see ourselves and our relationships to other human beings and societies in a different light. The advantage of seeing through this lens is to highlight our gifts, privileges, talents, and advantages. We can agree that the uneven distribution of talents, privileges, and resources across individuals and nations is in tension with the notion of equal value. Yet, if we think people are equal in value before some absolute standard, then we have to query the basis and implication of such uneven distributions. Too often the nod toward equality stops short of this additional step. We assume equality means only an aspiration toward equal opportunity. What to do about the unequal distribution of wealth and resources is a difficult problem, because there may be different approaches and the advantages and disadvantages of each may not be so readily apparent. We shall return to this key problem below, for it is a place in which the early moderns did not think deeply enough.

We should agree, I am arguing, to a common founding assumption in the organization of modern societies. And that assumption is that we wish to dedicate ourselves to working out the implications of seeing all human beings as of equal value. This is our vision, our moral compass, and our contribution to the development of the human species. This founding assumption can be seen as compatible with and in fact developing what are arguably the best strands of moral commitments within Western religious tradition. It is one of the moral commitments that distinguishes the West in some sense from some other traditions. It is also a moral commitment that is distinctively modern and differentiates the modern inclination from some of its earlier Judeo-Christian incarnations. The proposition that we are all of equal value is also one that nonreligious people can get behind without a commitment to God or a particular religious tradition. It is an assumption that can cross "the religious/atheist" line.

If we accept equal value as a starting point, the question then becomes how we work out the implications of what it means to organize society around that founding principle. What does this aspiration for equal value mean for the purposes of government, the way we manage our economies, our relations with other nations, and each other? In America, how does it help us to understand the trajectory of our Constitution and interpret the framers' vision and intent? There will be debate around these questions, to be sure. And the disagreements around what equal value means will proliferate. Liberty-first advocates may respond in a couple of different ways. They may argue that "equal value" should not have priority over rights. But if so, then we can identify that point as the foundation of our disagreement. We are the equality party; they are the rights party. They may also argue that "equal value" was not the intent of the framers. But we have seen that the language of equality was as fundamental to the vision of the Declaration as the emphasis on rights. Clearly the conviction of equality in some sense was core to their vision as well. Liberty-first advocates may also argue that even if we accept "equal value" as the founding principle, the implications of the idea differ from those implications I am going to derive from it. They may argue that to endorse "equal value" is to be "socialist" or "communist" and those ideologies failed. I argue that "equal value" doesn't have to end up in socialism or communism, and there is a way to have republican (small *r*) and democratic (small *d*) values that rest on the equal value of human beings. Indeed, one can argue that equality rather than rights is the animating impulse of liberty itself.

Equality in value has to have some meaning that is translated into power, resources, wealth, and opportunity. In America we have tended to interpret equality before God or equality with each other to mean "equal opportunity." Not only is equal opportunity impossible to achieve, but it is an inadequate interpretation of equal value. We cannot give everyone equal opportunity, because there is no way to achieve a level playing field in life. People do differ in talents, circumstances, and history. Resources have already been distributed based on thousands of years of history. We enter a game that has been ongoing for hundreds and thousands of generations. Equal opportunity is thus a flawed way of thinking about equal value and doesn't really address the question at hand.

The question at hand is this: How much of what we have, in our talents, in our historical circumstance, in the efforts of our parents and our ancestors, do we deserve because of who we are and our own efforts? It seems like a fair question, but one that we are no longer permitted to ask. If we do dare to ask the question, we are accused of undermining liberty, of demotivating individuals from working hard, seeking to better themselves, making new discoveries, and being entrepreneurial.[55] If we even ask the question of whether individuals deserve everything they have, we are accused of undermining all the advances of human society. We are the enemies of progress. We shall come back to these charges, which are nonsense.

We can grant that there are very positive consequences that flow from individual motivation. Yet we do not have to agree that individuals care only about financial and material reward. Humans have many motivations: ego, care, love, compassion, competition, desire, and so forth. People are not motivated solely by financial remuneration. Who does not rejoice at winning a race for which there is no award except approbation? And who does not enjoy remembering or knowing something that no one else does? Who does not take pleasure from giving an unexpected gift to someone who is surprised by it? And how many people fill up with tears when hearing about great works of compassion that some people perform? Human nature is complex. We have egos, and we love approbation. We have intellects and creativity, and we love to think and explore. We create not just for the financial reward, but because we love to create and we love to receive recognition for what we have achieved. How else to explain why some people choose to become teachers, academics, nurses, police officers, all careers in which financial remuneration is clearly not the determinative driver. Those who see humans as only motivated by material success and by rational, pragmatic goals have an impoverished, one-dimensional view of what the human being is. I shall return to this question again in chapter 9 below.[56]

I am not saying that there should be no financial reward for hard work and training, for creativity and brilliance, for natural talents, and for entrepreneurial risk. Instead, I am saying that the results we achieve should be shared. As I have argued in chapter 3, we stand on the shoulders of countless men and women who have come before us. We do not take our place on a clean slate. The slate is anything but clean. We build on the efforts and sacrifices of thousands who came before us, in our ability to stand upright, to grasp objects with opposable thumbs, in our vocal abilities to speak, and thanks to our cortical functions that let us imagine and think abstractly. We stand on the shoulders of others who have created fire, iron, medicines, and electricity.

If we take this view of history and equal value into account, we come to a different notion of what government and property should be all about. It is to the ramifications of equality for property and government that we now turn.

Chapter 6
On Private Property Rights and Equality

Property is one of those concepts and institutions whose origins and justification most people don't bother to think about. Property simply is assumed to be protected by our liberties. But if we delve into the ideas about property among those early modern thinkers who fashioned our modern notions of rights, we find some surprising convictions that should give us pause and help us rethink our basic assumptions about the allocation of resources, ownership, and our own responsibilities.

Among many advocates of liberty today, it is an unquestioned assumption that anything that we have in our possession or anything that we come by through our efforts, work, labor, and luck become and are part of our property. That view assumes that we own the results of our labor and what came to us through any accidents of history. Anything that we create, produce, and achieve is ours alone. For the same reason, anything our parents and ancestors have created was theirs alone. Anything that comes into our hands through inheritance or through the activity of our lives is our private property. This conception of property is intimately tied into our notions about what liberty is and means. Liberty includes the right to own the results of our labor and efforts and to be recognized for our talents.

These early modern notions of property are deeply tied conceptually to notions of "propriety," "proper," and "proprietor," as the etymology of the words reflect. In fact, early modern philosophers sometimes used the words interchangeably and said "propriety" where today we would say "property," and they used the word "property" also to describe all our rights, including our lives and liberties and not just our material possessions.[1] These notions are not easily pried apart in the modern Western tradition, illustrating just how deeply our notion of property is tied to our notions of what's right and proper.

In what follows, we explore this entanglement of property and propriety by looking at some of the forgotten assumptions that shaped our modern conceptions. In doing so, we discover grounds for rethinking what we hold to be right and proper. It is fascinating and somewhat startling to see the particular ideas on which our modern notions of property are grounded. Most of these ideas have long since been forgotten except by a narrow range of academics who still read the seventeenth-century classics. But they were the foundation for institutions and ideas about rights and property that still shape our lives, our language, and our way of thinking. Finding that our modern notions stand on such unusual foundations rattles the edifice on which they were built, a secret that very few want to acknowledge, let alone talk about. Indeed this is why even some liberty-first adherents have fled from a "rights" justification of property and turned to utilitarian justifications, as we shall see later.[2] Since property was and is ultimately about what's proper, it would be only reasonable that our own notions of what's right should reshape our relationship to property. We shall find in these early modern discussions the roots for other more productive ways to think about property that have subsequently disappeared or been forgotten.

For some readers, it will be interesting and perhaps even surprising to know that at the dawn of human time, the world and its resources were given "in common" to all humanity, according to our modern natural rights thinkers. Precisely what in common meant and how private property arose subsequently were points of disagreement. The debate turned on a variety of historical, philosophical, and religious questions. Why, when, and how did private property emerge? Was private property a natural right or a human convention? If the world was given in common, how did property become private, and what turned it private? If humans are equal, why is property distributed unevenly? These questions had their religious variations as well. What specifically did God give to Adam, the first human, in particular? Was the world Adam's alone or was it a gift to humankind in general? How did private property emerge out of that original gift to Adam?

For the most part, there was a general consensus among our early moderns that the institution of private property did *not* exist in the beginning of human time and emerged later in ways to be discussed. Only some royalists, such as Robert Filmer, tried to argue that private property started at human creation and that all property rights were inheritances of the property given to the first human ancestor, Adam. How these thinkers knew what happened in the beginning of time is part of the interesting story. For them, evidence of the early human situation came from scripture, which was identified not only with the word of God, but the historical record of early human history. They also found evidence of early human history and institutions in the practices of "simpler" peoples that European explorers believed they were encountering in the Americas. As Locke famously put it, "in the beginning all the World was *America* [italics in original]," meaning that humankind lived in the beginning of time like the American Indian tribes reported by explorers of his day, a view that dominated European anthropology until the end of the nineteenth century.[3] The early natural state of humans was thought to be still visible in the practices of non-European peoples, above whom the more civilized European Christians had progressed.

The idea that the world's resources were given in common is a good launching point for our discussion of property. Underlying this view is a set of interesting assumptions about the nature of history, human character, God, and morality. The core conviction is that the world was intended in some sense to benefit and sustain human beings equally. There are two key assumptions here that both need some examination.

The first is that either nature or God (which, for some thinkers, were one and the same) intended the natural world for human use and purpose. This is a teleological and religious perspective. It assumes that the purpose of creation was human oriented and in service of humanity. Humans were understood as the pinnacle of creation, and the rest of the natural world was created at least in part to serve human purposes. This is an assumption we can and should rethink, for it would seem reasonable to question, from both a religious and secular ecological perspective, whether this human-centered philosophy now appears to be arrogant. If the planet and resources were not given for human purposes, or were given in some more limited way, or were not "given" or "intended" at all, then the founding assumption that the world is for human use is problematic.

Doubts about this view already are hinted at in the writings of the early moderns, some of whom argued that God ultimately has property in everything, and human property rights are therefore only secondary to God's ultimate ownership.[4] If we today see ourselves as part of nature, instead of above nature, then the very question of what right we have in natural resources intensifies, a position that ecologically oriented secular and religious thinkers have made in emphasizing the obligation of stewardship.[5] Furthermore, these early moderns in some ways anticipated a view I wish to develop further below. That view holds that nature and God gave humans only the use of nature's resources at the beginning, but not private property rights per se. We shall come back to the question below of what it would mean to see humans as having only temporary use rights and not permanent property rights.

The second justification of the common nature of resources flows from reason: given the natural human instinct to self-preservation and the corresponding right to life, there must be an obvious means for humans to be able to sustain their lives. The idea here is that God gave humans a means of sustenance and that nature provided humans both the instinct to life and the means to fulfill it.[6] In this perspective, the world's resources were part of that human provisioning, and humans were fulfilling their nature by utilizing natural resources. For some thinkers, this provisioning had a distinctively religious foundation to it. God intended the world's resources as sustenance for human life through a special gift of the world's resources. This was evident in scripture itself when God blesses the first human beings:

God blessed them and God said to them, "Be fertile and increase, fill the earth and master it; and rule the fish of the sea, the birds of the sky, and all the living things that creep on the earth." God said, "See, I give you every seed-bearing plant that is upon all the earth, and every tree that has seed-bearing fruit; they shall be yours for food" (Gen. 1:28–29).[7]

According to Genesis, the permission to use vegetation as human food was given by God at creation. Initially, humans were told to subdue the earth and were given dominion over creatures, but this did not give them the right to take animals' lives and eat them. The permission to eat flesh was given to Noah in a dispensation after the flood, at which point God says, "Every moving thing that liveth shall be meat for you; even as the green herb have I given you all things. But flesh with the life thereof, *which* is the blood thereof, shall ye not eat." (Gen. 9:3-4)[8] [italics in original]

There are a number of key ambiguities in these scriptural verses that provided grist for debate among both religious scholars and early modern philosophers alike. These scriptural interpretations were at the heart of the debate over the nature of property rights and specifically over whom and for what purpose God gave the world's resources. Though scripture was central to the debate on property, others played down the religious overtones and assumed that one could infer the right of humans to *use* the world's resources from the human instinct for self-preservation, even without appealing to the idea of God. As Locke put it, "Whether we consider natural *Reason* which tells us, that Men, being once born, have a right to their Preservation and consequently to Meat and Drink, and such other things, as Nature affords for their Subsistence, or *Revelation,* which gives us account of those Grants God made of the World to *Adam*, and to *Noah*, and his Sons, "tis very clear, that God…[has] given it to mankind in common."[9] In either derivation of property, there was no attempt to differentiate ownership of resources by human status or human hierarchies at the inception of creation. What was given by God via revelation, or by nature via reason, was given in common.

The assumption that natural resources were in common aligns well with the emerging modern conviction that humans were equal in value with each other, a topic covered in the previous chapter. From this equality in value or basic human capabilities flowed the conviction that resources should not be preallocated in a way that privileged some human beings over others. Equality implied that resources were conferred equally by God or by nature in the beginning of human time. Without the conviction that humans were equal in value, early modern philosophers would have read scripture and human history differently. The idea that human equality implied "resources in common" at the beginning would help support the growing seventeenth-century repudiation of the divine right of kings, which gave the monarchs divine justification for their authority, though not necessarily unlimited power over their subjects and the properties of the kingdom.[10]

For the early moderns, the idea that natural resources were given or held in common at the beginning of time was thus a core conviction that was tied into their assumption of human equality. In the previous chapter, I suggested that the assertion of human equality can be taken as a core modern moral conviction, not something that is self-evident in nature. If we see modernity as trying to work out and embrace the implications of this founding assumption, then it is plausible to argue that our conception of property should also be shaped by our conception of human equality. This linkage between original human equality and the common ownership of property was already intuited by our earlier modern philosophers. Before pondering this connection for ourselves, let us see how they came to grips with what they considered an end of this original human condition of equality and common ownership and the emergence of private property and inequality.[11]

• • •

The claim that humans received the world and its resources in common had several meanings. For some, in common meant what we now would call "tenants in common," meaning that everyone has equal rights together.[12] On this view, all humans shared ownership equally in the world's resources, and no one could do anything without the permission of all other property owners. The other view holds that resources in common was intended exclusively, meaning that all resources were treated like the air and the ocean today and given for use to everyone, but that *no one had property rights over anything in particular.*[13]

The view that the world's resources were given in common was tied in with a particular reading of scripture. In Genesis 1, God can be understood to be talking about the creation not of Adam, the individual man, but Adam, the ancestor or prototype of humankind. Indeed, "Adam" in Hebrew can either be a proper name, Adam, or mean "human being," like the English word "man."[14] That God is bestowing the right "to subdue" or "to master" the world on more than just a single male is suggested by the vacillation from singular to plural in the instructions: "So God created man in his own image, in the image of God created he *him*; male and female created he *them*. And God blessed *them*, and God said unto *them*, Be fruitful, and multiply, and replenish the earth, and subdue it: and have dominion over the fish of the sea, and over the fowl of the air, and over every living thing that moveth upon the earth.[15] (Gen. 1:28–29) [emphasis mine]

Over the centuries, interpreters of Genesis have argued about the meaning of the plurals in this passage. What does scripture mean in saying that "male and female he created *them*"? There are many possibilities here. One traditional interpretation understands Adam to be the first human being created and male. A second interpretation understands the language as symbolic, seeing Adam, the first ancestor, as a representation of all humanity. Another approach interprets the word "Adam" like the English "man" as including human beings, and the word "them" refers to the first human pair. Still another possibility is that the first Adam was beyond or before the differentiation of the sexes (i.e., androgynous or sexless) and thus in God's image (which is beyond sex).[16] Adam, as the first human entity created, was a generic human with no sex or both sexes until Eve was later split off, at which point the male and female sexes were differentiated from the original sexless human entity. Adam, the first human, represents humanity writ large, and God's instructions to Adam are expressions of God's purpose for humankind in general.

This first human entity is instructed to replenish and subdue the earth and have dominion over the creatures of the earth.[17] For Robert Filmer, the author of *Patriarcha*, this instruction was the basis for the private property of Adam, the original male, and the ultimate foundation of the divine right of kings. Adam passed his property rights over the world and over people to his male heirs who became the kings.

Other early modern interpreters wanted to avoid the conclusion that property rights had been given to only a single individual at creation. Instead, they understood God's action at creation as granting the first human the right to *use* the world's resources, but not necessarily the right to have private property.

In either the religious or more rationalist positions described above, there was no private property at creation. For all of these thinkers, *it thus became a problem to explain how private property came to exist in the first place*. Locke puts this problem quite dramatically: "it seems to some a very great difficulty, how any one should ever come to have a *Property* in any thing."[18] The origin of private property was both a problem for and point of contention between early modern thinkers and highlights the fact that their notions of property did not sit easily with their notion of an equal creation and an equal value of human beings. Instead, they saw a tension between these two different sets of convictions. And in some sense their work can be understood as an attempt to work through these incompatible impulses. How could they argue both for the equal value of human beings before God or death yet also account for the emergence of private property and an uneven distribution of God's creation? One can see the debate about human beginnings as the foundation or original condition of their moral thinking. It was their point of departure. Given that humans were equal in value, how could they understand and justify private property and ultimately the uneven distribution of the world's resources? Is this what God or nature intended?

There were two basic answers to the question, with some variations on each. The first view is quite intriguing, since it attributes the introduction of private property to human convention and compact. According to this view, humans for various reasons came to an agreement that they would embrace private property, which did not exist at creation. Private property was thus an artifact of human society, not nature. A second view, by contrast, held that the mechanisms to create private property were already implicit in and available at creation, and humans simply exercised and implemented those mechanisms that already existed. Both views thus shared the assumption that the institution of private property arose after human creation. But they differed on how private property in fact began and whether it was a purely human convention or already authorized by nature or God. The differences are significant and interesting for our discussion and show that there was not a single perspective on the origin of property. After summarizing the two main positions on property, we shall rethink their implications for our own notion of what's right and proper.

Consider first the perspective that private property was introduced by human convention and compact or civil law.[19] In this view, private property is *not* comparable with the right to life and liberty, which were in nature or God-given, but was rather an institution or practice agreed upon by human beings.[20] In this view, we may have natural rights to life and liberty but not to property. From the beginning of human creation there was a natural right to *use* the world's resources, but there was no notion of legal ownership. This right of use was thought to arise from either a gift of God (as told by scripture) or the fact that humans had a right and instinct to self-preservation and thus to use resources for sustaining life (as inferred from reason). *Using* resources was qualitatively different from having property rights. A right to use resources may have entitled Adam to eat fruit from a tree but not to put a fence around the tree, keep others away from it, hoard the fruit from it, or sell it. Use was limited to what an individual needed to sustain his or her life, but it did not entitle individuals to own or accumulate more than they needed.

Thus when things were "in common," people could use resources for life's basic needs but not rightfully accumulate them beyond what they needed. The ability to accumulate was an artifact of property rights and human civilization.

This property-free condition in which people lived off the land was thought by some to be the simple state of humankind, in which people lived closer to nature, without clothing, in caves, and had no practice of private property.[21] As evidence, thinkers pointed not only to the biblical story about the naked Adam and Eve, but also to what they perceived as simpler living arrangements and social organizations in the practices of the non-European peoples that European explorers had encountered. As we shall see later, this equation of non-European peoples with simpler societies would be among the justifications used by Europeans for settling on and occupying the lands in the Americas. In any case, these thinkers concluded that the development of property was historical, not natural, and the result of human convention, either through explicit agreement or through tacit consent to new social arrangements. Why did this arrangement emerge? The historical development of private property occurred in response to the nature of human character, the development of the human species, and pressures of population growth, and was part of what differentiated the early simple societies from more complex later ones and what even differentiated humans in their early natural state from their more advanced state. Private property was thus a good and perhaps inevitable human invention that was part of the foundation of civilization.[22]

This view of property has intriguing implications. If private property rights are the result of human social convention, they cannot be part of a natural law that is protected in the same way that life and liberty would be protected. Private property is instead the result of a "contract" that human beings made with each other. And like other institutions that result from human convention, property rights could potentially be rethought and under certain conditions could revert to their prior natural state. In this sense, private property is analogous to political institutions and government, which are created by human compact and therefore subject to human control, change, and ultimately revision. And just as the compact that creates government can be overturned under certain conditions that violate the underlying intent and rights of the original parties, some thinkers believed that property rights would be undone and revert back to the state of nature in the face of "extreme necessity."[23]

The assumption here was that the parties to the original agreement (or agreements) codifying the idea of property entered with an implicit understanding that everyone would have sufficient basic resources needed for their sustenance. Since this was the tacit intent of the "original contract(s)," the case of starvation or other forms of extreme necessity could override the convention and revert matters back to the condition prior to the agreement. As one Dutch thinker put it, "My Calamity doth not give me a right to those things, to which I had none before; but the extremity of my Danger makes that Condition cease, under which I gave up my first Right."[24] Under extreme circumstances, one could take another's property without the action falling into the category of theft. My conventional right to property does not supersede another person's right to preserve his or her life.

What, then, led humans to adopt private property arrangements? Private property was regarded as a reasonable and even a necessary response to the growth of human civilization and the nature of human character. Property rights provided a way to "preserve peace" and avoid "discord" and "infinite clashings."[25] What provoked this tendency toward discord or even war was the nature of human character itself. The fact that humans were equal in character meant they desired and expected the same goods, were driven by ambition, and competed for resources as a result of population growth.[26]

According to some, the transition to private property occurred over a period of time as humans spread out across the earth and came to multiple agreements on property rights among smaller groups.[27] There was not a single contract with all humanity. Instead the arrangements emerged among groups of the expanding human population. Sometimes the agreements were explicit, as groups settled on new land and divvied it up by property rights. Sometimes the agreements were tacit, as when people spread out and settled on new land, tacitly accepting that there was a first-come-first-served basis to appropriating goods and lands.

Some thought "seizure" was the means by which the original humans exercised their "right" to own what had been given in common, while others disagreed.[28] Even seizure of property only constituted rightful ownership because humans had come to agree to abide by private property rights and identify seizure as the conventional mechanism to secure them.[29] God had given the resources for human use, but neither God nor nature had defined how the resources should be allocated.[30] According to some, property rights thus emerged along with the very concept of right and wrong and thus were implicit in the human step out of nature itself.[31] Others argued that humans accepted the notion of private property rights in recognition that most human goods came into being only through human labor and effort. For reasons of fairness, the individual who expended effort and labor thus deserved the value created by that labor and effort. As one writer put it, "Again, many Things stand in need of Human Labour and Culture, either for their Production, or to fit and prepare them for Use. But here, it was very inconvenient that a person who had taken no pains about a Thing should have an equal Right to it with another, by whose Industry it was either first rais'd, or exactly wrought and fram'd, to render it of farther service."[32] A number of thinkers also recognized the positive benefits of private property, which made humans more industrious and improved their character.[33]

To summarize, then, the first view understands private property as a human convention or arrangement that emerged for many good reasons from the challenges of human character, competition, ambition, and recognition of human effort. In this view, property is not among the natural rights on the same plane as "life and liberty." Instead, humans invented the institution of private property for some good reasons. But because it is a human invention and not a right in nature, it is theoretically revisable. One advantage of this view of property is that it better aligns with the probable history of human development. The institution of property is lost in history; it evolved over thousands of years in different ways in different cultures. No one can prove how private property arose originally.

A second view of property attempts to push property rights back to God and creation in order to avoid the implication that property rights were "conventional." In this view, property was a right in nature.[34] John Locke is the most important proponent of this position, and it is his view of property rights and their origins that in many ways shaped and continue to shape our modern perceptions.[35] By locating the origin of property rights back closer to creation, Locke was walking a fine line. On the one hand, he was trying to avoid the claim that property rights were just "human conventions" and wanted to position property more like "life and liberty," as rights authorized in nature. In doing so, however, Locke also had to avoid the royalist position of those like Robert Filmer, who had argued that God had given property rights at creation to Adam, and those rights had been inherited by Adam's descendants, who were the kings.

Locke made his intellectual move by claiming that it is *human labor* that creates private property rights. As noted already, some thinkers before Locke had already argued that persons who expend labor should, out of fairness, be recognized with property rights for their efforts. Yet there was a crucial difference. Those same thinkers had argued that treating labor as the source of property rights was a convention adopted by human beings, not a right of nature, as Locke argued. Let's follow Locke in his thinking.

Like others before him, Locke argued that the right to use the world's resources was evident from both revelation and reason. Revelation taught that God had given the world to humans in common (and not to just to the first man, Adam, as Filmer and others had argued). Reason also made evident that humans who were given the right to life and instinct to self-preservation (derived from the idea of God) must also be given the right to sustain themselves.[36] Indeed, they were forbidden to take their own lives for the same reason. So far Locke is not so different than the other early moderns writing in the same tradition.

But here is where Locke makes an intellectual move different from several of his predecessors. He argues that there must be a natural way to create property rights, because the world was given in common. If there was no way to make something "mine," how else could a person take food or resources that were held in common? Would it not be stealing if I took acorns from a tree that had been owned in common? There must be something that turns that which is given in common into something over which I have private rights and can eat. "The Fruit, or Venison, which nourishes the wild *Indian*, who knows no Inclosure, and is still a Tenant in common, must be his, and so his, *i.e.* a part of him, that another can no longer have any right to it, before it can do him any good for the support of his Life."[37]

To make this intellectual move, Locke takes for granted that in the beginning all humans were "tenants in common" and that one must remove resources from that common status in order to use them.[38] Thus, in the beginning, everything was like the air or the ocean, to which all people had rights jointly. We have seen that not all thinkers understood the common status of resources this way. Some believed that resources were in common in the "negative sense," meaning that no one owned anything at all but had only the right to use what he or she needed. Those who held this view of resources would not have struggled with or recognized Locke's conceptual puzzle. If no one owned anything at all (it was all in common), there would be no problem taking anything for one's personal use. Like fish from the ocean, everyone could take without infringing the rights of others.[39] Locke thus based his argument on a conceptual problem that not all thinkers had or recognized. Nor did he explicitly defend his view that God or reason had given everything as co-owned instead of owned by no one.

In any case, Locke reasons that it is human labor that in the beginning turns what is owned in common into what is mine. Since my labor belongs to me, when I labor I mix what is mine into what is common and thereby create my private property. Locke's theory has become known as the "labor theory of value."[40] As Locke puts it,

Though the Earth, and all inferior Creatures, be common to all men, yet every Man has a *Property* in his own *Person*: this no Body has any Right to but himself. The *Labour* of his Body, and the *Work* of his Hands we may say, are properly his. Whatsoever then he removes out of the State that Nature hath provided, and left it in, he hath mixed his *Labour* with, and joyned to it something that is his own, and thereby makes it his *Property*. It being by him removed from the common state Nature hath placed it in, it hath by this *labour* something annexed to it, that excludes the common right of other Men: for this *Labour* being the unquestioned property of the Labourer, no Man but he can have a right to what that is once joyned to, at least where there is enough, and as good, left in common for others.[41]

There are a number of assumptions here that still permeate our own contemporary views of property. If we scrutinize them, we see a number of perplexing questions. First, it is interesting that Locke says that human labor belongs to the individual. Elsewhere, he also writes that "man is proprietor of his own person."[42] On the surface, this is a perplexing assertion by Locke, since he has already argued that individuals are the workmanship of God and God's property.[43] As we have seen earlier, the fact that we are God's workmanship and God's property is the basis for Locke's argument that a person is not allowed to commit suicide, since to do so would be to end his or her life, which does not belong to him or her but to God.[44] In addition, even our basic rights to protection of "life, liberty, health, and possessions" come from the fact that we are the workmanship of God and thus equal before each other. But if we are God's workmanship, then from where do we get the right of property from our labor? Does not our labor belong to God too?

One possibility is that Locke holds that we have property "in ourselves" and not over ourselves, meaning we are proprietors over the exercise of our will, and thus by extension our labor belongs to us, since it is the outcome of our will. This is what he means by saying that we have a "property in" our own person.[45] It is thus our labor, which belongs to us, and that creates our rights over property, even though we are God's property, and our bodies and selves are God's property. Locke assumes that the fact that labor has the capacity to create private property rights is obvious from both reason and revelation. He writes, for example, that "the Condition of Humane life, which requires Labour and Materials to work on, necessarily introduces *private Possessions* [italics in original]."[46] Or as he puts it more theologically in his *First Treatise on Government*:

> Man had a right to a use of the Creatures, by the Will and Grant of God. For the desire, strong desire of Preserving his Life and Being, having been Planted in him as a principle of action by God himself, Reason, *which was the Voice of God in him*, could not but teach him and assure him, that pursuing that Natural Inclination he had to preserve his Being, he followed the will of his Maker, and therefore had a right to make use of those Creatures, which by his Reason or Senses he could discover would be serviceable thereunto. And thus Man's *Property* in the Creatures was founded upon the right he had, to make use of those things that were necessary or useful to his Being.[47] [italics in original]

Locke thus argues that in giving humans an instinct and right to self-preservation, we know by reason (which is the voice of God inside humans) that we have a right to use creatures.[48] Furthermore, if we have the right to use resources, we must also have the right to remove them from rights in common and by definition have the ability to make them "mine" and not "yours." Locke assumes that this conclusion is also known from revelation and God's command to Adam to subdue the earth, which sets an expectation that humans will labor. The fact that labor creates property rights is thus both a "law of reason" and a "law of nature," the voice of God within the human, and not a human convention as others had argued.[49]

• • •

To step back and take stock, we have so far summarized two major positions in the early modern period regarding the origins and rights of private property. In many ways, these positions broadly characterize the arguments that have continued forward to our own time in late modernity. The position of the "conventionalists" is principally an argument from human contract (what academics describe as "contractarian") or history, because it argues that private property arose from earlier human agreements or conventional arrangements. It is also utilitarian in flavor as well, arguing that the motivation and justification of private property was to improve human life by avoiding conflict and improve human character. By contrast, Locke's natural rights justification of private property locates private property in nature and makes individual labor the trigger that creates private rights in common resources. As we have seen, both positions were trying to answer the principal problem of how private property could have arisen and been morally justified if the world's resources were first given in common. The foundational assumption that resources were given in common was itself based on the prior conviction that humans were created equal in value in nature and before God and that humans needed resources to preserve their lives. In nature at creation, in other words, there were no inherent kings nor queens, no masters and slaves, no leaders and followers, no aristocracy nor commoners. From the original equality in human value and equal human rights to the world's resources flowed the question of how property came about and how an uneven distribution of wealth could have arisen.

I believe the early moderns posed a deep and troubling question for modernity in asking how the disparity of wealth and resources could be reconciled with a conviction of equality. They were aware of the problem and grappling with it. And the question is one with which we collectively still have not sufficiently come to terms. At the start of the modern period, they had grasped and posited what I am taking as the fundamental founding assumption of modernity: that humans are equal in value before the absolute—call it nature, death, or God. They thought this truth was self-evident in nature, even though equality in value is not natural and instead should be seen as a compelling modern conviction by which to organize ourselves and our relations. Some of the early moderns saw that this conviction of equality had the power to undermine the divine right of kings and to justify the transfer of power away from absolute governments into the hands of the people.[50] In this insight, their perspicacity was profound, and they fundamentally began the process by which we in the West conceptualize human value. At the same time, their ideal of equality also called into question how private property could have arisen and how resources that were given in common could have come to be so unevenly distributed among individuals. Is this what God, nature, or both intended? Or is this the product of human conventions, and if so, why did it get this way? It is in response to these latter questions that their answers fell short and did not go far enough in digesting the implications of their own founding insight. It is to the limitations of their answers that we now turn.

Limitations in the Conception of Property

To understand the limitations in the early modern conceptions of property, let us turn again to Locke's justification of private property, for it is the more prominent and entrenched view of property today.[51] Locke's position gives grounding to the conviction that the results of both our efforts and those of our direct ancestors are our own. At the core of this natural rights view is the assumption that the industriousness or labor of one person will not have a negative impact on or injure another. This core conviction, however, makes sense only on the premise that natural resources are inexhaustible and that one person's labor does not limit another's. This assumption is critical for Locke's natural rights argument and constitutes a blind spot in Locke's justification of private property, as it does for others such as Pufendorf before him.[52] Locke assumes that there is an inexhaustible supply of resources, land, and opportunities for every individual and that the decisions and activities of those who came earlier do not limit or affect the opportunity of those who follow. If resources are not sufficient or inexhaustible for everyone's needs, then by what right could God or nature privilege the first laborers over later ones if all were equal in value? We can see this blind spot more clearly by considering the following analogy.

Suppose that at the beginning of time there were five hundred people and only five hundred square miles of land. And suppose in the beginning everyone was wandering the planet and eating acorns and fruit from the trees and living off the earth, and there was no private property. Now imagine that one hundred individuals got a head start, and each enclosed and labored on five square miles, tilling the soil, growing wheat, and involving themselves in productive engagements with the land. All five hundred square miles in the world would now be private property according to the labor theory. There would be none left for the other four hundred individuals who wanted to labor later. Simply because they got a slow start, the remaining four hundred individuals and their descendants would now be forced to work for the first one hundred individuals or to start their own businesses somehow, because they didn't take advantage of the first-mover advantage. The other four hundred might be creative enough to find alternative ways to build their wealth, but they would need more industriousness to avoid simply selling their labor to those who own the land. In this case, the labor of the first individuals circumscribes and limits the opportunity of the latter individuals. And it does so because land and resources are not unlimited.

Because Locke assumes resources are plentiful and inexhaustible, he does not see how the labor of one person could injure the rights of another *in a condition of scarcity*. Where resources are limited, the labor of the earlier individuals can negatively affect the rights of other or later individuals. There might not be as many natural resources available for another laborer.

It is easy, for example, to see how Locke and other early moderns made the assumption of abundance about the earliest human ancestors. In the beginning of human time, when a person took something from the common stock, no one else was damaged or hurt, for there was always plenty more to go around. Here is this assumption in Locke's words:

> Nor was this *appropriation* of any parcel of *Land*, by improving it, any prejudice to any other Man, since there was still enough, and as good left; and more than the yet unprovided could use. So that, in effect, there was never the less left for others because of his inclosure for himself; for he leaves as much as another can make use of, does as good as take nothing at all. No Body could think himself injur'd by the drinking of another Man, though he took a good Draught, who had a whole River of the same Water left him to quench his thirst; and the Case of Land and Water, where there is enough of both, is perfectly the same.[53]

If one person claimed a piece of land, another could readily move elsewhere and find arable land or lands to hunt. If one drank from the river, there was plenty left to quench the thirst of another.

While it is easy to see how seventeenth-century thinkers projected an unlimited abundance back into the early history before humans had greatly populated the earth, it is more difficult, though still understandable, that they drew this same conclusion in the seventeenth century, when the human population in Europe had begun to expand. The seventeenth century was still a century before the Industrial Revolution with the kinds of inventions such as the steam engine and the spinning jenny that would transform the means of production and the size of cities. The population in England by 1600 was estimated to be four million people, and London's population had grown to two hundred fifty thousand, though other towns were quite smaller.[54] To the early modern thinkers, it is understandable how natural resources still looked sufficiently abundant and unlimited. Locke noted that though "the Race of Men have now spread themselves to all the corners of the world and do infinitely exceed the small number [which] was at the beginning," yet it is still possible to find "vacant places" in America.[55] Locke thought he was being bold when he claimed that even if every individual had as much land as "he could make use of," there was still sufficient land in the world for double the world's population at his time. He could not imagine that the population might reach more than seven billion, as it has today.

Locke's optimism about the inexhaustible abundance of nature came in large part from what is an extremely thoughtful understanding of human labor. It is labor that unlocks natural resources and creates abundance, at least in comparison with "nature unworked." Nature provides the basic raw resources and some basic resources on which humans can subsist. Locke is eloquent and insightful in detailing how human labor transformed and expanded the benefits of natural resources. Labor was so powerful, according to Locke, that nine-tenths of goods produced for human consumption were produced through labor and did not come unmediated from nature.[56] As evidence, he noted too that Americans (natives) are "rich in Land, and poor in the Comforts of Life" and that though Americans have much land, "yet for want of improving it by labour, have not one hundreth part of the Conveniences we enjoy: And a King of a large and fruitful Territory there [in America], feeds, lodges, and is clad worse than a day-Labourer in *England*."[57] It is not the amount of land itself that determines whether it produces abundantly, but the amount of labor upon it. Locke concludes, "This shews, how much numbers of men are to be preferd to largenesse of dominions, and that the increase of lands, and the right imploying of them is the great art of government."[58]

In this way, Locke rightfully anticipated that human labor and industriousness had the power to expand nature's bounty dramatically. To Locke, the world's resources looked inexhaustible. Labor could continue to unlock infinite resources of the planet, and an industrious person could always find ways to satisfy his or her needs. For one who wanted to labor, there was always ample opportunity. In this sense, humans fulfilled God's purpose to "subdue" the earth, which Locke interpreted to mean "improve it for the benefit of life."[59] Labor on the land was the fulfillment of the earth's potential and God's will, and for this reason uncultivated land could not be owned, for it had not yet been worked. Similar assumptions about labor helped justify European colonialism and conquest of America, as we shall see.[60]

Locke's insights about labor gave him confidence that the creation of private property rights would expand rather than limit the resources available for the human species. It was this confidence that led him to the moral position that one individual's labor and creation of property rights does not limit or injure the opportunities of the next person.[61] For Locke, the situation at creation before private property existed was really no different from the situation later in human history in his own day. There was always a limitless supply of natural resources on which human labor could be expended. The pie grew and grew and did not diminish.

Today, with the hindsight of more than three hundred years since Locke, many of us can see this as an understandable blind spot in Locke's theory. Most of us realize today that without care, the planet's basic resources are exhaustible. I do not need to enumerate the number of animal and plant species that have disappeared, the bodies of water and air polluted, the number of forests depleted, the ozone that is thinning out, and countless other examples of the way in which nature has been depleted. The question before us is thus different from the one before the architects of natural rights. For we can see that without constraints, labor on nature can have a detrimental impact on others' rights. Nature is not an ever-expanding pie. There are only so many pieces to go around, and the right thing to do is to share them with everyone at the table. Without constraints, the natural resources on which we can labor and through which we can create abundance can and will be depleted. Indeed, my labor can create damaging effects on nature through what economists have called "externalities," such as pollution, restricting and limiting your possibility of limitless abundance. In a situation of scarcity, the people who labor first are privileged over those who labor later. A natural rights theory of property thus falls apart when there is in fact an exhaustible supply of resources. With scarcity or a limitation on resources, the first movers who grab and labor on the property benefit more than those who come later and find less available.

This brings me to a second critique of Locke's natural rights theory of property. As noted earlier, Locke assumes that a person is a proprietor of his or her own person and therefore owns his or her own labor and the fruits of that labor. This all makes some sense only when we imagine labor in the beginning of civilization, as in the examples Locke uses. It makes some sense to say, using Locke's examples, that the Indian who kills the deer or takes fish or ambergris from the ocean, or the person who gathers acorns from the tree, should get the full results of his or her labor.[62] But if we talk about labor later in the development of civilization, it is much harder to see how all of my labor belongs exclusively to me when I am not laboring directly on unmediated nature.[63] I have explored this issue previously, in chapter 3, arguing that we stand on the shoulders of countless people before us, whose insights and inventions provide the platform on which we live our lives. We don't labor on a blank slate of nature in the same way the very first theoretical ancestors may have, though even distant ancestors benefited from early discoveries of tools, fire, and an upright posture. As soon as we labor and transform nature, humans produce a new platform through which they engage nature. Human labor and inventiveness created fire, domesticated animals, invented steel, made parchment and paper, built spinning jennies and steam engines, discovered penicillin, and created light bulbs, electricity, automobiles, computers, and so on. Those who follow earlier laborers benefit from their prior labors. The knowledge of the predecessors gets embodied in the output of their labor and is taken up and assumed by those who labor later. What grows is a shared human knowledge that is the platform on which later humans labor. Indeed, humans are distinctive in the amount of knowledge they accumulate and pass on to descendants through learning and culture. The output of this shared human endeavor actually changed the very nature of the human animal over time and made us what we are.

Locke to some extent anticipated this insight but did not draw out its full moral implications. He talks eloquently about what investment of labor goes into making even a simple loaf of bread, making the point that it is labor invested in countless other products that stand behind even the simplest commodity:

> "Twould be a strange *Catalog of things, that industry provided and made use of, about* [i.e., in the making of] *every Loaf of Bread,* before it came to our use, if we could trace them; Iron, Wood, Leather, Bark, Timber, Stone, Bricks, Coals, Lime, Cloth, Dying-drugs,

Pitch, Tar, Masts, Ropes, and all the Materials made use of in the Ship, that bought any of the Commodities made use of by any of the Workmen, to any part of the Work all which, "twould be almost impossible, at least too long, to reckon up."[64]

In seeing how any product is in fact the outcome of many other prior investments of labor, Locke here anticipates an insight that is core to Adam Smith's *Wealth of Nations* and modern economics, a topic to which we return later.[65] If we take Locke's insight here to its logical conclusions, then it is difficult to see how my labor can or should belong exclusively to me.[66] If I invent a cure for cancer because someone earlier created a microscope, or if I make bread because someone else learned to create yeast, build ships, and transport wheat, then countless outcomes of labor in the human community make possible the abundance that follows an individual's labor. It is hard to see how the results of an individual's labor should belong only to him or her alone.[67] While it might make sense to say a person is a proprietor of his or her own person, it is more difficult to see how all of my labor should be my own when I work on gifts bequeathed by others before me. Every type of labor I perform leverages the efforts of countless other people who labored before me. How are their labors not also embedded into mine? The key here, as in the previous point, is that no humans besides the theoretical first ancestral pair labor on a blank slate of nature. We labor instead within a human world that has already transformed nature, and we bring to bear in our labor collective knowledge that the human community has gathered, remembered, and shared. How can the outcome of my labors belong only to me when I labor with knowledge of countless others before me? How can I borrow from the bank of human knowledge without paying back a fee or interest for that use?

There is a third critical hole in the modern labor theory of property that has to do with the fairness of labor as the only mechanism to create private property. The labor theory of property assumes that labor invested is always proportional to outcome. That is why Locke, like predecessors such as Pufendorf, says that labor creates private property, because he sees it as a fair way in which what was in common became private. Locke assumes it is fair because of the ever-expanding theory of natural resources. If there are always more possibilities for resources and human inventiveness, then my labor can theoretically always find an outlet that produces an outcome proportional to my investment of labor.

There are several problems with this theory. If resources are not always expandable, or they are not easily accessible, or there are dwindling resources, then my efforts may not be proportional to the outcomes, for I may have to expend more labor than another person to achieve the same results. In other words, the labor theory of property assumes that individuals should be rewarded for their effort and labor, and that makes them work hard and fulfill God's vision that resources were given to humans to expand. And that view fits with the starting assumption that everyone is more or less equal and starts out on a level playing field with equal access to resources. The problem is that while it may theoretically be a level playing field in the beginning of time—though that point is debatable too—it is not a level playing field as the human population expands and resources come under ownership. A proportional outcome matches effort expended only on a level playing field with the same rules of the game for everyone and when everyone gets to start the game at the same time. In the real world, effort is not always proportional to outcome. This is because access to resources may vary, and because talents and circumstances enter into the outcome, and because not everyone plays the same game. A better analogy would be a relay race in which subsequent runners are already hindered or advantaged by the outcome of their earlier teammates or even those who are not on their team.

Indeed, the labor theory of property does not adequately take account of the differences between effort, talents, or circumstances. Not everyone's equal effort is the same. People are born with different talents and capabilities. Not everyone has the same starting point by definition. While hard work and training can go a long way in maximizing a person's capabilities, neutralizing inborn deficits, and maximizing inborn talents, differences in skills and capabilities do affect outcome, no matter how big a person's effort. In addition, a person's circumstances, including not just the talents they are born with, but where they are born geographically, to which parents and culture, and in which epoch, all will shape and affect the outcome of their individual effort. The question is whether a theory of property should or could recognize variations in talents and circumstances.

Let's start first with the question of talents. There is no question that human variations exist among people. Some are smarter, some better looking, others are better singers, or taller for basketball, or able to run faster, etc. And there is no question too that this variation has been beneficial to the human species as a whole, for like nature in general, the proliferation of differences helps create new varieties of species. So while we can see the benefits to everyone of each person pursuing his or her own course and talents, the benefits may not ultimately be fair to the individual him- or herself. We do not all start with the same skills, capabilities, circumstances. Was this what God wanted, for those who believe in God? Did God give us varying talents so that some of us could live in poverty, and others in a rich abundance of resources? Is there an understanding of God that would have wanted some humans to have radically more resources than others? One suspects this was not God's intent, at least the kind God that some would want to believe in.

One can see how the differentiation of humans into rich and poor might be what humans produce naturally. And one could argue from nature that the uneven distribution of resources is itself natural. But the question before us, as humans who start with the hypothesis or quest for equality, is whether we are content with what nature naturally produces. Isn't the notion of human equality a vision that contests nature's natural course and that tries to have us live according to a human ideal and aspiration? Isn't that what we think and wish is different about humans, that is to say, that we can live by an ethical center that moves beyond instinct? In some ways that was at the heart of the vision of the modern natural rights thinkers, who argued that humans had distinctive burdens among the animals species and thus distinctive responsibilities to identify and realize a moral law.

For all of these reasons, it is hard to see how a labor-only theory of property would be a fair way to distribute resources. On the contrary, if equality suggests that all natural resources were (or should have been) given to humanity in common, then it would seem that relying on labor alone to create private property would be a fundamental violation of that founding conviction. While it is easy to see how we might want an individual's effort to be a key factor in his or her outcomes, and why we might want to motivate people to pursue their individual interests, it is hard to see how the equality of human beings can justly mesh with a radically uneven distribution of natural resources. By what right should some people have radically more than others, if all resources were or should have been given in common in our imagined beginning or because we wish to embrace the pursuit of equality?

That this tension exists in the labor theory of property is evident from Locke himself, who sensed some of the inherent problems in his theory of natural property and who attempted to argue that there were natural and reasonable limits on what an individual could accumulate through labor, at least in the beginning of human history. Specifically, Locke says that in the beginning of human history, a person's labor created property rights only in what could be used without spoiling. A person could *not* hoard up resources and let them go to waste, though he or she could destroy property as long as it was while using it, as, for example, when one eats food.[68] These were constraints imposed by God, nature, and reason, at least in early human history. In the beginning, therefore, property distribution was fair, for no one could or would take more than was needed or could be used. There was a *natural* inherent limit on accumulation, reinforced by God and reason's command not to let anything spoil.

> As much as any one can make use of to any advantage of life before it spoils, so much he may by his labour fix a Property in: Whatever is beyond this, is more than his share, and belongs to others. Nothing was made by God for man to spoil or destroy. And thus, considering the plenty of natural Provisions there was

a long time in the World, and the few spenders; and to how small a part of that provision the industry of one Man could extend itself, and ingross it to the prejudice of others; especially keeping within the *bounds*, set by reason, of what might serve for his *use;* there could be then little room for Quarrels or Contentions about Property so established.[69]

In Locke's mind, property rights had built-in, natural, inherent limits, and there was sufficient abundance that ensured one person's labor and property rights did not harm the rights of others. People did not live in a state of war with each other, because there was plenty to go around, and no one hoarded anything.[70] All was well as long as nature was governing things.

This natural equilibrium broke down, however, when humans invented money. With the agreement to use something like gold as a medium of exchange in transactions, humans could now accumulate wealth without worrying about spoilage. They could thus satisfy the human desire to accumulate while meeting the expectation of God and reason that nothing should go to waste. This is why precisely those types of things that did not spoil (such as gold) came to serve as money. Prior to the invention of money, spoiling was a built-in, natural mechanism that prevented people from accumulating much more than they could use or exchange. With the invention of money, which by its very nature would not spoil, individuals could accumulate more than they needed without disrupting the equilibrium of nature. Here is Locke again: "This I dare boldly affirm, That the same *Rule of propriety*, (*viz.*) that every Man should have as much as he could make use of, would hold still in the World, without straitning [i.e., without bothering] any body; since there is Land enough in the world to suffice double the Inhabitants, had not the *Invention of Money*, and the tacit agreement of Men to put a value on it, introduced (by Consent) larger possessions, and a Right to them; which, how it has done, I shall, by and by shew more at large."[71]

If we pause here, we can see that Locke is in some ways wanting to eat his cake and have it too. On the one hand, he wants to argue that property is a natural right intended by God and made evident by reason from the natural desire for self-preservation.[72] In that natural state of simpler societies, people do not accumulate more than they can use. He also acknowledges that industriousness differs across individuals and therefore that a labor theory of property means some people accumulate more than others. On the other hand, he also wants to say the uneven distribution of wealth is not entirely natural; it is the outcome of the human invention of money and the human desire for more than what people need. In nature, there is equality and a kind of natural equilibrium in which people have no mechanism to accumulate much more than they can use. The human desire for more and the ability to store wealth with money destroyed the natural equilibrium and ended the equality of resources that nature maintained. Although the right to property from labor by itself leads to uneven accumulation, it is in part humanity's fault, and not entirely God's or nature's, that there is such an unequal distribution of resources.[73]

This is ultimately a tension in Locke's theory, and it exposes the fundamental problem we are here exploring. Can you argue that property is a natural right but not also see the uneven distributions of resources as also from nature? Locke tries to slip around the problem by blaming material inequality partially on the invention of money, which was born of the human desire for more than what people need.[74] Inequality of wealth was in part the outcome of human convention, not entirely from God or nature itself, which had a more natural equilibrium and balance. While it is clear that Locke celebrates labor and private property, it is not completely clear how Locke feels about the unequal allocation of resources that arises from human convention. Locke seems to be saying it was inevitable, given the nature of human desire and the origin of property in labor. Some view Locke as essentially providing an early justification of a capitalist economy, which was just developing.[75] Yet it also appears that Locke sees the modern human state as a kind of fall from an earlier natural state in which people lived in balance with nature with enough resources to go around before the invention of money.[76] And if he does see the fall into inequality as a corruption of the original human state, then why does he not argue for a way to correct it? These are questions that, standing three hundred years after Locke, we will need to ask in his place.

In trying to pawn off responsibility for the inequitable distribution of wealth in part to the invention of money and human desires, Locke ends up offering an answer that looks like that of the conventionalists, who had argued that private property itself was a human invention. In their view and Locke's, the unequal allocation of resources is ultimately a result of human decisions—whether the invention of private property or the invention of money. On neither view is the unequal distribution of resources entirely implicit in nature itself, even if property exists in the natural state. It is a consequence of who humans are and how they have chosen to live. And if that is so, then we have the right, if not the obligation, to think about that ideal human state, which may never have existed in nature, but which may serve as a regulative idea to which we aspire and by which we measure our present circumstances.[77]

• • •

My intent in looking at early modern positions on private property was to call into question those assumptions that continue to inform our modern notions of property and, more specifically, the relentless ideas that 1) private property is a natural right, like life and liberty, and 2) that our labor belongs exclusively to us. These assumptions are taken for granted today without thinking about their philosophical foundations, which rest on debatable and even untenable assumptions. As we have seen, the conception that property is a natural right is mistaken in several ways. It is mistaken not only because it is part of a notions of rights that, as previously discussed, is fuzzy, but also because it assumes the understandable but mistaken notion that the world's resources are inexhaustible and that anyone who labors will find access to as much natural resource as is necessary to sustain him- or herself. There was a certain fairness taken for granted in the conception of property as a natural right that collapses when there is a limited supply of resources. With limited resources, the first movers in time and history are the beneficiaries of nature's bounty, and the equal value of human beings is undermined by this right, which is supposed to be natural.

Furthermore, the notion of private property rests on the problematic assumption that the output of our labor should be completely our own. I have questioned this assumption in previous chapters showing that everything we labor on, and the knowledge we labor with, is also given to us by the labor of others. We labor not in a vacuum at the beginning of time, but on a platform created by the human species before us. And thus the outcome of our labor should belong partly to ourselves but also partly to humanity, who has enabled us. Finally, we have seen that with limited or inaccessible resources the justice that private property was trying to create is not achieved. Without a level playing field, we aren't playing the same game, and my efforts or talents don't have the same chances as yours, and vice versa.

What all of this means, practically speaking, is not a simple problem to address, but it is one that matters. The first step is to realize that the outcome of our labor should *not* belong 100 percent to each of us individually. With the starting point that resources are limited and exhaustible, and that the outcome of our labor is due in part to the efforts of many others before us, we can no longer see our moral responsibilities as fulfilled by our own labor and the expansion of nature's capabilities. Limited resources means that anything we consume can potentially harm a contemporary or a future human being, if we do not have the means to conserve or expand resources and distribute access to those resources fairly. The pie is not infinitely expanding, at least as we now understand it. And until we can prove that our consumption of resources is not a deprivation and harm to others, then we have to assume that any use has to be compensated by a payback to the general fund with interest.

The original intellectual instinct of the natural rights thinkers—that everything was given in common and that nature was given for humans to use—was on the right path. And the attempt to link human initiative, labor, and private property with those assumptions about equality and resources makes sense. But what those early modern thinkers failed to do was set any limits. Some limits should arise, because we can do harm through the consumption of resources, both through the depletion of nature but also through the uneven distribution of nature across human populations and individuals. In light of our current understanding of nature, it would make more sense to see the use of natural resources more like a bank loan or business capitalization rather than like a free gift: we are granted something on the condition we pay back more—either interest or a percentage of the benefits. Such a notion would be more compatible with the idea of natural resources given in common, which flows from the conception of human basic equality. After all, if resources were owned in common, why would any of us agree to let people use them without contributing something back and paying for their use? Would a bank give away its resources for nothing? Any use of the natural environment should be understood to come with a cost that should be paid back to the common shareholders. Why should our relationship to nature be any less responsible than our relationship to our banker or our investor? We can see property rights, then, not as individual rights, but as a contract between human individuals and the Bank of Nature (or, if you prefer, God), for whom the human species as a whole are the shareholders. Arguably, we will also want to expand the notion of shareholders to include all stakeholders, not just ourselves, but all living species, to also go beyond the view that nature was given to human beings alone and for their purposes only.

We should also now see ourselves as having natural responsibilities to conserve resources and to think about accessibility to resources across human populations. Since resources are exhaustible and since resources were given or intended for human beings in general, then it would be stealing both from one's human contemporaries and future individuals to take too much of nature's resources. Since resources are exhaustible, *their overuse constitutes stealing from others.* In a context where supply is exhaustible and opportunities are limited, a much more rigorous model of sharing and conserving should be part of how humans think of their rights, since their rights arise, after all, from the notion that we are equal in value. If we don't want to allocate resources more fairly, then we should just abandon the modern quest to live in light of the idea that "all people are created equal." After all, as discussed before, duties and responsibilities are often the flip side of rights.

What this approach restores is a sense that the notion of property rights comes with a set of duties and debt to the human species as a whole. Some of the natural rights thinkers articulated this broader conception of obligation to humanity in general and, contrary to popular opinion, did not just focus on the individual's rights. Even Locke, who is often cited as the champion of individual rights par excellence, argued that the law of nature "willeth the Peace and *Preservation of Mankind*." One who violates the law of nature is "dangerous to Mankind" and has committed a "trespass against the whole Species." Such a person has "quit the principles of human nature," "committed war against all mankind," and become like a "Lyon or a Tyger." I have a right to punish or execute such a person, because as an individual I have "a right to preserve mankind in general."[78]

Locke implicitly connected this obligation to preserve humankind with his theory of labor, which he saw as expanding the human population and human resources and thus fulfilling the vision of protecting humankind. Given our vantage point in time, we can go beyond Locke and see that preserving the natural resources and sharing the benefits of our labor are natural responsibilities that are embedded in our rights that we wish to make natural.

I have argued that the "natural rights" understanding of private property is flawed in critical ways and needs to be revised. The fact that private property should *not* be treated as a natural right was already obvious to some of the early moderns who argued it was a human institution created for pragmatic human purposes. On this latter view, the question arises as to how binding on the present are human institutions developed in the past and how much pragmatic, utilitarian goals should override moral convictions such as the equal value of humans before the absolute. Even within natural rights theory, human institutions are by definition revisable, because people's opinions change and because they don't like or foresee the consequences of what they instituted. Indeed, the ability to change is the very hallmark of the liberal conception of government: people can revise the laws because they created the original contract, as long as they don't infringe what are the natural rights. If private property rules arose hundreds or thousands of years before us, what obligation do we have to honor them precisely as they are? And to what extent are these earlier practices binding if their consequences were and remain unfair? If these were human conventions and contracts intended to solve human problems, then it logically follows that humans can agree to revise their terms and conditions, and this is especially pressing if the consequences of those earlier agreements produce consequences that were not intended or expected or that have proven morally disturbing.

At issue, in other words, is how much we should be stuck with an institution of private property in exactly the form as it currently exists simply because it was thought to be reasonable in the past. Is not the difference between a natural right and a contract precisely in the fact that the latter is thought to be revisable? Furthermore, if the key and compelling founding assumption of modernity is that humans are equal in value, then the fact that resources are so unevenly distributed both among individuals and among nations should be seen as a moral problem that we aspire to address, even if we cannot practically eradicate it. The uneven distribution of resources cannot be justified by appeal to either a natural right or a long-ago convention of human beings.

What alternatives do we have, given this history? I shall take up this question in a subsequent chapter, where I argue that it is precisely government's responsibility to be umpire, to seek fairness among individuals, and to help level the playing field, and that as individuals we have a natural responsibility or duty to contribute to that goal. Socialism, of course, was a failed attempt to institutionalize the equal value of human beings. It didn't work because it destroyed human initiative by making personal efforts irrelevant and by trying to manage an economy centrally. But why should a failure to actualize our commitment to the equal value of human beings mean we give up completely and abandon the moral responsibility?

Indeed, there remains no moral foundation ultimately for the argument that it is right for one person to have more than another if *both have labored equally hard with all their talents.* The practical problem, of course, is that it is impossible to rank how hard people have worked or how to rank their talents. Talents come in a wide variety, and a person may excel in one area but not in another. Today, we let the market take care of solving that problem. People seek to find their place based on their particular interests, talents, and resources. Yet since those pursuits of happiness are already constrained by thousands of years of private property and by dwindling resources, there is no fairness in the game. The game is stacked for and against certain players because of the historical allocation of resources, which defines how widely they can pursue their talents. That is the moral problem that remains. Natural rights in private property do not make it go away. In the vision of modernity that sought to place equal value on human beings, no one should have been privileged from the start with access to more resources. The question before us is how best to take that commitment seriously now and how much to let pragmatic utilitarian concerns and the decisions of the past deviate us from that goal.

Chapter 7
The Original Theft and the Wealth of Nations

Why should one nation have more wealth than other nations? This question is related to the prior question of why one individual should have more than another. This is a question that is almost never asked here in the United States today, where we simply take for granted our vast resources and our right to have them. Instead, political rhetoric focuses on how to preserve the wealth and position of the United States in the world and how government's purpose is to prevent the United States from losing its power and prestige in the world and to ensure its people are prosperous and happy. We have had such a privileged position as a country that few people stop to think about what right there is that our nation is so blessed with wealth and resources. But if liberty is all about rights, as many liberty-first advocates argue, then by what right does America have such wealth and so much land? Is there a moral justification that legitimates our country's wealth compared to another? How does a nation legitimately acquire wealth, and how is that related to individuals' rights to property?

As we might anticipate, the issue of national wealth has been inextricably linked in the modern period to the property rights of individuals. In fact, an important if not the central purpose of government is often understood as protecting citizens' rights to life, liberty, and property. Locke, representing the view that has come to dominate, is often quoted to the effect that "The great and *chief end* therefore, of Mens uniting into Commonwealths, and putting themselves under Government, *is the Preservation of their Property"* and the *"enjoyment of their Properties in peace and safety."*[1] For Locke, "property" means more than just material possessions, since people unite into political societies "for the mutual *Preservation* of their Lives, Liberties and Estates, which I call by the general name, *Property."*[2] Since the purpose of government is the protection of property broadly construed, the *"Supreme Power cannot take* from any Man any part of his *property* without his own consent. For the preservation of Property being the end of Government, and that for which men enter into society."[3] In this view of government, we can see that the distribution of resources among nations is intimately related to the question of property's distribution among individuals as well as the role of government itself in protecting rights.

Popular discussion of individual rights often overlooks and ignores this larger question of a nation's moral foundation and its jurisdiction over resources and land, as if this latter problem does not exist. Debates tend to focus only on the internal-facing question of whether government is overstepping its bounds by infringing the rights of individuals inside the nation. In asking that question only, we take for granted that our nation has the rights to the land and resources over which it watches. Little attention is paid to the flip side of the same coin, namely, the external question of how my government has the power to command control over the extensive resources and territories over which its laws extend. This is one of the deep, hidden problems in rights theories that liberty-first advocates don't want to acknowledge or talk about.

But we will acknowledge it here. The notion of a nation's wealth is built on top of the notion of individual property rights, which we have previously discovered needs to be substantially revised. In the classic natural rights theory, political institutions emerged as individuals came together to form larger communities with political institutions called "commonwealths." Not all kinds of social groups or communities are political in this way. A political society or "commonwealth" differs from other types of communities, such as a church group, club, or other informal community, by having a sovereign power that creates and judges law and enforces its rules through punishment of its members. It is this "sovereign" power to enforce law that distinguishes a political community from one that is not.

In the modern period, as natural rights theories emerged and reshaped the understanding of nations, the state's authority over lands needed justification and could no longer be attributed to the divine right of kings. In the modern version of the natural rights theory, states or political communities emerged when individuals explicitly or tacitly agreed to form one body and live under one set of rules that could be enforced by a sovereign political power. This was the classic "social contract" theory, in which individuals made voluntary decisions to live life under a commonwealth with its rules and regulations and to forgo life outside a commonwealth in the "state of nature." In the view that individuals already acquired legitimate rights to property in nature, the commonwealth or political state represented an extension of individual property rights and the raison d'être of the state was at least in part to protect an individual's property. Everything fit nicely together. The story went something like this:

Individuals first spread across the earth, legitimately acquiring their property rights through labor or by agreement and consent. Living as individuals, however, was unsatisfying for a variety of reasons, including fear that one would or could lose one's life, liberty, and property. The fear arose because there was no overarching power that could protect their lives and property from others who used power to steal and plunder.[4] There also was no impartial judicial system, with the result that justice was not meted out fairly.[5] People also lived together in informal communities out of a desire for sociability and because God made the human being as a creature who was not intended to be alone and "put him under strong Obligations of Necessity, Convenience, and Inclination to drive him into Society as well as fitted him with Understanding and Language to continue to enjoy it."[6] To protect their lives and property, however, people quickly developed political institutions that could protect themselves and their properties and enforce justice fairly.[7] The development of political power was thus thought to be in line with the law of nature and natural reason, because living without a political power was dangerous, fearful, and threatening to one's life, liberty, and property.[8]

There were two complementary theories about how states came into being, and both explained how the state legitimately had jurisdiction over the territory that it oversaw. According to the first theory, commonwealths came to have power over the land that their citizens had legitimately and rightfully acquired as individuals. The state's territory thus became coextensive with the properties originally owned already by its citizens. Since the citizens acquired their property legitimately, either through labor or through human convention, the territorial boundaries of the state were themselves thought to be legitimate and defined by individual property rights.[9]

In a second complementary theory of commonwealth development, individuals came together as a group and together moved into and settled what had been previously uninhabited lands. In this case, the whole community as a body took possession of vacant lands and then divided the territory up among individuals based on laws in the commonwealth.[10]

The first commonwealths were often thought to be those of the patriarchal family, since the father somewhat naturally fell into the role of leader in the early clans.[11] These grew into hereditary or elective kingdoms not because the father had political power mandated by God or nature, but simply somewhat organically, since clans naturally chose the father as the patriarchal leader of the clan. Smaller commonwealths that were legitimately formed in either of these ways merged with other commonwealths until larger political bodies or states were formed.

In all of these cases, even though the individuals who formed or joined commonwealths continued to own their own properties, the commonwealth itself now had a supervisory power or jurisdiction over their lands and properties. That was the deal that individuals made when they entered into a social contract. They would turn over the right to set laws about property to the commonwealth. The power to rule and punish for harm to property was part of what political sovereignty involved. Individuals gained the protection of the commonwealth but only on the condition that they would abide by the rules that the state would create to govern land and property. Indeed, it was through oversight of the land that states exercised control over individuals. While individuals were free to enter and leave the commonwealth if they were not citizens, they had to obey a state's rules in general if they enjoyed benefits from the property that was under the state's control.[12] If individuals chose to leave the state, they could not take their lands with them, since the lands belonged to the state. Some theorists even denied them the right to leave a commonwealth once they explicitly assented to the social contract.[13] In either of these theories of state formation, the boundaries of the state are legitimate. In the one theory, the state's territory is identical with the lands of the individuals who originally formed those political entities. In the other theory, the state comes into being as a group of individuals together settled vacant lands.

This close relationship of the individual, the land, and the state is not thought about very deeply today by many of those who speak about protecting their rights. The state exists as a fait accompli, and people argue about their rights within the state, forgetting the equally important question of what the foundation of the state's right to exist and control its territories is. In what follows, I want to probe this relationship between individuals, the land, and the state in several different ways.

First, I want to extend my argument from the previous chapter and ask about the legitimacy of the state's jurisdiction over its lands and the distribution of wealth among nations. Since the state's power over land is derived from the logically prior notions of private property, our reconceptualization of private property inevitably must alter the very notion of a state's ownership of wealth and resources. As a result, it will become apparent that the state's jurisdiction over property is not an absolute right, but a temporary right, and more like an executor of a will than an owner of property. That conclusion becomes evident from our realization in the previous chapter that the individual does not have exclusive rights in his or her own labor and also has duties that come from being a member of the human family.

As a corollary, I want to explore the relationship of the individual to the state and consider the proper expectations individuals should have of the state and the state should have of individuals. In the rhetoric of the "liberty-only" platform, government should be concerned only with protecting an individual's rights and property, and there is little responsibility of the individual to the state. But it shall become evident that the relationship of the individual to government is more complicated than that, for even in the early modern theory of rights, a sacrifice or compromise is thought to occur when an individual agrees to live within a commonwealth and gives up some freedoms for the benefits of sociability and security of living in society. A certain kind of mutual obligation arises that makes individuals subject to the state and thus responsible to the state and the purposes of the community. But neither the state nor the individual is the exclusive focus of moral obligation, which also belongs to the species as a whole.

The State, Land, and Rights

If a thief steals property and resells it, does that property belong to the person who unknowingly bought it? And what if that person now sells it to someone else, and that person sells it to someone else again? And what if none of these buyers knew that the original seller was a thief? Does each of the subsequent people in line legitimately own his or her property? How does the original theft affect the legitimate rights of those who come later?

One may be able to excuse the subsequent individual for not knowing the original property was stolen. But what if the subsequent individual did know or could have known about the original theft? The fact that an act of theft occurred at the beginning of those transactions raises questions about the legitimacy of the property rights of each of those subsequent property holders. Had the theft not occurred, some other sequence of buying and selling transactions would have happened, and other distributions of property would have arisen that were founded on legitimate ownership. And what if the original theft is pervasive, and all private property that exists today ultimately descended from some original theft?

This problem of the original theft is analogous to the situation of how nations came to have jurisdiction over their lands. It is a fiction that nations' lands and resources are nothing more than the aggregate of the properties that their individual citizens legitimately acquired or that the states themselves came into existence legitimately when a group of people settled vacant lands. It is fiction because there have been few nations that ever came into existence through a social contract among their citizens in the way that is presupposed by natural rights theory.[14] And even in the case of nations that supposedly did come about in something close to this ideal way, such as our United States, it is not the case that the original citizens' acquisition of property was legitimate, reaching back all the way to the beginning of time.

There are thus two separate issues here. The first is whether nation-states come into existence through agreement and social contract. The second is whether individuals who came together to form the state legitimately own their properties and, if not, whether the state has arisen in vacant territories. This is a double-decker problem, but the two issues are intimately related to each other. Let us take up each in turn.

We start first with those individuals who theoretically volunteered to join the commonwealth or state. Let us suppose, following the ideal assumptions of natural rights theory, that the first commonwealths really did form out of a voluntary social contract of the individuals who became members. For the commonwealth to legitimately have jurisdiction over its territory, all the members of the voluntary association must have acquired their properties legitimately. But if they or their ancestors did not legitimately acquire their properties, then the state's territory cannot be thought to be legitimate either.

In the previous chapter, I showed some of the reasons that we cannot suppose that individuals' acquisitions of property rights can be thought to be exclusively their own. Without repeating my argument in detail here, I argued that we labor within a world of knowledge that we received from our human predecessors and thus stand on the shoulders of giants when we labor. I concluded that anything that we create is also at least in part a product of humanity in general, and it would be stealing from humanity in general to say that the entire output of our labor is our own. So even if the commonwealth was in fact created voluntarily by individuals, those individuals really do not have the right to give their states the exclusive jurisdiction of their property, since the property cannot belong exclusively to them in the first place. Thus the very core claim that the state's purpose is to protect individual property rights is flawed from the outset. It may be true that the individuals who come together to form the state may be doing so at least in part to protect their properties. But those properties do not belong exclusively to them. These individuals are at least in part stewards of property for humanity in general. And while their motivations in joining or affirming the power of the state may be in their own selfish interests, to protect their lives, their liberties, and their properties, the fact is that they do not legitimately have exclusive title to those properties they are wishing to protect. Thus, if we accept the refined notion of private property discussed earlier, we have to also conclude that one purpose of the state goes beyond protecting individual self-interests, for the state also has fiduciary jurisdiction over lands that in part belong to humanity itself, and not to individuals only. There are thus responsibilities that fall to the state, implicit in the individual ownership of the property, that involve duties to the human species as a whole. And just as the state has no right to take what belongs to the individual, so it does not have a right to abuse the property that belongs to the human species as a whole. The state thus has an obligation to balance the responsibilities to individuals under its purview with the responsibilities to humankind as an abstract whole.

To be sure, it may be impossible to say what part or percentage of an individual's property is his or her own versus that which belongs to humanity in general. I shall come back to that difficult practical question again. But saying that this separation is difficult does not do away with the moral insight that both individuals and the state have property that belongs to humanity in general. That is the core point of departure for the very notion of rights that start with the insight that we are all equal in some deep human way.

This reconceptualization of the state dovetails with a second flaw we discovered in natural rights theory: natural rights theory assumed there was an inexhaustible supply of resources in nature and that a later person's opportunity would not be limited or harmed by the efforts of an earlier or contemporaneous laborer. The early modern thinkers thought there was always more vacant land in America. Since we know clearly now that nature can be and is being depleted, the notion that everyone has the same opportunity for success through his or her labor is mistaken. With that knowledge, it is not clear that the majority of reasonable people standing in the "original condition" would have agreed to the convention of private property and a labor theory of value.[15] For if they did not know in which centuries they or their children would live, or they knew that the future would deplete resources, reasonable people would not self-evidently have agreed to let earlier generations consume all the land, air, fish, and species of the planet before they or their children's children had a chance to live. Instead, reasonable people standing in the original situation would have insisted there be conservation of resources among those who are allowed to use resources before either them or their descendants. They would *not* have alighted on or agreed to the notion of private property that sees the outcome of my labor as strictly my own to control as I wish. Instead, they would have understood, as we now understand, that private property carries a responsibility of stewardship to conserve resources. As individuals appropriate resources, a responsibility devolves upon them to both give something back to the bank of the human species as well as to conserve resources for peers and future generations. These responsibilities that fall on the individual become part of the state's responsibility if, as natural rights theory contends, the state is a creation of individuals. My claim, then, is that even if we work within a natural rights theory and language, we see that the very formation of the state involves a transfer to the state of not simply rights, but also responsibilities that had already devolved on individuals through their labor and in their appropriation of natural resources.

That the state's oversight of its wealth and resources cannot be completely legitimate is evident, ironically, from a contradiction already inherent in natural rights theory itself. On the one hand, natural rights theory assumes the commonwealth or state is really just an aggregation of properties that individuals or groups of individuals have rightfully acquired. On the other hand, the theory also takes for granted that the proper distribution of property is *disturbed* in nature by human theft, plundering, murder, and conquest. It is, after all, the fear for their properties, lives, and liberties that supposedly drive individuals into a commonwealth or state and lead them to relinquish police powers to that government. In this way, the natural rights theory of the state assumes that the rightful and just alignment of properties based on individual labor, efforts, and convention was frequently disturbed in nature before the commonwealth was created.[16] Otherwise, there would have been no need to join a state at all.

What we see, then, is that the natural rights theory of the state has a deep contradiction in it. It assumes the state has legitimate ownership over properties because the individuals or group who formed the state acquired their rights legitimately, through labor or convention and not force, and they voluntarily joined their political commonwealths. Yet at the same time the theory assumes the state exists as a remediation for the fact that human ambition and desire led many individuals to plunder and steal property and thereby disrupt the rightful and fair allocation based on labor or first occupation of vacant lands. The state, according to traditional theory, is the best way to remediate this inherent problem in nature.[17] In this view, the state or commonwealth represents an attempt to create and protect a just allocation of land and resources and to prevent further erosion of a rightful alignment of labor, efforts, and property.

What seems right about the perspective we have been exploring here is that it seems to align more closely with the actual messiness of history. If we take a historical perspective, commonwealths and nations appear to have come into being in many different and complex ways that often involved power and conquest, among other historical forces. The natural rights theorists were not naïve in this regard. Looking back into earlier human history as well as at the periods in which they were writing—with religious wars and an emerging European colonialism and empire building—they recognized that political conquest was a recurring historical phenomenon. But in recognizing that political conquest and war existed, the natural rights tradition undermined its own contention that nations had a rightful control of their territories. For if conquest and theft occurred regularly, as the theory presupposes, the allocation of resources among individuals and nations was invariably disrupted from what should have been a proper and legitimate allocation of resources among peoples. It is irrelevant if the individuals among the vanquished agree after the fact to become members of the political entity that emerged postconquest.[18] The dislocations of property and resources and the loss of life caused by conquest and war make clear that the supposed neat alignment of property distribution among individuals based on labor or human convention is fundamentally a myth. We cannot see the boundaries of nations as natural or rightful, as natural rights theorists wanted, but rather as pragmatic consequences of historical forces that are complex, multifaceted, and frequently if not usually unjust in some fundamental ways.

It is not possible to get around this problem, as both Locke and many of his modern interpreters try, by claiming that in the ideal case, *rightful and peaceful* government involves the consent of the people. For even in the ideal situation of consent by the parties to the state, the properties those individuals bring to the state have a history behind them that involved theft and conquest. There is almost always some figurative theft or act of violence lurking historically in the background of any piece of property. The consent of individuals to a state does not absolve either the state or those individuals of the moral burden of history and the history of the human species. Even if the majority of individuals acted in good faith in purchasing property according to the law, the historical backdrop against which those transactions have taken place is already sullied invariably by a history of violence, conquest, theft, and war. One transacts in waters that are not clear.[19]

While there might be significant pragmatic obstacles to the reallocation of wealth and resources between individuals and nations, that does not remove a moral burden of our realizing that we live in a world that does not live up to its own aspirations and its own language of rights.[20] In other words, we have to see ourselves in a "fallen state" or "nonelevated" state from where we would like to be. This notion of a fallen state, of course, resonates with a Catholic view of the human world after the Fall and with a view of other religious traditions, such as Jewish Kabbalah, which assume the world needs *tikkun, or* repair, after the fragmentation of light in the Creation. One need not see this in religious terms, nor do we have to see ourselves as "fallen," but simply as not yet having achieved our aspiration of equality. The argument is that our vision of what's right and good is not yet where we would like it and feel it should be. This is in fact the burden of individuals who live in states: the protections that the state offers of our properties and our lives have to be understood with moral duties that the state has to humans in general, both present and future, and to the historical insight and burden that all property has an element of theft lying behind it.

On Native Rights and the Conquest of America

The moral burden that surfaces but is not fully explored or appreciated in natural rights theory is one that includes but also goes beyond the question of native rights.[21] When we realize that the property we own was touched by theft and conquest, the question naturally arises as to who are the rightful owners for which piece of land.

Some of the rights thinkers, such as Locke, sensed part of this problem, with Locke claiming that

> The *Inhabitants* of any Countrey, who are descended, and derive a Title to their Estates from those, who are subdued, and had a Government forced upon them against their free consents, *retain a Right to the Possession of their Ancestors*, though they consent not freely to the Government, whose hard Conditions were by force imposed on the Possessors of that country. For the first *Conqueror never* having *had a Title to the Land of that Country*, the People who are the Descendants of, or claim under those, who were forced to submit to the yoke of a Government by constraint, have always a Right to shake it off and free themselves from the Usurpation, or Tyranny, which the Sword hath brought in upon them.[22]

Locke here exposes the problem at the root of a theory of property and statehood. He must argue that native populations do not lose the right to their land in a conquest, for his whole theory of the state rests on labor being the means to acquire property. In doing so, he rejects the views of those who held that just war can justify taking away a native population's land, at least if they have settled upon it and cultivated it. And thus in this line of thinking, native populations reserve the rights to their ancestral lands.

But Locke apparently did not see or work through the full implications of his insight. Had he thought more deeply about conquest, he might have seen that any notion of rightful ownership of property and the territorial sovereignty of most states was thrown in doubt. While there is something that feels right about recognizing native populations' prior claim to the land, the problem is more complex, since it is hard to see where the native right begins and with whom. While natives were natives before Europeans, if we look all the way back in history, we are unable to get back to the beginning and trace the true descendants from Adam and Eve or from Lucy (to invoke a Darwinian theory of evolution that most of us believe in) into the currently living populations. We cannot, in other words, get back to the true original natives. While some may argue this means that we cannot do anything about the history of conquest at all, I would argue that, on the contrary, it means we all are complicit in the problem and all bear the burden, though some may bear the burden more than others. The moral burden of the theft is shared and distributed. It certainly belongs to colonial powers, as we shall see, but it also belongs to native populations, who themselves stole and invaded the lands of natives who lived contemporaneous with them. Conquest, theft, and invasion have been with us all the way back in time to the beginning.[23] It is a shared human problem that conflicts with our aspirations and ideas.

Americans will find it particularly difficult to swallow the perspective put forward above. After all, Americans know that our nation was one of the first to be founded on an individual's rights of "life, liberty, and the pursuit of happiness." While many nations may have come about through conquest in the past, Americans have always seen themselves as having created a state that was founded on consent and a social contract. America, in American minds, is the nation par excellence, created for and by the people. It is thus the nation that, in the view of many, first lived up to the vision of the natural rights tradition.

This story, however, is misleading in some critical ways, some of which I have explored in another context. It is true that the American founders were influenced significantly by the natural rights tradition and may have been influenced most by John Locke's theory of government, though they also had doubts about natural rights theory and were aware of European intellectual critiques of such theories from figures such as David Hume.[24] The American founders were also aware that anyone's rights had to originate ultimately in the right to the land. If they did not have a right to the lands they lived on, then by what right could they create a state that had sovereignty over their territories? At issue in the entitlement of Americans to their lands was not only the relationship of the American colonists to the British government, but also and less obviously their rhetoric to the native populations of America. The former problem overshadowed the latter question and for this reason obscured and hid the issue of how Americans came to have a right to their lands in the first place. This is one of the hidden dilemmas in the American myth about liberty.

The colonization and conquest of the Americas was part of European expansion and colonialism in general in the sixteenth and seventeenth centuries.[25] Yet by the time the Americans were debating their rights under British rule in the 1760s, the colonies were already well populated and secure on the east coast of the North American continent, though they had not yet expanded far westward into the interior. The question of what gave the European settlers the rights to have property on this American continent was not one that had a great deal of prominence for the colonists at this point in time, though the problem had been voiced in the early period of settlement. By the time Americans asked about their own identities and rights as colonies, the logically prior question of the settlers' rights to American lands had already been decided in many ways by a fait accompli and was peripheral to their concerns. They were focused instead on themselves as colonists being suppressed by an existing sovereignty. They did not think as deeply about themselves as a colonizing and conquering people and thus were able to avoid facing that question, since the European powers had already settled and conquered American lands, at least those along the Eastern seaboard. Lands further inland would remain for Americans themselves to conquer without the benefit of being able to hide behind what European colonizers had already done. By the time the American colonists broke away from Great Britain and declared their independence, they did not examine as carefully the question of how they came to have rights in the American lands in the first place. In some sense, the downplaying or disappearance of the original theft or conquest from the thinking of the American founders is itself a metaphor for all of us who each have forgotten all the murders, conquests, and thefts that reach back into early history and on whose backs our current rights properly sit. This history must somehow figure into what we name as our rights.

It is clear that to some extent the American founders were aware that this thorny question lurked in the background of their own search for American rights. This is part of a much larger and morally disheartening story that cannot be fully told here.[26] But the story is relevant to the construction of rights in America, for if the acquisition of land was not legitimate and rightful in the first place, then on what basis can subsequent descendants claim their rights under their governments to their property? What is the nature of rights, if they rest on an earlier theft and conquest?[27]

To briefly summarize the main themes, the colonists themselves debated the basis of their own American rights. Some argued they had rights because they were British subjects and therefore entitled to the rights and duties of British citizens. On this view, the settlers came to the Americas under British auspices and with full British rights. Another less popular position, espoused by Thomas Jefferson, among others, held that the settlers were not British subjects at all but were independent Europeans settlers who had come to America and started new states under their own sovereignty.[28] Such states were *not* beholden to the British Parliament, though the settlers had voluntarily chosen to adopt the British king as their elected executive. They were British subjects of the king but not under the authority of British Parliament. A third position emphasized the natural rights of all people and justified the American resistance to British rule on that basis.

While each of these positions justified American rights vis-à-vis the rule of British Parliament, the American thinkers also took for granted a background theory of how the settlers came to have rights in the lands they now occupied. They knew that rights, property, and sovereignty were all tied together. These background assumptions were mentioned in passing in the founding literature in the decade leading up to 1776 but were not examined nearly as deeply as other dimensions of their rights, for some obvious reasons.

There were a couple of ways to justify American rights to the lands on the North American continent. First, some founders assumed that it was through a rightful conquest that the European settlers had acquired a right to their lands. That conquest, they believed, was either under the auspices of the British, who led the conquest, or under the initiative of the settlers themselves. In fact, part of the debate between the colonists and the British was precisely over who had sacrificed the most blood and resources to create the new settlements and thus who owned the benefits of the conquest. What legitimized the conquest in the first place was not discussed as openly, though we can discern reasons hovering in the background of their second justification.

The second justification rested on the assumption that American lands were uncultivated and therefore in a state of nature. Since they were "vacant" and uncultivated, the founders assumed they could be settled on a first-come-first-served basis, just as in the original state of the world, when land was in given in common to all humankind. On this view, American natives were thought to lack any rights to the land since they were nomadic and moved with the herds and did not cultivate the land. Since natural rights theory held that nature had been given in common and only became property when it was seized, settled, or cultivated, depending on one's theory, the American lands were understood to be available rightfully to any who would settle and cultivate them.

A third position articulated by the founders was a blend of the first two. This position assumed that a conquest of the Indians was justifiable because the Indians lacked rights to the lands. Since they had not settled on or cultivated the land, they were wrong to resist the colonists or settlers who landed on their shores and wanted to settle the land. Those uncultivated lands belonged to everyone in common. The conquest of the Indians was therefore understood to be morally right, since the Indians were defending property that did not belong to them. It was they and not the colonists who were in the wrong.

These natural rights rationales for taking American lands had a number of similarities to earlier Catholic religious justifications for the Spanish conquest of the Indians in the Southern Hemisphere in the previous century. In fact, the British Puritan colonizers of North America had learned much from and saw themselves as competitors with the Spanish Catholic colonizers of Latin and South America. This was the historical backdrop when the American founders, 150 years into the British colonization of America, began to write about their rights.[29]

Let us take a deeper look at a few of the American founders' positions. The view that American lands were conquered was one theme that runs through the writings of the founders in the period leading up to 1776. Thomas Jefferson, for example, held the view that the settlers' rights to lands came via a conquest through their own blood. It was this conquest, and not any official activity of the British government, that gave the settlers the rights to the land that they occupied and thus grounded their rights to create political territories on those lands. In Jefferson's view, the settlers' rights to create new states rested not just on the natural right to leave their countries of origin but on their legitimate claim to the land that they conquered through their own efforts.[30] The emphasis was that the settlers had spilled their own blood to occupy American lands without the financing and help from the British Crown. Here is how Jefferson put it in his first major piece of political writing, called *A Summary View,* which was written in 1774 and was intended for the meeting of the First

Continental Congress, only two years before he wrote the Declaration of Independence. This essay established the young Jefferson as a respected intellectual of caliber among his political peers. Although Jefferson was too ill to attend in person, he sent his essay on to Congress to share with this colleagues. In the essay, Jefferson has this to say:

> America was conquered, and her settlements made and firmly established, at the expense of individuals, and not of the British public. Their own blood was spilt in acquiring lands for their settlement, their own fortunes expended in making that settlement effectual. For themselves they fought, for themselves they conquered, and for themselves alone they have right to hold.[31]

Jefferson's intent is clearly to show that the settlers did not come to North America under British auspices, expense, or sacrifice, and consequently should not be understood to be under the rule of British Parliament. To make this claim, he argues that it was the settlers as free individuals and not as British subjects who conquered the North American lands.

In Jefferson's view, the settlers' claims to the land flowed from the fact that the conquest was at their own effort and sacrifice. On the land that they rightfully occupied, they set up a society with political and civil institutions. "From the nature and purpose of civil institutions, all the lands within the limits which any particular society has circumscribed around itself, are assumed by that society, and subject to their allotment only."[32] Jefferson is here alluding to the supposition discussed earlier that if individuals had legitimately acquired the rights to the land, or a group of people had settled on unsettled land, then the society they erected around themselves has jurisdiction over those lands. In articulating this view, Jefferson was rejecting the British claims that they had planted, financed, and protected the settlements, and therefore the conquest was under British auspices and that the settlers were thus "colonies" under British rule. The argument over who "owned" the conquest of North America, therefore, was an argument within colonial theory about whether the Americans were British subjects conquering America or independent individuals risking their lives to settle in and conquer new lands.

In this first major foray into political writing, Jefferson was silent on the question of why the settlers' conquest gave them rights to the lands, even though we know Jefferson was intimately familiar with some of the natural rights thinkers who had written on the subject of conquest and just war, to which we return below.[33] In this essay, Jefferson does not *explicitly* acknowledge the presence of the natives in America, though in passing at one point he describes the "settlements having been thus effected in the wilds of America" as if to imply that the lands were unoccupied and thus up for grabs, consistent with the natural rights theory assumption that lands that had not been settled or cultivated were still in a state of nature and were owned in common.

Only a few years before writing the Declaration of Independence, which was the public justification to the world for the American Revolution, we see two different presuppositions in Jefferson's justification of American rights: there was a right based on conquest and a right based on settlement. We can surmise that the two positions were not incompatible for Jefferson. If the lands were unsettled and uncultivated, then Europeans had a right to settle them, at least according to one stream of thinking in natural rights theory. And if the natives resisted, Europeans had a right to take the land by force. The conquest itself was justified.

Jefferson was not the only American founder to pause over the American right to the native lands. A similar concern is evident in the early writing of James Wilson, one of the brightest legal minds in the founding generation and on a par with John Adams. Wilson served in the Continental Congress, was a signer of the Declaration of Independence, was a key contributor to the Constitutional Convention, and eventually was appointed by George Washington as one of the original justices of the Supreme Court. Wilson touched on the question of conquest in writing one of the earliest important pamphlets on American rights.

The pamphlet, *Considerations on the Nature and Extent of the Legislative Authority of the British Parliament,* may have been written as early as

1768 but was not published until 1774. In it, Wilson drew an analogy between the conquests of America and Ireland. He argued that if the Irish, who had been conquered, were not under the authority of British Parliament, certainly the American colonists should not be either. As we shall see below, the English Protestants in fact had first developed and tried out their colonizing practices in the conquest of the Catholic Irish and would later transfer and expand that theorizing to the colonization of America. Wilson was therefore leveraging a well-understood analogy that was already familiar to the British public. Wilson does note in passing his own doubt about whether the conquest of Ireland was just. He writes: "If the idea of conquest must be taken into consideration when we examine into the title by which America is held, that idea, so far as it can operate, will operate in favour of the colonists, and not against them. Permitted and commissioned by the Crown, they undertook, at their own expenses, expeditions to this distant country, took possession of it, planted it, and cultivated it."[34]

Wilson is clearly less comfortable than the young Jefferson in justifying the American rights on the basis of conquest. But in some sense he felt he had no choice. If the idea of conquest must frame the terms of the debate, he says, then it operates in favor of the colonists' rights, since they took possession and cultivated the distant country at their own expense. Those who funded the conquest and took the risk deserve the fruits of its reward. Though uncomfortable arguing on the basis of conquest, Wilson feels compelled to do so, for his opponents argued that British powers over the colonies derived from the British sponsorship and investment in the conquest.

In contrast to Jefferson, who sees the settlers as independent Europeans who conquered America, Wilson views the American settlers as British subjects who colonized on behalf of and under the auspices of the British Crown. "Secure under the protection of their king, they grew and multiplied, and diffused British freedom and British spirit, wherever they came." Since for Wilson the conquerors acted on behalf of and under the auspices of Great Britain, they were entitled to all the rights and privileges of British subjects. How and why the British were justified in that conquest is not a question that Wilson takes up in this context, though he signals his discomfort with reasons justifying the conquest of Ireland.

It is clear from Wilson's language that he feels uncomfortable arguing that American rights derive from a conquest. He thus picks up more clearly on the second justification in the natural rights tradition, that people have a right to settle and claim as their own any uncultivated land. The colonists undertook "expeditions to this distant country, took possession of it, planted it, and cultivated it." The theme of possessing, planting, and cultivating alludes to the view that any uncultivated lands are still held in common and up for grabs by the first to settle and cultivate them. Wilson's views, like Jefferson's, were firmly rooted in the natural rights justification of property.

Another important American founder, John Adams, expressed still more discomfort with the theme of conquest than did James Wilson and actually went so far as to recognize the Indians' rights to property. Like Wilson, Adams was one of the key intellectuals in the colonies, and he participated in the First Continental Congress, edited Jefferson's Declaration of Independence, participated in the Constitutional Convention, went on to be the first vice president of the United States, and eventually second president of the United States. A year before James Wilson published the essay quoted above, Adams offered one of the more profound statements on the moral question at stake. The larger context is a 1773 essay that Adams wrote in response to the claim of the Massachusetts governor, Thomas Hutchinson, who claimed that the colonies were under the supreme authority of the British Parliament. Hutchinson wrote that "at the Time that our Predecessors took Possession of this Plantation or Colony, under a Grant and Charter from the Crown of England, it was their Sense, and the Sense of the Kingdom, that they were to remain subject to the Supreme Authority of Parliament."[35] Although Adams uses pejorative language to describe Native Americans in his response to this claim, he makes several telling points showing his discomfort with a justification based on conquest.

First, Adams takes a position against one stream of the natural rights tradition, arguing that the natives had rights to their lands even though they had not settled on or agriculturally developed them.[36] If that is the case, Adams wonders, then on what basis is there a legitimate foundation for the conquest of the natives? Adams first casts doubt on the "papal" views used extensively in the preceding centuries that justified conquests against heathen and barbarous people. Adams was no doubt also aware that many of the English Puritans who settled Massachusetts often offered similar religious justifications for destroying the Indian heathen. Indeed, the British colonial project had been modeled in some respects after the Spanish Catholic one, as we shall see. In rejecting the justice of a conquest and in arguing that the Indians were rightful owners of their land, Adams implicitly denies that the British Parliament should have any jurisdiction over the American colonists.

Furthermore, Adams argues that even if we assume that the conquest was justified, it would mean that the *Crown of England* (i.e., the king), and not the *British Parliament*, had jurisdiction over the Massachusetts territory and people. In saying this, Adams means that the conquered lands would belong to the Crown (the sponsoring sovereign) but would not come under the supervision of Parliament, the legislative body. Adams here is arguing a technical point in the law of conquest about what rights the Crown and Parliament each had over conquered and colonized territories. As discussed below, there were differing views in the natural rights tradition about the rights to conquered territories and peoples. Here are Adams's words in his own language, referring to the charter granted to the colony of Massachusetts.

> We would take a View of the State of the English North American Continent at the Time when and after Possession was first taken of any Part of it, by the Europeans. It was then possessed by Heathen and Barbarous People, *who had nevertheless all that Right to the Soil and Sovereignty in and over the Lands they possessed, which God had originally given to Man.* Whether their being Heathen, inferred any Right or Authority to Christian Princes, a Right which had long been assumed by the Pope, to dispose of their Lands to others, we will leave to your Excellency or any one of

Understanding and impartial Judgment to consider. It is certain they had in no other Sense forfeited them to any Power in Europe. Should the Doctrine be admitted that the Discovery of Lands owned and possessed by Pagan People, gives to any Christian Prince a Right and Title to the Dominion and Property, still it is vested in the Crown alone. It was an Acquisition of Foreign Territory, not annexed to the Realm of England, and therefore at the absolute Disposal of the Crown. For we take it to be a settled Point, that the King has a constitutional Prerogative to dispose of and alienate any Part of his Territories not annexed to the Realm.[37] [italics added]

Though Adams's primary intent is to argue that Parliament did not have absolute authority over the colonies, he grasps that the real question of the settlers' rights turns on the prior question of who has legitimate entitlement to American lands in the first place. Adams's language goes further than either of his colleagues in recognizing native American ownership over their lands. Adams was clearly going against the grain of one strong stream of natural rights tradition in assuming that natives did have legitimate ownership over their lands, and probably, given the breadth of his scholarship, in full knowledge that he was doing so.

All three positions described above were articulated just a few years before the Declaration of Independence was penned by Jefferson in June 1776. When the First Continental Congress met in September 1774, the focus was on debating the foundation of American rights, and Congress issued a series of "resolves," which at the time were called "the American Bill of Rights." After debating those resolves for over a month, Congress rejected Jefferson's theory of American rights and chose instead that of Wilson and Adams, holding that the American colonists came to North America as British subjects and thus with all the rights and obligations of "natural-born subjects within the realm of England." In this first American Bill of Rights, Congress was completely silent on the underlying question of why the settlers had a right to the land in the first place. Was it a conquest or a settlement, and what reasons justified the Americans' rights to the land? The question of the colonists' rights to the land was also passed over in silence in the Declaration of Independence itself, the document justifying American rights and the right to revolution against their oppressors.[38] This silence was characteristic of many American colonists, who were focused on their rights vis-à-vis the British and who turned a self-serving blind eye to the question of their rights with respect to the natives. They looked "up," in other words, at their oppressors, but didn't look "down" at the way they and their predecessors were oppressors themselves. The same issue, of course, was true of slavery itself, with the founders arguing for liberty from British oppression, but many, though not all, thinking slavery was compatible with their own appeal to natural rights.[39] This silence on the actual history of what happened is something that we have to now, rightfully, peel away. It matters how we acquired our American lands, even according to the very theories by which we claimed to make it our own. A brief look at the historical background of the American conquest is thus in order to situate the various American declarations of rights in a broader historical context. Claims about rights have a history, and there are often positives and negatives of that history that have to be examined and talked about.

Conquest and the Right of Taking Land

The American founders, of course, were not inventing their justifications to American lands. Their positions were in line with various strands in the natural rights tradition as it had emerged in the seventeenth century. We know, for example, that Jefferson was familiar with the positions of Hugo Grotius, who at the start of the seventeenth century had argued that "just wars" included those against people who were committing grievous acts against the laws of nature.[40] In taking this stance, Grotius was in fact refining a position analogous to what had already been articulated by the Catholic Church, reaching back to Pope Innocent IV and heavily influencing the Crusades. On the one side, Grotius rejected the earlier Catholic position that a just war could be "for no other Reason but because they reject the Laws of Christianity." On the other hand, Grotius did justify just wars against those who violated the laws of nature.[41] Violations of the law of nature replaced the prior violation of Christianity as a justification for war. As examples of grievous violations of natural law, Grotius identifies people who are "inhuman to their Parents" and "those who eat human Flesh," ways incidentally in which Europeans were often characterizing the Indian populations from the time of Columbus. Grotius thus concluded that the "justest War is that which is undertaken against wild rapacious Beasts, and next to it is that against Men who are like Beasts."[42] By the time Grotius penned these words, Spanish conquerors had for over a century decimated Indian populations, justified, at least in part, by the fact that they were not Christian and no better than wild animals. Grotius also argued that the conquerors in a just war could keep the properties they conquered, a position that the Church had also earlier taken. "But now as Property, or Right to the Goods of an Enemy, may be acquired by a lawful War, the Word *Lawful* being taken in the Sense I had before mentioned, so may also Civil Dominion, or an absolute right to command and govern the Enemy."[43] On Grotius's theory, then, a just war ends with the victor taking the property of the vanquished and also acquiring the right to rule.[44] Grotius's views were key in shaping the tradition that provided the younger Jefferson with a justification of the American conquest of Indians. Yet Jefferson was also a reader of others in the natural rights tradition, such as Pufendorf and Locke, who were more circumspect in their views of conquest. Pufendorf, for example, rejected the European view that Indians could be conquered because of their barbarous practices:

> My Lord *Bacon*, in his *Advancement of Learning*, gives this for a *sufficient Reason* to make War upon the *Americans*, which I must confess, I cannot agree with him in: "That they be look'd upon as People proscribed by the Law of Nature, because they had a barbarous Custom of sacrificing Men, and fed upon Man's Flesh. For it ought to be distinctly considered, whether a Christian Prince might invade those *Indians*, as People proscribed by Nature, only because they made Man's Flesh their common Food? Or because

they us'd to eat the Bodies of those of their own Religion? Or
because they devoured Strangers and Foreigners? And then again,
it must be asked, whether those Strangers [i.e., Europeans] came
as Enemies, and Robbers? Or as innocent Guests and Travellers,
or for'd by Stress of Weather? For this last case only, and none of
the others, can give any *Right of War* against them, and this to
those only whose Subjects have been used with that Inhumanity
by them?[45]

Pufendorf takes the position that Europeans have no right to conquer
Indians simply because their practices deviate from natural law. Barbarity
alone does not justify conquest. In taking this position, Pufendorf also
notes that European visitors didn't come as innocent guests or travel-
ers lost in a storm. They came with a purpose of settling and taking
land. Only in cases where Europeans were forced onto American lands by
storms could they justify a right of war if so needed to protect their own
lives.

If barbarity did not justify conquest, lack of property rights was
another possible justification. The claim that Indians did not have property in their lands was tied into the natural rights arguments about the
origin and nature of property and human history.[46] As we have discussed
earlier, natural rights thinkers had discussed the rightful way in which
various people had come to have their rights to territories. They had
assumed that in the early state of humankind, there had been a division of property based on either human agreement or through individual
labor that cultivated land and provided the basis for property. By general
accounts, lands that had not been allocated in the original division of
land were vacant spaces that could be subsequently taken in one of two
ways: either by individuals who settled on and cultivated the land or by
groups of people who together moved into a vacant territory and formed
political communities. If a group of people settle a territory together, all
lands within that settlement belong to the community as a whole and
are under the control of the sovereign. The one exception is land that
remains uncultivated. Such vacant lands could still be rightfully taken

by outsiders, even if such lands were inside the sovereign territory of a people.[47]

Natural rights thinkers pointed to the American Indians as examples par excellence of a people still living in a state of nature, taking natural resources as needed but never settling on and cultivating the land.[48] Since cultivation was the key to making property one's own, the Indians never achieved private property rights that were characteristic of more advanced societies. Speaking about the early history of humans, Grotius again provides an early example of this line of thought.

> From hence it was, that every Man converted what he would to his own Use, and consumed whatever was to be consumed; and such a Use of the Right common to all Men did at that Time supply the Place of Property, for no Man could justly take from another, what he had thus first taken to himself; which is well illustrated by that Simile of *Cicero, Tho the Theatre is common for any Body that comes, yet the Place that every one sits in is properly his own.* And this State of Things must have continued till now, had Men persisted in their primitive Simplicity, or lived together in perfect Friendship. A Confirmation of the first of these is the Account we have of some People of *America*, who by the extraordinary Simplicity of their Manners, have without the least Inconvenience observed the same Method of Living for many Ages.[49]

Grotius is here arguing that private property did not exist in the beginning of human civilization and "use" fulfilled the role that would later be enlarged to "ownership." A similar perspective was espoused by Pufendorf and Locke, among others. Locke, we recall, had said that "Thus in the beginning all the World was America," meaning that in early human history, people lived simple lives in the state of nature like the American Indians without the invention of money.[50] On the one hand, Locke also had an idealized view of these peoples who lived closer to nature. For "want of power and money," they had no "temptation to enlarge their possessions of land." Yet on the other hand, Locke assumes that Europeans had the right, and possibly even a kind of duty, to take these lands and cultivate them.

Recall that Locke cites the vacant lands in America as proof that even in his day anyone could still have lands who wanted them.[51] He also implies that a person who settles and cultivates vacant property actually does good for humanity by increasing nature's bounty. "And therefore he, that incloses Land, and has a greater plenty of the conveniencys of life from ten acres, than he could have from an hundred left to Nature, may truly be said, to give ninety acres to Mankind."[52] Locke is making the point that by taking uncultivated land and making it into private property, individuals benefit humanity. His rhetoric may also suggest that there is a moral duty to actually cultivate vacant lands. Here again is Locke: "God gave the World to Men in Common; but since he gave it them for their benefit, and the greatest Conveniencies of Life, they were capable to draw from it, it cannot be supposed he meant it should always remain common and uncultivated. He gave it to the use of the Industrious and Rational, (and Labour was to be *his Title* to it)."[53]

In 1759, nearly a century after Locke had written the above statements, Swiss philosopher, legalist, and philosopher Emer de Vattel had this to say in his influential *Law of Nations*, a book that James Wilson, James Otis, and others read and quoted:

> There is another celebrated question, to which the discovery of the new world has principally given rise. It is asked whether a nation may lawfully take possession of some part of a vast country, in which there are none but erratic nations, whose scanty population is incapable of occupying the whole? We have already observed (§ 81), in establishing the obligation to cultivate the earth, that those nations cannot exclusively appropriate to themselves more land than they have occasion for, or more than they are able to settle and cultivate. Their unsettled habitation in those immense regions cannot be accounted a true and legal possession; and the people of Europe, too closely pent up at home, finding land of which the savages stood in no particular need,

and of which they made no actual and constant use, were lawfully entitled to take possession of it, and settle it with colonies. The earth, as we have already observed, belongs to mankind in general, and was designed to furnish them with subsistence: if each nation had from the beginning resolved to appropriate to itself a vast country, that the people might live only by hunting, fishing, and wild fruits, our globe would not be sufficient to maintain a tenth part of its present inhabitants.[54]

To summarize, we have thus seen that those American founders who did not feel comfortable justifying American rights to land on the basis of conquest could appeal to the theory of the vacant and uncultivated land. In European theory, even if the American Indians claimed the land as their own property, their claims would have been meaningless, since in European eyes they left it uncultivated, though we shall see below that even this view is a distortion and misrepresentation of Indian culture and practice. In European Christian views, humans were intended to expand on the earth and the resources of nature were given for their support and nourishment. Leaving land uncultivated wasted what God and nature had given. It was these sorts of views that hovered in the background of Jefferson's and Wilson's claims that the American lands could be taken by Europeans who settled and cultivated them.

History Versus Philosophy of Conquest

Having looked at how some of the important founders thought about their rights to the land, and the European philosophical positions that hovered behind them, it is important to ask about the actual history since, as I have said, theft and conquest are often everywhere lurking in the past. For those who know something about the history of European colonization, it is appropriate to use the word "conquest" and, according to some, even "holocaust" to describe what the Spanish, British, and eventually Americans did to Native American populations.[55] Starting with Spain in the late fifteenth and continuing throughout the sixteenth century, conquerors beginning with Columbus had decimated Indian populations throughout what became South and Latin America. Through a combination of European diseases, such as smallpox, and wholesale slaughter by the European conquerors, Indian populations were reduced by as much as 90 percent or more in only a matter of a few decades.

The conquest was justified originally by a series of Catholic papal bulls giving Spain ownership of the lands of South America. As early as the thirteenth century, Pope Innocent IV had written a legal commentary on the question of when Christians could legitimately take away the political authority and property of pagan peoples. Innocent was one of the first great medieval legal theorists who attempted to systematically address the questions raised by Christian contact with non-Christian nations. He defined the essential terms of the debate by providing European legal theory with a fully elaborated legal discourse for determining the rights and status of pagan people.[56]

Papal authority over infidels, he wrote, applied to those instances where it was clearly necessary for the pope to intervene in order to protect the infidels' spiritual well-being. Such circumstances obtained when infidels clearly violated natural law and their rulers refused to punish them, as required by God's divine law.[57] For example, those peoples who were sexually promiscuous or who worshipped idols could be compelled by secular force and conquest to obey the laws of nature, which were understood to be synonymous with the Catholic vision of civilization. Natural law and Catholicism were understood to be one and the same.

In 1492, the basic framework articulated by Pope Innocent in the thirteenth century was extended to the discoveries in America in a series of three papal bulls issued by Pope Alexander IV (originally the Spaniard Rodrigo Borgia) confirming Spain's title to Columbus's discoveries.[58] The bulls granted Spain virtually all of North and South America and blessed the expansion of Christian rule. Motivated in part by a search for gold and slaves, and justified in the name of Christ, the conquest of Indians was both religiously and racially justified. Following closely on the heels of the Spanish Inquisition of the Jews, and using some of the same rhetoric by which Jews, witches, and Moors had been demonized by the Catholic

Church reaching back to the Crusades and earlier, the Spaniards justified the savage ravaging of Indian men, women, and children.[59] When Columbus could not find the gold he expected to find, which would have justified his expeditions, he began enslaving Indians as the only resource he could export back to Spain. For the action, Columbus lost his governorship, and the queen forcibly recalled him. But the Castilian Crown was unable to stifle the conquerors' impulse to enslave Indians. The outcome was a political system called "encomienda," which justified coerced labor and the enslavement of Indians as part of the civilizing and conversion process. Only by denying the Indians their freedom and appropriating their labor could the work of Christianization take place.[60]

Columbus initiated and framed the European discourse on the Indians by describing the backward state of their civilization and practices. He characterized the Indians as being uncivilized, naked, lacking private property and religion, and not having iron and steel weapons. In his rhetorical tropes, Columbus set out many of the themes to dominate European discourse for the decades and centuries to follow. The view that Indians lacked property, of course, played into the European view that uncultivated land was available for the taking, even in God's eyes. Of course, no one understood at first that the people who had been discovered occupied a "new world" that was unknown to Europeans. Nonetheless, as Spanish accounts of Indians developed over the sixteenth century, Indians were at times portrayed as barbaric heathens who ate human flesh, had promiscuous sexual behaviors, worshipped the devil, or had no religion at all. For some Europeans, the Indians were thought to be the ten lost tribes of Israel (thus explaining why they didn't have a more sophisticated religious understanding but did have practices, such as sacrifice, and food taboos that resembled those of the Jews).[61] A pernicious racial theory also developed that portrayed the Indians as a separate type of animal created by God, somewhere on the hierarchical tree of being between apes and humans. This type of "beast" was not descended from Adam and Eve, according to some, but was created by God to be a beast of burden, a view that dovetailed nicely with Aristotle's position that some people were natural slaves. The horrific tales of Spanish slaughter, torture, rape, and enslavement cannot with justice be recounted adequately in this context and has been done more ably by others.[62]

Through the first half of the sixteenth century, while Indians were being decimated and the continent was being conquered, Spanish Catholics were periodically debating whether the Indians were sufficiently rational to be entitled to the protections of natural rights. The view that the Indians' heathenism justified their enslavement and torture dominated Spanish practice. There were some notable Dominican challenges beginning in 1511, when a Dominican friar named Antonio de Montesinos gave a sermon challenging the prevailing views and prompting King Ferdinand to convene a council in the Spanish town of Burgos to deliberate on the question of whether Indians could be saved in ways other than being enslaved. Debate focused on whether the Indians had sufficient reason to be governed by the laws of nature, which are only discernible through reason, and on the possible applicability of Aristotle's notion of "natural slaves" to the natives. The council promulgated seven propositions and a legal code by which Spaniards were to manage the domination of Indians. The code mandated peaceful means by which to Christianize the Indians unless peaceful means failed, in which case the code authorized the use of force. The debate over the right way to Christianize the Indians, and the debate over the applicability of natural law and reason to them, continued throughout the first half of the sixteenth century and reached its peak in the 1550s.

Of particular note for our purposes was an emerging intellectual countercurrent articulated by Spanish Dominican scholar Franciscus de Victoria (1480–1546). Inspired by an interpretation of natural law by the Catholic theologian Thomas Aquinas, Victoria challenged the justification of the Indian enslavement and conquest under papal authority. His most important work on Indian rights was a three-part lecture in 1532 called "On the Indians Lately Discovered." On the one hand, Victoria challenged the stream of thought that said Indians lacked rationality. On the other hand, he provided a new, more secularized justification for Indian conquest, under the umbrella of natural law and the emerging laws of nations that he helped conceptualize.[63] This justification of conquest on a foundation of natural rights would be taken up by seventeenth-century natural rights philosophers and British colonizers.

To begin with, Victoria challenged the Spanish view that the Indians lacked reason and therefore could not own property or run their own government. Running counter to dominant Spanish colonial views, he thus argued that the Indians had just ownership over the territory they possessed, and he rejected the Spanish Catholic view that "discovery" of American lands gave Europeans possession of them. We saw echoes of a similar view in the writings of John Adams, who had similar doubts about the papal association of discovery and property. By the time Victoria wrote, of course, Columbus had already claimed ownership of discovered lands on behalf of Spain, and the tradition continued throughout the next two centuries with both Spanish and British explorers claiming ownership for their respective Crowns on the basis of discovery.[64] The association of discovery with possession would be a position that ultimately was made into the law of the land by the early American Supreme Court, as it contemplated the very question of how Americans had rights to Indians lands.[65]

If, on the one side, Victoria challenged the Spanish Catholic portrayal of Indians as irrational beings and natural slaves, he nonetheless found grounds for the European conquest of the Americas based on natural law.[66] Victoria argued that the relationship between all peoples was governed by a universal law of nations that was derived from natural law and was obligatory on both Indians and Spaniards alike. If the Indians violated the law of nations, Spain would have a right to use force against them. Although Victoria rejected the papal justification of conquest, he still recognized a Christian duty for Christians to preach the gospel in barbarian lands and instruct those who are ignorant of civilized Christian faith.[67] Seemingly unaware of what appears as a contradiction today, Victoria concluded that the pope had the authority to assign the role of educator to the Spanish nation, which thus had the authority to bring the gospel to the Indians. If the Indian princes created barriers to this mission, they had put up an obstacle against what was naturally right. The natives' resistance to being educated in the Christian faith thus furnished the Spaniards with a justification to make war and seize their lands.

The debate over whether the Indians were natural slaves and rational creatures reached a peak intensity in 1550 when the controversy became so intense that Spanish King and Holy Roman Emperor Charles V suspended all expeditions to the Americas and called a group of leading theologians, jurists, and officials to the royal capital of Valladolid to listen to the arguments between Las Casas and the scholar Sepúlveda on the nature of the Indians.

Since 1519, Bartolemé de Las Casas had been a leading Dominican spokesperson for the view that Indians were rational men "not demented or mistakes of nature, nor lacking in sufficient reason to govern themselves." And he was guided by the view that "our Christian relation is suitable for and may be adapted to all the nations of the world, and all alike may receive it; and no one may be deprived of his liberty, nor may he be enslaved on the excuse that he is a natural slave."[68] In 1527, La Casas had started a compendium on Indian customs called *Apologetic History*, in which he advanced the idea that astonished Spaniards of his day: that the American Indians compared favorably to the peoples of ancient times, were rational creatures, and met Aristotle's criteria of living a good life.[69] In 1547 at the age of seventy-three, Las Casas was back in Spain after spending most of his life involved in Indian affairs.

What prompted the debate in 1550 was a treatise written by the respected Aristotelian scholar Juan Ginés de Sepúlveda, who argued that wars against the Indians were just and even necessary as a preliminary first step to their Christianization. Sepúlveda was a leading, well-respected scholar of his day, enjoyed great prestige with the royal court, and was involved in the European intellectual recovery of Aristotle and a translator of Aristotle's *Politics*. Las Casas's challenge to Sepúlveda's manuscript prompted King Charles V to summon a council of fourteen scholars and jurists to Valladolid to consider the question, "Is it lawful for the king of Spain to wage war on the Indians before preaching the faith to them in order to subject them to his rule, so that afterward they may be more easily instructed in the faith?"[70]

Las Casas spoke for five days, and the judges had to assign one of their members to boil down his arguments into a succinct summary to which Sepúlveda could answer. Sepúlveda, for his part, had taken the position that wars may be waged justly when their cause is just and that the war with the Indians was just due to their idolatries, the gravity of sins against nature, and in order to protect the weak among the natives themselves. Drawing on Aristotle and appealing to the rudeness of the Indians' natures, Sepúlveda argued that the Indians were examples of Aristotle's natural slaves and that Spaniards had the right to rule over them because of Spanish superiority. Las Casas, for his part, took the position he had held throughout the century. He argued that to treat Indians like natural slaves and torture them into conversion was immoral and offended God. Since 1512, he had been promoting the position that Indians should be won to Christianity by peace, love, and good example, when no danger threatened. The council members took the summaries of the debate home with them and agreed to reconvene in early 1551 for a final vote. The judges, however, never issued a formal decision and left the question over the Indians' nature unresolved.[71]

For our purposes, there are a number of insights to draw from this fascinating yet disturbing historical moment in 1550–1551. On the one hand, one can be encouraged that ideas of the natural law tradition were beginning to resist and challenge pernicious views of Indians that had been based on Aristotle's notion of natural slaves and the views of the Roman Catholic Church, which justified conquests, enslavement, and torturing of other peoples because their religions and cultures differed. Remember, this was still more than a hundred years before early moderns such as John Locke had fully articulated the modern natural rights theory of the seventeenth century, as we understand it today. But lest we naïvely conclude that the light of natural reason was beginning to triumph over the darkness of Catholic orthodoxy, we should remember that the natural rights tradition was itself being shaped so as to provide a new justification for the conquest of America. In that justification, though the Indians were rational creatures and had rights of nature, Europeans had rights to conquer them and to take their lands.

Lest we blame Spain's Catholics alone for the conquest of the Indians, it is important to realize that British Puritan settlers would use very similar kinds of justifications in their settlement of North America in the seventeenth century and in fact were influenced by Spanish Catholic thinking a century earlier. The British Puritan settlers were relative latecomers, arriving after the Spanish had spent a century decimating Indians in much of what is now Latin and South America. Diseases introduced farther south had already spread to the North American continent, where they continued to destroy Indian populations even before the British settlers arrived. Encountering already weakened Indian populations, the British settlers in North America were also brutal to the Indians.[72] Like their Spanish predecessors, they too justified the murder of native populations in religious terms, this time fueled not by Catholic religious sentiments, but by a Puritan Christian zeal to eliminate the heathens.

In fact, the British understood their colonial settlements in North America as part of the competition not only between Spain and England as European nations, but between Catholicism and the reformed Protestant Church of England, which had broken from the Catholic Church during the Reformation. English translations and abridgements of the writings by Spanish and Portuguese explorers and historians of the Spanish conquest, such as explorer Amerigo Vespucci, introduced the British public to stories about the strange new world inhabited by flesh-eating barbarous peoples who had no laws, manners, or civilized religion.[73] Vespucci had described the Indians in themes already familiar from Columbus as lacking money and desiring only what they needed. Early historians of the conquest, such as Pietro Martire, had described the Indians as lacking core concepts of "Mine and Thine" (i.e., they lacked the conceptual foundation for property).

The British people themselves were already developing their own framework for dealing with what they regarded as rude and backward peoples in their conquest of the Irish.[74] Ireland had been part of the realm since the Norman invasion, and as Catholics, the Irish provided a nearby opportunity to work out the beginning of England's own colonial empire building framework. Under Protestant Queen Elizabeth's rule, British discovery and colonialism began in earnest in the 1570s. Rejecting Spain's papal justification of conquest, Elizabeth asserted the right of her subjects, based on the law of nations, to establish colonies in any region of the world not inhabited by Spain. In essence, discovery became the justification of colonization among competing European powers.

British writers justified the overseas colonization based on a number of factors, including economic opportunity, an outlet for natural resources, and advancing the true version of Christianity (Protestant, not Catholic) to the savages of America, and thereby countering the influence of Spain in the New World. Thus the two themes of Indian conversion and anti-Catholic/-Spanish sentiment were merged into a single discourse justifying the British Puritan colonization.

Early descriptions of Indians emanating from the early colonies, such as those sponsored by Sir Walter Raleigh, portrayed the Indians as using their land inefficiently. Throughout the early settlement days and what amounted to a British invasion sponsored by the Virginia Company, Indian "idolatry" and their reported failure to settle and cultivate the earth served as biblically sanctioned justifications for the British settlers to take their land and in many cases to massacre them.[75] The claim that Indians lacked the idea of private property reached back to Columbus and continued throughout the North American conquest, even though Indian tribes did live in settled villages surrounded by agricultural plots and the British colonists would have starved in early days of the colonies without the help of food grown by Indians.[76] Ironically, it was the Indians who knew how to live off the land, not the early colonists.

In the early British colonies, there were debates on whether the Indians owned their land, and these debates continued throughout the first hundred years of colonization. The Virginia Company, which sponsored the settlement of Jamestown, decided not to publish a justification of the colonization in part because colonization of an inhabited land was controversial. In general, however, the theory of sovereignty by which the English government embarked on colonization assumed that the land in North America was unowned and available for the taking.[77] One can find contradictory positions among the settlers themselves on their rights to

Indian land, and the position that Indians lacked land ownership was not a unanimous position. Some, like William Crashaw in a sermon in 1609, pondered "the doubt of lawfulness of the action" and concluded that the colonists must "take nothing from the Savages by power nor pillage" but "we will *exchange* with them for that which *they may spare*, and we doe need."[78] Other sermons, such as that by William Symonds, argued that conquest was legitimate and that human history is full of invasions and wars, with the winners taking the land of the losers.[79]

There is substantial evidence that in practice, colonial policy treated Indian land as though the Indians indeed owned their property, and therefore Europeans purchased land from them.[80] But the context of the purchases was complex. Often Indians were pressured to sell under increasing expansion of European settlers, especially as colonization proceeded; the Indians felt in some sense as if they had no choice, since settlers would take the land from them anyway. In addition, the Indians had a different concept of property that did not match precisely the European one, and therefore the meaning of the transaction was often understood differently by the parties. There were numerous instances as well of trickery and deceit involved in these transactions, to the loss of the Indians. Often individual Indians and individual colonists would try to sidestep the rules of both the tribes and of the British and colonial governments to conclude a transaction. In part because of such problems and because Britain was trying to limit colonial expansion westward before the American Revolution, colonists were restricted from purchasing land directly from Indians without government authorization. Intended to protect the Indians, this law ironically undermined the natives' ability to get a fair price by limiting real market competition. Furthermore, colonists would often simply ignore the rules and sometimes simply move onto the land. Neither colonial authorities nor the British government had the capacity to stop them. On the verge of the Revolution, when Jefferson, Wilson, and Adams referred to the status of American lands, there was still not a settled position on the origin of the colonies' rights to their lands. Eventually, the view that European discovery entailed ownership of land would be codified as the official position of the United States in the 1823 decision of the Supreme Court that based American claims to land on the European discovery doctrine.[81]

The conquest of America was thus complex and proceeded in stages. Jefferson's characterization of the settlements of America as a conquest is historically accurate, if completely understated, and unjustified. We do know that by the time Jefferson wrote *Notes on the State of Virginia* in 1781, he held the view that the extensive documentary record of Indian land sales demonstrated that Virginia had been taken from the Indians not by conquest but rather "by purchases made in the most unexceptionable form," though he qualified it with the comment "that these purchases were sometimes made with the price in one hand and the sword in the other," a point he crossed out before publishing.[82]

It would be wrong and too simplistic to say that Americans stole Indian property. But it would be a mistake to characterize this process as a simple set of straightforward purchases. In some sense, the Indians had no choice, especially as the coercive context grew more apparent as the settlements expanded, and it became clear that turning European expansion back was impossible. Furthermore, the ideology that the lands were uncultivated and available did inform and help justify colonization from the start.

This abbreviated overview of the Spanish and British conquests of America hardly does justice to the details or complexity of the story. But it does provide sufficient background for us to return to the question of rights and their relationship to land that was stolen and conquered in America, our original theft.

Theft All the Way Down

I began this chapter arguing that rights under a state are intelligible only if that state has rights to oversee the territories over which it has jurisdiction. I suggested that the ideal alignment of individual property and the state's territorial sovereignty is and has always been problematic. Individuals do not have exclusive rights to the properties they own or inherit. Their labor is partly their own and partly that of the human species as a whole. Thus even if individuals did aggregate their individual properties to form a state, even then the state would oversee property that did not belong only to those individuals who formed the state, since no one can own all of his or her labor. The state would always also be a guardian of property that belonged to humanity in general. Even were this not the case, the actual messiness of history suggests that murder, theft, and other forms of violence were critically important in shaping both the historical allocation of resources among individuals and the boundaries and territories of states.

My intent in discussing the European conquest of America was to show that even in the country that understands itself par excellence to be founded on a social contract and the consent of the people, even here a theft and conquest are at the foundation of the nation. Anywhere we look there is a past that includes conquest, murder, and theft, which have shaped the distribution of resources across the human species. There is no innocent nation that does not have this problem of violence and domination somewhere in its past. And even the native populations that preceded the development of states gathered their lands at times by power and conquest as well. It was not just European nations, Christians, or Americans who have conquered and murdered. Conquest, murder, and theft go all the way back in time. Parts of the native populations themselves have a history of violence one to another.

The question of rights and entitlement to resources has ultimately to deal with this fact of history and the violent past of the human species. There is an "original theft" or conquest at some point behind every state and every individual's private possession. No nation gets off morally scot-free from this burden of history. At the very least, any person who wants to insist on his or her rights and demand protection from the hands of a powerful and overreaching government must also accept the burden of history for the creation of that state. For any property we do have at this moment in time is not simply the result of the efforts of the smart and hardworking people that we are. It includes also the collective result and inheritance of thousands of other persons who labored before us, who contributed their knowledge to us, and on which we built our efforts.

And this piece of land that is temporarily mine in this big nation that is temporarily ours in this larger world that belongs to us all for now is but a temporary place that I occupy that has landed at my feet, after all the thousands of murders and conquests and thefts that have disappeared, lost in time. If we pretend anything else, we are erecting a myth that justifies some notion of ourselves, our religions, and our nations. The question is, what should we do about this truth that has always been present but that our myth of natural rights so conveniently wants to hide?

Chapter 8
The Myth of the Social Contract

Time has now come in our discussion to take a hard look at the purposes of what the early moderns called the political "commonwealth," or what later became "the state" or "nation-state." Why do we all live in nations anyway? Why bother with political institutions that set laws and have powers to punish us, jail us, and take away our liberty, or even put us to death? Surely people who celebrate liberty should prefer to have no constraints and live with as much freedom as possible. So why choose to live in a state rather than in a state of nature? This paradox has been obvious to modern thinkers in the rights tradition from the beginning. As Locke said, "IF Man in the State of Nature be so free, as has been said; If he be absolute Lord of his own Person and Possessions, equal to the greatest, and subject to no Body, why will he part with his Freedom? Why will he give up this Empire, and subject himself to the Dominion and Controul of any other Power?"[1]

According to the early modern thinkers, humans create political commonwealths and states to protect their lives, liberties, and properties as well as take advantage of the range of benefits of social life afforded by peace. If we did not feel insecure, live in a state of fear, or find inconveniences in nature, humans would not have submitted themselves to the power of a government at all.[2] The purpose of government is thus to protect our properties, construed broadly as including also our rights of life and liberty. In this theory, human beings chose voluntarily to live under the power of the state because it was better than the envisioned alternative. This is the classic theory of what is typically called "the social contract."

In the social contract theory of the state, individuals joined together voluntarily in an agreement to live by a set of common laws, which they collectively created in exchange for the benefits of social life and the protection of lives, liberties, and properties. The state's powers were thus understood to be derivative from the rights that individuals originally held in nature prior to joining the contract. The state's rights to create and enforce laws and to punish offenders all derive from the contracting individuals' original natural rights to protect their own lives, liberties, and properties. The state gets some but not all of the rights and powers that belonged to individuals in their natural state.

Liberty-first advocates build on this understanding of the state to criticize the way that the American government is repeatedly overstepping the appropriate bounds of its power and infringing on the freedom of individual rights. In their understanding, government abuses its powers in a variety of ways: by taxing individuals too much, by overregulating business and the economy, and by creating rules to govern individual behavior, an area where government has no business being. The nature of liberty requires government to be as minimalist as possible and to stay out of people's lives.[3]

And yet there is something very deeply wrong historically and morally about the conception of the state as a social contract that is rarely if ever talked about anymore.[4] We will talk about it here. The idea of the state as a social contract is a myth. It hides and trivializes both the actual histories of violence in human history that preceded the formation of any state as well as the inequalities of human life caused by the accidents of history and the violent nature of some human beings. We got here, to the place we are now, in whatever state we now live and with whatever property we now own, through a long series of events that were neither entirely fair nor equitable nor exclusively our own efforts. This is a critical insight that gets buried in the image of the state as a social contract. The idea of a contract carries with it the idea that everyone joins voluntarily and within a framework that is more or less fair to all.

As discussed in the previous chapter, in most cases there was never a clean or clear original contract that founded a state, and most states have some history of violence and conquest in their past by which some people conquered and took land from some other people.[5] That history of violence itself calls into question the image of the state as deriving its just powers from the individuals who comprised it. For if the state acquired its territories through violence and conquest, rather than through some rightful means, then the properties that it regulates and protects on behalf of its citizens were never theirs rightfully to own.

Neither is it just the violence in the state's own past that undermines the claim that its duties are only to protect the lives, liberties, and properties of its citizens. Even had there been an idyllic "social contract" in the beginning of the state, as the United States likes to claim about its own past, those who stood at the original social contract did not possess all the rights that they supposedly collected together when the state was created. We live within a framework of a mess that we have inherited from the past, no matter how righteous or ethical any of us is. And even had there been no violence ever, it would still be wrong to say that the properties the individuals bring into the state are exclusively their own, as we have discussed before. We all labor on the backs of thousands of people before us who created the platform on which we all live. There is thus a debt of inheritance to the past of those who contributed to our success. Whether or not a state came about through conquest and violence, the state's responsibilities cannot be simply summarized as protecting the lives, liberties, and properties of its citizens. To define the state in that narrow way is to ignore history, human nature, and the moral burden of seeing humans as equal in value. Let us dig into these points in more detail to understand why the modern natural rights understanding of the state, and the one that informs the United States' self-understanding, is flawed, and why it needs to be rethought.

If we take seriously the fact that the use of violence, power, and manipulation have been present throughout the history of the human species, then the social contract crumbles as a valid idea. Here's why: If the allocation of properties and resources has not been fair in human history, then the individuals who come to the table to create a social contract cannot have the rights they claim they want the state to protect. It is an invalid contract. If a person contracts with a thief to buy a car that was stolen, the thief does not have the right to enter into the contract to make the deal. The buyer who entered into the contract was thus cheated and entered the contract on false premises. And if the buyer entered the deal knowing the car was stolen, then the buyer is morally implicated too.

The same must be true at the founding contract of every state, since there must be some or many thieves or their heirs standing there participating in the social contract. If the state derives its powers from the contract between the individuals who comprise the state, then the state must have its powers illegitimately, since those who stood at the original contract did not all have the rights they claimed to bring into the contract. So too, the people who were moral and not thieves, or descendants of moral people, stand at the social contract shortchanged by the abuse of others who lived earlier.

It is deeply ironic that the social contract theory of the state actually takes the history of human violence as its own conceptual starting point. In doing so, the theory misses how the assumption of human violence destroys the very notion of the state that it seeks to defend. As noted earlier, modern natural rights theory holds that the state comes about because it is necessary to end violence, create peace, and eliminate the inconveniences of living in a state of nature. The state of nature is thought to be unsatisfactory for human beings because no one is secure from the violence of others and because everyone has the right to judge and enforce the law individually.[6] In all of these cases, the state plays a key role in ending violence or injustice. In fact, that is why individuals are said to prefer losing some of their rights in nature and living under the power and authority of the state. Individuals relinquish some of their rights so that they get this benefit of the state's power and authority.

As is evident, the assumption is that people took properties and lives inappropriately from one another in nature and that the commonwealth or state as an institution arose as a remediation to this situation. The state is thus portrayed as a way to transform the human animal into more civilized beings by reducing the power, violence, and partiality that otherwise structure human relations.

By implication, this understanding implies that those who enter into the state at a particular moment of time do not have in their possession what they might rightfully deserve, and some may have more than they deserve. At that moment in time, everyone's possessions are the results of a history that reaches back into the past in which violence and power shaped the distribution of property and resources. Thus there are people standing at the original contract who lack what they deserve and others who possess what they did not themselves earn or who inherited from ancestors who took by force, stealth, and power. If the state just imposes fairness and equality moving forward, it essentially freezes in place a structure of inequality that already exists in the history of the human species. And while the state may be increasing fairness going forward, that fairness is already based on a set of inequities that existed in nature or in prior states. However, playing a game fairly from an unfair starting point is hardly a fair game. The modern natural rights thinkers and their "liberty-first" heirs did not see this problem or think it was relevant. They assumed that the past was the past, and all the inequalities and injustices of the past were either wiped clean by the adoption of the social contract or were simply too problematic and complicated to weigh.

The problem is not just that a history of violence and injustice are concretized in the distribution of properties and resources that are brought by individuals into the state. Many states themselves do not come about historically through a social contract but instead are founded on a history of conquest and violence. As discussed in the previous chapter, even the United States, which claims to be one of the first to create a "social contract," had a history of violence and conquest entangled in its formation prior to the social contract on which it was founded. Natural rights theorists were aware of this objection, for critics of the modern natural rights theory, including some in the founding American context, argued that states always came about through conquest and not through a social contract.[7]

In response to such criticisms, modern defenders of social contract theory have argued that even if the state was not really founded through a social contract, the ideal state *should act as if it was*.[8] In other words, the social contract is an ideal toward which a state should aspire even if it did not begin that way. *The moral or just state acts as if all citizens were at an original contract and gives them equal representation in founding the state's laws*. It was already obvious to the classic natural rights thinkers that not everyone was present at the original contract.[9] Critics had noted that descendants of the original contractors clearly did not participate in the original social contract. Natural rights theorists responded to the criticism by arguing that the social contract is renewed and reaffirmed by every individual at maturity. Descendants of the original contractors are said to have a choice whether to affirm the social contract at their own maturity by choosing to leave the state or staying within it at their own choice, and no longer at their parents' discretion.[10] The claim is that every person in essence makes a choice at adulthood whether to voluntarily consent to the state and reaffirm the original contract that was originally founded. In making that affirmation at maturity, every individual becomes subject to the same laws and privileges and has the right to shape the ongoing evolution of the social contract.

This view that treats the social contract as an ideal, rather than a reality, tries to rescue the morality of the state by discounting the past and the actual history of human violence that may have founded the state and that structured individual relationships throughout history. It ignores anything that happened prior to the development of the social contract.

Defenders of natural rights and the idea of social contract might respond pragmatically that this ideal state is the best human beings can hope to achieve. We cannot go back and disentangle the inequality embedded in the fabric of human history. The only possible moral stance is to impose fairness moving forward. On this view, the liberal state's purpose is to impose equity and fairness based on the starting point at which the state begins or at the point in time at which it becomes moral. This has been one way for natural rights theorists and their modern interpreters to "get out of jail free" with respect to the moral problem of human violence.

If we accept such a pragmatic position, however, we are essentially saying we have no moral obligation to the past history of our species and to the uneven distribution of resources both globally and within our own states. It is that position that seems morally untenable and needs to be challenged. For if the whole premise of rights flows from the moral proposition that humans are equal in value and had a right to equal access to common resources at the beginning, then by what right do we say we can take advantage of what we have now, no matter how it came to us? It is an impossible contradiction that no one apparently wants to discuss.

My claim here is that we inherit a moral burden from history that is unavoidable if we rely on the notion of rights. Or, to put it another way, the very notion of a right seems to carry with it a claim from history. The claim that I own or have a right to my property and that the state must protect it rests on a moral proposition that this property has come to me rightfully and that I have an exclusive claim to it. We have seen how natural rights theorists felt this pressure to trace "rightness" back to Adam and Eve and respond to the claim of kings who grounded their right in history and the divine will as well. But the truth is that we have no way of knowing that the property came to us morally or rightfully. We can only see actions one or two generations back at best, and we have no way of knowing how and why the situation of our earlier ancestors came to be the way it was. In fact, there is a great deal of evidence that what came into our hands did so through a long sequence of actions and events that were both moral and immoral in character. There are no "undamaged goods." Everything is tainted. The idea that we own property rests on assumptions that are precisely the opposite. It is a moral claim that pretends as if history has been just. It assumes that no one else has a claim to the very same object or land in our possession. It assumes that anyone else's claim to the same properties can be rejected. There is no moral basis for such a position.

I have talked in earlier chapters about another kind of affirmative moral burden that we inherit from history. Even those of us who try to act morally and who labor hard can hardly claim that everything we have belongs to us alone. The outcome of our efforts is not necessarily directly proportional to our labor, no matter how hard we work or how creative we are. As argued earlier, we stand on the shoulders of many thousands of people before us who gave us the human platform on which we labor. Our labor is not only our own. We have become who we are through the labor of humans before us, and everything we do takes for granted their efforts in history. There is nothing that any of us can claim is ours exclusively. And while many of us work hard and contribute as well, everything that we own is a product of a long history of human labor that preceded us. Nothing is ours alone. This is the affirmative moral burden that we have to the past, to our ancestors who gave us the platform on which we carry out our lives, and to the thousands of inventors who left us with capabilities and inventions with which we build our lives. As I argued previously, we are like the entrepreneur who borrows from the bank or in whom the capitalist has invested. We are obligated to provide a return on the investment they have made in us and the debt we have inherited.

Thus far we have identified several ways in which the idea of the state as a social contract is flawed and simply a myth. Those who join the social contract or affirm the state do not rightfully own what they have in their possession. Human violence and conquest distorted the distribution of properties that would have been based exclusively on the rightful and fair labor of individuals. Some people have what they or their ancestors never earned rightfully. And some people do not have what they or their ancestors should have rightfully. These are the facts that we learn from history. Even apart from the history of violence, no one rightfully owns all of his or her own property. For everyone's labor already assumes the contribution of thousands of others who contributed earlier. And thus when we come to join together in the social contract, or participate in the state, we do not have the complete rights to the properties we own, even if we reaffirm the state on our own at maturity.

Reconceptualizing the Moral Purposes of the State

The conception that the state's primary purpose is to protect our rights essentially hides the fact that the state is freezing and protecting a set of property relations that were not fair or right to begin with. Even if fairness is imposed going forward, which is itself debatable, as we see in the next chapter, the very fact that the process must have started from an unjust starting point undermines the rightness of what follows. An analogy might be useful here. Often government is compared to an "umpire" that ensures the game is played fairly by the rules.[11] To extend the analogy here, we would be saying that the parties who join the game each come in to the start of the game with different scores, whether they deserved those scores or not. The umpire ensures the game is played fairly by the rules from that point forward. However, since there was not a level playing field to begin with, the enforcement of the rules evenly can hardly justify calling the game fair or moral. Instead, the umpire is in fact unwittingly enforcing an immoral situation by not questioning the starting point of those who join the game. Who would choose to play a football game if one started three touchdowns behind? The football season starts over with no wins and losses every year, making irrelevant the history of wins and losses from previous years. No one wants to play a game that is not fair and that does not give one a chance to win, which is why golfers with different skills give each other a "handicap." What makes a game fair is that competition is fair.

Understanding that the state is essentially immoral when it simply sees its role as protecting the lives, liberties, and properties of individuals as they now exist is a critical insight for those of us who want to move forward morally in this world of late capitalism. This insight both builds on the assumptions of the natural rights tradition and draws out its implicit moral implications that were left unrealized. The notion that we have rights at all, as we have seen, is a modern hypothesis that flows from the conviction that we are all equal in value before some absolute standard, however we may define it. The proposition that human beings are equal in value is not a fact in nature, but a founding aspiration of modernity. On the interpretation of that aspiration offered here, the purpose of the state is not simply to protect the lives, liberties, and properties of its citizens, but to step toward a vision of human equality and attempt to counteract the unfairness of history, and the immorality of human nature, and pay back our debt to the past. For the truth is that nature never was fair or equal, and power and violence always played an important role in the evolution of the human species. That is our legacy and part of our debt.

What I am offering is a conception of the state that is very different from the one that typically is associated with the idea of rights. In the view here, we bring into the state not just rights of protection, but responsibilities and debts that were incurred before we were born. In both of these conceptions, the state is a human invention intended to improve the human condition and counteract the tendencies of human beings to use of violence and power. Still, there is a significant difference between the two views. On the original modern natural rights view, the state is intended to improve only the lot of those who come together under its contract. Its purpose is to end the violence in nature between those individuals and reduce the power that is used among them. The state has no obligation to any of those people who lived previously or who live elsewhere. States are themselves said to be in a state of nature toward one another and, until they make treaties with each other, they are like individuals in a state of nature.[12]

According to the alternative conception developed here, the ideal state is also a cultural invention of human beings, but its purpose goes beyond helping protect individuals' lives, liberties, and properties. Its purpose is also to help lift us up as human beings, and as a human species, by trying to redeem ourselves and by making improvements and repairs to the human condition. While the traditional modern notion of the state has always recognized its possibility of improving human life for those humans who leave nature, it has not recognized the duty of repair and reparation that goes with it. If as individuals we carry this burden of the past with us, then the states we live in do as well.

We are all debtors to the past in some fundamental way. And we have all been harmed and benefited from the history of the species. None of us are rightful owners of all our properties. And thus if we come together to live under a state, we do so with the recognition that we all bring with us a debt or moral burden that must be paid back and to which we all must contribute. The relative burden or debt depends on our individual and national situations. Our economic situation and our place in the world give us benefits or liabilities that we all carry with us. We are not discrete individuals with no moral obligations when we join a state or when we are born. Unless we were Adam and Eve, we are born into a world that was made by others before us and in which acts of violence and kindness shaped our own destinies. There is no clean slate when we are born. Though we have done nothing morally in the world at birth, we are born into a set of histories and facts that have moral implications because we are human. If we embrace the aspiration that we are all equal before the absolute, then we come into the world understanding the world has not lived up to our ultimate vision of what we want to be as humans beings. Indeed, historically speaking, the proposition that we are all equal in value was not an idea that humans had in the beginning of time and for much of human history, and arguably it is one distinctive modern perspective since the Enlightenment. This is a relatively new human aspiration and one that we treat as a moral commitment by which to judge our actions and those of our fellows.

One might attack the above conception of the state as too idealistic and impractical. Indeed, one can reasonably argue that the wrongs and violence of the past are too hopelessly complex to sort through and disentangle. There is no way we can figure out "who harmed whom" and "who owes what to whom." Perhaps my ancestors worked morally and much harder than yours, or vice versa. We'll never know. Therefore, one could argue, the best we can do is impose fairness going forward. Furthermore, one might even argue that the violence used by our ancestors may have arisen because they were acting according to mistaken moral convictions, if not deep tendencies and instincts in the human species. Some might even argue that humans were living out their natures as God had created them.

All of this could be true. While it is impossible to sort out the history of unfairness that may have existed in the past, this difficulty does not relieve us of all the burden of responsibility for that history. For the question before us is, what is the best we can do moving forward, and should the best we can do take any account of history? If we say history is too complex to sort through, does that mean we simply ignore history altogether? And on what grounds should our states simply protect our properties that we have in our hands now?

This is the heart of the debate with those who say that the purpose of the state is just to protect our lives, liberties, and properties. The alternative is that the state has a debt, both financial and moral in character, which is born from history and inherited from our human predecessors. The financial debt comes from the fact that each individual stands on the shoulders of those who came earlier. As I argued previously in chapter 3, everything we accomplish ourselves assumes the contributions and inventions of those who came before us. We labor on their backs and with their capital investments. Like the entrepreneur who borrows from the capitalist, we all have investments from our ancestors. These investments in us should be thought of as loans on which a return or interest is expected. Though those human capitalists who preceded and invested in us are no longer alive to collect the debt, their beneficiaries and descendants are our peer human beings. Our human peers are at least partly the beneficiaries, as are we, of the growth of whatever capital occurred. This would be the ultimate fulfillment of that vision that we are all the children of Adam and Eve (or, if one prefers, of Lucy) and that we all once owned resources in common. We have a moral debt as well that derives from the nature of our human species. Historically, we have spread across this earth not just laboring and staying constrained in the plots of land and with the properties each of us has rightfully earned. The history of our species is marked by violence and warfare, theft and power.

What would it mean for a state to pay attention to the debt and burden of history? It means that the state bears two kinds of responsibilities beyond protection, safety, and regulation. One of those responsibilities is inward looking, toward its own citizens, and the other is outward looking, toward the citizens of other nations. Both focus the state and its purposes on values beyond the maintenance of the status quo and the protection of property as it now is. Both rest on an understanding of the claim of history and equality on our moral selves. Both see part of the state's purpose as involved in not the redistribution of wealth and resources, but the payment of debt to capitalist investors.

Consider first the inward-looking perspective. We should recognize that within our states there are massive discrepancies of wealth, education, and opportunities between the individuals who participate in the ideal of the social contract. Inequalities have in fact gotten worse over the last three decades in the United States.[13] We know that these differences come from many sources: luck, history, self-initiative, persecution, and so forth. The United States has given many individuals the opportunity to overcome their histories and pull themselves up by their bootstraps. Some have "bootstrapped" themselves to the middle or upper class. The bootstrap philosophy, however, doesn't recognize the fact that not everyone has bootstraps, let alone shoes. While a small percentage of people do, it depends on a number of factors beyond self-initiative, including the economic situation at the time, the opportunities and resources available, and luck.

The United States celebrates the bootstrap philosophy because so many immigrants were able to remake themselves in the United States. Indeed, America was a land of opportunity in part because it was relatively unpopulated and undeveloped. In its early history, the United States offered vast resources and opportunities that were not as readily available in their countries of origin for immigrating Europeans. That early European expansion into the Americas, as we noted, was in part built upon a conquest, seizure, and purchase of land from the Indians. Subsequent waves of European settlers could take advantage of a vast continent of resources and what seemed like unlimited opportunity and growth. Now that the United States is fully developed and populated, the opportunities to pull oneself up by one's bootstraps are fewer and far between, though still possible in certain sectors of the economy, such as high tech, green energy, and so forth. There is always room for some brilliant entrepreneurs who are there at the right time and place to strike it rich. But many are still impoverished, and wealth is concentrated in the hands of an even smaller number. Many are descended from people who were enslaved or marginalized earlier in history.[14] Indeed, inequality has gotten worse over the last thirty years. From the perspective developed here, the possibility of some people bootstrapping themselves does not relieve the rest of us from the duty to the others. They too are descendants of our common ancestors. They too should be beneficiaries of what was built on the backs of their ancestors. My labor and success capitalize on the investments their ancestors made too, and they too should benefit from the results of my labor. My labor is not entirely my own and belongs at least in part to humanity in general.

From this perspective, the state has a duty to return some of my earnings and benefits to those who earn and benefit less. This government action is not theft. On the contrary, it would be theft were I to keep all my earnings. Everyone owns a piece of my earnings. Instead of thinking of this payment as a "transfer of wealth," it should be thought of more as a payback on a loan or return on an investment that was made to us. It is not charity. It is an obligation born of a loan or investment given to us from the past.

To be sure, this understanding does not relieve any individual from the responsibility to care for his or her basic needs. Every individual has his or her own obligation to take the investments from our ancestors and try to enlarge them for the benefit of all. One cannot take a loan without a commitment to pay it back with interest. Thus a person who is lazy or who does not try hard does not deserve the same benefits as one who does. And the contributions should be in proportion to the resources that one has. The state's purpose in all this is precisely to help in the monitoring of this intergenerational loan and the responsibility of sharing one's success that devolves on every individual in proportion to his or her success.

This perspective should not be lumped together with a Marxist socialist vision. In the view offered here, not all capital is the property of the state or collectively of the people. On the contrary, we are using capitalist concepts of loans, investments, and return on investment to explain this debt we owe to others. In this model, individuals still own private property but have in their assets value that should be paid back to others in the state. With a loan or capitalist investment, the terms of payback are clear. A percentage must be paid back on the loan or a percentage of the company is owned by the investor and the investor's heirs. A similar obligation arises here.

One of the central purposes of the state is to regulate the management of this intergenerational payback and obligation. Through the liberal state's democratic process, it should set a target percentage payback that occurs in any year. The state is a bank or capitalist writ large with the fiscal duty to monitor the intergenerational loan and investment. That responsibility should be treated as fundamental as any right that individuals have, including life, liberty, and property. And the duty to repay a percentage of one's income or wealth should be codified into the Constitution as much as any of the civil or natural rights. In my view, there is no right of a state to exist if its mission is simply to codify the relations that exist at the time of its founding. Such a state, as I have been arguing, is an immoral state, for it imagines that the properties of those who enter the social contract have exclusive ownership of their assets.

We shift now from an internal-looking to an external-looking view. That view starts with the recognition that the boundaries of the state itself are arbitrarily drawn and depend on arbitrary facts of history themselves. If the rightful allocation of resources should have been done via labor and effort only, and had the peoples of the earth spread across the earth in just ways, then there is no telling what the boundaries of states would now be. Thus the first insight is that the state itself is a problematic institution that cannot really justify its existence as a moral entity. This view of the state takes us a further step beyond that early modern realization that God did not pick kings or popes to express the divine will in the form of political power. We go further and acknowledge what everyone has really known all along, namely, that the state within its current boundaries is an arbitrary artifact of history too. What, then, is the purpose, if anything, of the state?

For those of us who feel a moral burden to the past and to the human species as a whole, for all the reasons that this book has talked about, the state has to be one of the vehicles through which we try to transform and improve the human situation and attempt to respond to our moral burden. We can think of other complementary means to do so, such as religious traditions, nonprofit agencies, transformation of business practices, and our own individual acts of kindness. It is easy too to see how states often fail dismally to be this power for reparation, especially with some of the ideologies that came out of the modern period. States, as well as religions, have all the same possibilities for violence that human beings themselves possess. The original claim that the purpose of the state is to end violence is ironic, since most if not all states have actually perpetuated violence of one kind or another at some time or another.

Still, there are reasons to see the liberal state, somewhat redefined, as offering our one hope as a species that is trying to live morally on this planet. Most people would agree that without some sort of police power that is broader than individuals, those who are more powerful, wealthy, or charismatic will take power into their own hands, and we will end up with a set of relations based on the will of the powerful, the economically wealthy, or both. Getting rid of the state, therefore, does not seem like it will solve the problem of violence, power, or uneven distribution of resources. The liberal theory of the state does not adequately address the financial debt and moral burden we inherit from the past. Instead, the classic liberal theory describes the power of the state as a means to protect the interests and concerns of its citizens only and their lives, liberties, and properties. In conceptualizing power this way, the tradition theory freezes and supports a set of relations that benefit the group of people who already have the resources.

On what grounds can we claim that the liberal state's obligation is broader and more complex than protection of its citizens only? If the state just protects us and our properties, the state is in fact aiding and abetting an accidental and immoral distribution of wealth based on past violence and accidents of history. While the liberal state as traditionally under-stood has the positive impact of reducing the use of violence and power among its citizens under the rule of law and protecting them from other peoples or states that may harm them, it is also using its power to retain the status quo or expand the territories and power of its citizens. This is why in classic natural rights theory some theorists said states are in a "state of war" or "state of nature" with respect to one another. Seen from inside the state, the protection of citizens and the end of violence inside the state is a moral good. From outside the state looking in, however, the use of the state's power has the effect of hardening the distribution of resources between states as they are, based on their histories of violence and power, and of course in some cases power is used to expand the state's resources.

We all live on the horns of this dilemma. The same balance that we all recognize when it comes to interpersonal relationships also applies to the state that acts in our name. Were we to lay down all powers of the state, then we would have no protection of ourselves and our lives. Were we to focus only on our state and not the rest of the world, then we are for ourselves alone. We would, moreover, be thieves.

The moral liberal state (contrasting it with the immoral liberal state) has an obligation to those beyond its borders. It has a duty to go beyond the interests of its own citizens and attempt to repay the debt and level the playing field, to some extent. The Marxist vision of the state, of course, envisioned a leveling of the playing field within the state through the shared ownership of the means of production. The moral vision here is broader than that, seeing the disparities of wealth and resources across the species, and thus across states, as morally unfounded. What that means practically speaking is now something that we must discuss.

The Moral Liberal State

It is neither practical nor even desirable to completely level the play-ing field within a state or between states. We know that there are good reasons to link outcomes of individual efforts and talents to reward. When

I am rewarded for my industriousness, I am more likely to labor hard, invent something new, and contribute to the stock of human knowledge. Private property thus helps make people industrious and improves their moral character in some critical respects.[15] We do not want to completely level the playing field and adopt state or communal ownership of the means of production. We have abundant evidence of how that approach has failed in practice.

Still, there is an intelligent position between these two extreme poles, despite the protestations of our opponents. On the one side, we have the instinct for and right to life and self-preservation. And we have the desire to improve our situation. On the other side, we have a moral compass, born from our histories and religious traditions and embedded in our psychologies. In its modern variation, that moral compass says that all human beings are equal in value and, as I have argued, the current distribution of wealth and resources across the human populations is neither fair nor consistent with that proposition. The only way to navigate between those pulls is to recognize an obligation of every individual and every state to shift some of its wealth and resources from those who have plenty to those who have less. As noted earlier, this should not be treated as a "transfer of wealth" but as a "payback of debt," since the former by its very language makes it sounds like it is an act of charity, whereas as we have seen, this is in fact more a return on a debt.[16] When we pay back the bank for a loan on a house or car, or when a capitalist sells his company and returns a hundredfold to his investors, this is not a negative "transfer of wealth." This is the completion of an obligation and contract. So too with the payback I am describing here. It is all relative, of course. But everyone is better off than someone else, and thus everyone has a duty to pay back some of his or her wealth to others. Let us now see what the basis is for this return of on investment.

The State, Taxes, and the Return of Wealth

We often think of everything that we earn as exclusively our own. If this were true, then why is a government allowed to tax us at all?

Why aren't all taxes defined as stealing our property, which a government is supposed to protect? The following statement from Locke illustrates what appears to be the modern rights conundrum:

> *Thirdly*, The *Supream Power* [of the state] *cannot take* from any Man any part of his *Property* without his own consent. For the preservation of Property being the end of Government, and that for which Men enter into Society....*Men* therefore *in Society having Property*, they have such a right to the goods, which by the Law of the Community are theirs, that no Body hath a right to take their substance, or any part of it from them, without their own consent; without this they have no *Property* at all.[17]

Despite this claim that the state cannot take a person's property without his or her consent, taxes have been understood to be a duty and obligation of citizens in exchange for what they receive from the state or as a cost of living in a social community. The assumption has been that an exchange in value takes place. The state offers something to the citizen, and in exchange the citizen owes something to the state. It is not a "taking," but a payment for services rendered. Many of these early modern convictions about taxes arose against the background of the seventeenth-century conflict in which English monarchs such as King Charles I were at frequent odds with Parliament over, among other things, the issue of raising taxes and revenues. For example, in what was a contentious move and one of the contributing factors to the English Civil Wars, King Charles I tried to make an end run around Parliament by raising revenues for the navy through "ship money," an old, contentious law that gave the Crown the right to tax communities for the navy without parliamentary approval.[18] The questions of who could raise taxes or revenues, under what conditions, and by what right were at the heart of the growing modern debate over the locus of authority and property in the early modern conceptions of the state.

As an example, one can see all the classic themes of the modern discussion on taxes already in play when Hobbes published *Leviathan* in

1651, after a decade of English civil war and only two years after King
Charles I was beheaded.[19] Hobbes positions taxes as a payment for the
debt that citizens incur for the safety and protection they receive from
the state. Since all subjects benefit equally from such safety and peace
provided by the state, Hobbes concludes that taxes should be equal across
subjects as well. This in his view is part of the equal justice that by the
law of nature must govern the state. "For the Impositions, that are layd
on the People by the Soveraign Power, are nothing else but the Wages,
due to them that hold the publique Sword, to defend private men in
the exercise of severall Trades, and Callings. Seeing then the benefit that
every one receiveth thereby, is the enjoyment of life, which is equally dear
to poor, and rich: the debt which a poor man oweth them that defense his
life, is the same which a rich man oweth for the defence of his; saving that
the rich, who have the services of the poor, may be debtors not onely for
their own persons, but for many more."[20]

Hobbes is saying that everyone benefits equally with protection of
his or her life and therefore the debt to society is the same, regardless of
one's personal wealth. And yet by safety Hobbes means more than "bare
Preservation, but also all other Contentments of life."

"Equall taxes," in Hobbes's view, however, does not mean taxing everyone at the same rate but based on a person's level of consumption. "For
what reason is there, that he which laboureth much, and sparing the
fruits of his labour, consumeth little, should be more charged, then he
that living idly, getteth little, and spendeth all he gets;…But when the
Impositions, are layd upon those things which men consume, every man
payeth equally for what he useth: Nor is the Common-wealth defrauded,
by the luxurious waste of private men."[21]

We see in Hobbes's position most of the themes that are still contentious today. First and foremost, Hobbes positions taxes as a debt, not only
for safety provided by the state but for the benefits of life that accrue from
safety. Hobbes argues that taxes should fall equally on persons, since the
benefits of safety fall equally to persons under the state. This is consistent with Hobbes's assumption, discussed earlier, that individuals would
never have agreed to be part of the state had the state's rules not been

applied equally and with equity. Taxes are thus another example of how equality should govern relations in the state.

But equality does not mean everyone pays the same amount. Hobbes argues that taxes should be tied to an individual's consumption, not based on total wealth. In linking the debt to society to the amount of enjoyment or consumption one has, Hobbes in essence equates debt with the benefits one receives through one's contentment in life. In this way, the state isn't "defrauded" by people who live in luxury but pay little, nor are those who have much wealth, but who spend little, punished by the state when they lead moderate lives. Taxes are proportionate to consumption.

Hobbes recognized a second purpose of taxes beyond payback for safety. Taxes were also to be used to care for the poor and indigent who were incapable of working. "And whereas many men, by accident unevitable, become unable to maintain themselves by their labour; they ought not to be left to the Charity of private persons; but to be provided for, (as far-forth as the necessities of Nature require, by the Lawes of the Common-wealth. For as it is Uncharitablenesse in any man, to neglect the impotent; so it is in the Soveraign of a Common-wealth, to expose them to the hazard of such uncertain Charity."[22] We thus see that the state's purposes includes taking care of those who cannot care for themselves because of some act of fate, and the assumption is that the state can legitimately tax for that purpose.

While Hobbes acknowledges the responsibility of the state to care for "the impotent," he insists, in anticipation of still current arguments, that idleness should be prevented and that able-bodied persons should not be supported by the state. Instead, those with strong bodies "are to be forced to work," though Hobbes does not explain whether he literally means people should be conscripted for labor. But Hobbes does see the state as responsible for helping to make opportunities available, and therefore "to avoid the excuse of not finding employment, there ought to be such Lawes, as may encourage all manner of Arts; as Navigation, Agriculture, Fishing, and all manner of Manifacture that requires labour." We see here the modern view that the state's duty is to create an economic environment that produces jobs and thus gives able-bodied people the opportunity to work and support themselves.

What if those state economic policies do not create sufficient jobs and individuals still cannot find work? Anticipating the view of Locke, who followed him, Hobbes goes on to say, "The multitude of poor, and yet strong people still increasing, they are to be transplanted into Countries not sufficiently inhabited, where neverthelesse, they are not to exterminate those they find there." Unlike Locke, who envisioned "unlimited resources" still available, Hobbes ends with a pessimistic and disturbing vision: "and when all the world is overcharged with Inhabitants, then the last remedy of all is Warre; which provideth for every man, by Victory, or Death."

It is true that Hobbes endorsed an absolutist view of the state, believing that the sovereign, represented by either the appointed assembly or the monarch, had absolute power to make laws and even decide beliefs. In this sense, he did not take the step of leaving the question of taxes up to the people. But he clearly anticipated all the major contentious themes surrounding taxes and government's role and posed the questions that continue to haunt us today.

John Locke, writing his *Second Treatise on Government* forty years later, was among those to take the final conceptual step that shifted the power on taxes from the sovereign to the people who comprised the state.[23] Locke provides a similar reason for why taxes are not considered theft. He notes that "governments cannot be supported without great charge, and it is fit every one who enjoys his share of the protection, should pay out of his estate his proportion for the maintenance of it." Like Hobbes, Locke sees taxes as in part an obligation for the protection offered by the state, though Locke also notes that governments require substantial financing. But then Locke explains why this tax is not theft. "But still it must be with his own consent, *i.e.* the consent of the majority, giving it either by themselves, or their representatives chosen for them: for if any one shall claim a *power to lay* and levy taxes on the people, by his own authority, and without such consent of the people, he thereby invades the *fundamental law of property,* and subverts the end of government: for what property have I in that, which another may by right take, when he pleases to himself?"[24]

It is interesting to see how Locke solves the conceptual dilemma of explaining how a government cannot take from anyone "any part of his property without his own consent" yet can forcibly take money in the form of taxes. Locke argues that if the majority or their representatives endorse the tax, it is not considered against an individual's will. Why not? Because Locke recognizes that taxes are really no different from any other kind of law that a society makes. No laws will be endorsed by everyone in the state. Thus any law adopted by the state will go against the will of some individuals. It would be impossible for the state to act at all if it tries to win the approval of every person. Locke therefore concludes that the conceptual agreement of those who have agreed to live in the state is to accept the vote of the majority or their representatives as the basis for the decision-making process.

> And thus every Man, by consenting with others to make one Body Politick under one Government, puts himself under an Obligation to every one of that Society, to submit to the determination of the *majority*, and to be concluded by it; or else this *original Compact*, whereby he with others incorporates into *one Society*, would signifie nothing, and be no Compact, if he be left free and under no other ties, then he was in before in the State of Nature. For what appearance would there be of any Compact? What new Engagement if he were no farther tied by any Decrees of the Society, then he himself thought fit, and did actually consent to? This would be still as great a liberty, as he himself had before his Compact.[25]

In this sense, there is an interesting similarity between Locke's liberal state and the absolute state of Hobbes, for Locke's liberal state also does not make everyone happy either nor give everyone individual consent. "Consent" in the liberal state is the will of the majority, which the individual has agreed to abide by as if it were his or her own consent. Thus

Locke sees compliance with laws and with taxes as taking place with one's consent, even if one does not individually agree.

In Locke's vision, an individual has a choice whether or not to live under the commonwealth. Yet making that choice at maturity, the individual has now bound him- or herself to the will of the majority, whether he or she likes the particular expression of that will or not. And thus the will of the majority by definition amounts to the consent of the individual.[26] This is the reason why, for Locke, one who enters society "divests himself of his Natural Liberty, and *puts on the bonds of Civil Society*."[27] Because individuals have consented to live in the state and because they have representation, the state is not stealing, even if it forcibly takes taxes that as individuals they do not affirm. The alternative fails, as Locke points out, for if everyone follows his or her own inclination, there is no state and individuals are thrown back into the predicament of the state of nature.

Locke is less explicit than Hobbes about the purposes for which taxes can be raised and leaves that question open ended, suggesting perhaps that the purposes of government can themselves be determined by the majority; the majority themselves can define the way taxes are implemented and for what purposes. Thus in his brief mention of taxes in his treatise on government, Locke does not take a position on how the state should deal with the question of poverty and unequal distribution of wealth. By his silence on the subject, he appears to leave that question up to the majority to decide and does not apparently see a need to set limits on which types of taxes are legitimate and which are not. It would seem to be a decision of the majority.

Unlike Hobbes, Locke does not here explicitly mandate that the state is to focus on job creation or how it should deal with the indigent and impoverished. Of course, we do know that he put tremendous emphasis on the value of labor and work. Thus it is not surprising that he would see the role of government to be the art of making people industrious:

> This shews, how much numbers of men are to be preferred to
> largenesse of dominions, and that the increase of lands, and the

right imploying of them is the great art of government. And that Prince, who shall be so wise and godlike as by established laws of liberty to secure protection and incouragement to the honest industry of Mankind, against the oppression of power and narrownesse of Party, will quickly be too hard for his neighbours: But this bye the bye.[28]

And yet there is another side of Locke's statements on inequality that makes it more difficult to say what his own position on poverty would be. For Locke also thought that the unequal distribution of wealth came about in part because of the invention of money, as previously discussed. Prior to the invention of money, Locke assumed that the relative balance of wealth was more naturally maintained, because the natural tendency of things to spoil prevented people from hoarding more than they could use. In the state of nature, "it was useless as well as dishonest to carve himself too much, or take more than he needed."[29]

Locke never says that the state has the responsibility to level out the inequality that humans had created. But one could construct a position around his views that does lead in that direction. Indeed, he does imply that ultimately extreme poverty overrides and suspends the law of property. For the ultimate purpose of resources as they were given by God in nature is for humans to sustain themselves and increase and multiply. In a discussion in his *First Treatise on Government*, in an argument about the nature of Creation and whether God had given Adam property over all the world, Locke had this to say:

> But we know God hath not left one Man so to the Mercy of another, that he may starve him if he please: God the Lord and Father of all, has given no one of his Children such a Property in his peculiar Portion of the things of this World, but that he has given his needy Brother a Right to the Surplusage of his Goods; so that it cannot justly be denied him, when his pressing Wants call for it: and therefore no man could ever have a just Power over the Life of another, by Right of property in Land or Possessions;

since "twould always be a Sin, in any Man of Estate, to let his Brother perish for want of affording him Relief out of his Plenty. As *Justice* gives every man a title to the product of his honest Industry, and the fair Acquisitions of his Ancestors descended to him; so *Charity* gives every man a title to so much out of another's Plenty, as will keep him from extream want, where he has no means to subsist otherwise.[30]

Locke does not draw out the possible conclusions of his position here for the obligations of the state. But one could argue, based on his position, that the right to the surplus of goods by a needy brother is brought into the state and is part of the state's obligations. This becomes all the more imperative when we realize that Locke's foundational assumption guiding his faith in industriousness was that land was limitless, and those who applied themselves could find ways to support themselves.

Original Debt and the Return of Wealth

To return to the argument I have been making, individuals in the state, and thus the state itself, carry an obligation to pay back a debt to humanity and the human species. The notion of debt or payback, as I said in the previous section, is already present in the natural rights tradition in the form of the idea of taxes. But it is a notion that was conceptualized as a debt between the individuals and the state. Individuals owed the state a debt for their safety and contentment. The state had a responsibility back to its members. The notion of debt I am insisting on in this discussion, however, is broader and wider than that between the state and its members. It is a debt to the human species as a whole, both past and present. This notion of debt exists prior to the creation of the state and thus is not limited by the relationship of the state and its members.

This expanded notion of debt derives from the revised notions of property and labor that we have uncovered in the course of this analysis. Property is never exclusively my own, since my investments already encode the investments and labors of thousands before me. Thus I carry a debt to the past and all those who contributed to the platform on which humans operate. That debt should be paid back to their living heirs, who are my contemporaneous human fellows, both those within my state and those without. This debt to my fellows thus arises as a responsibility on each individual and is handed off to the state, which carries the debt and helps execute its payback. Taxes are the mechanism by which this return on investment should be paid. Since the word "tax" has become synonymous with a bad word, it is worthwhile renaming this as a repayment on a debt.

I realize that the position I am articulating can be criticized as too idealistic and vague. What makes it vague, however, is only the fact that it has not yet been institutionalized. The very notion of a debt to society for safety and contentment is just as vague until it is quantified in some political and moral process that defines what that debt should be and how it should be paid off. Indeed, the very idea of a society founded on rights was a vague and idealistic idea when it was originally being developed. What transformed it from an idealistic conception to an institutionalized reality was a set of social transformations that changed the structure of government. It was equally vague to say society must defend us until we specified in some social and political institutions what that defense amounts to and should be. By the same token, all that is needed to take the "idealism" out of this conception of human debt is a transformation of practices by which we govern ourselves. To be sure, there is no loan document or terms of investment for our debt to the past as there would be between a bank and a borrower or a capitalist and an entrepreneur. And thus one of the responsibilities of the state is to forge a consensus on what this debt implies, based on the wealth of the nation.

We know, of course, that any decision-making process that is social and political in nature, like any discussion of taxes, will invariably be fraught with politics, debate, and power. So what else is new? If, however, we ensure that that the ideas of "payback" and "debt" are part of our conceptual framework that founds our constitutions and shapes our institutions, then we have shifted the debate from concern with government "stealing my property" to the question of "my responsibility as a human being." Imagine that.

If we do not embrace this conception of the state as carrying and executing our collective individual duties to pay off our historical obligations, then the state is nothing but a power for defending and expanding the properties and wealth of its citizens. It is nothing more than power and violence writ large. This conception of the state as seeking to develop a nation's wealth has in many ways been the guiding idea that has been aligned with the modern philosophy of rights and properties. While the political philosophy of rights was once a transformative and radical notion that subverted the power of the monarch, it has now been tamed and transformed into ideas that now support the status quo of violence. The idea that states have moral duties to mend the world, therefore, corresponds to the idea that individuals carry their own debts to the past.

For this conception of the state to win, or to have some influence, it will have to be taken up and become part of a political platform that adopts it and makes it a coherent position. In some ways, these ideas are already embedded in leftist and progressive notions of justice that point to moral obligations beyond ourselves and our states. What I have done, however, is ground such commitments in the very concepts of liberty, labor, and property, the key concepts in the political philosophy of the Right and the owners of wealth. The Left has made the mistake in the past of not taking on and contesting the conceptions of liberty and property of both those on the Right and of libertarians, and thereby weakened its own position. The Left thus looks like it does not embrace these seemingly important values and thus appears to abandon both the liberal traditions of modernity and of America. As I have been suggesting throughout this book, however, there is another and better way of understanding liberty that does not end up endorsing the view that everything for which I labor is mine and that the state is the institution of power that protects those rights.

If we succeed in this reunderstanding of liberty and learn to shift our focus to our responsibilities as much as our rights, and we understand our responsibility as arising from our obligations from the past, then we create a new kind of politics that can transform at least some of the purposes of our state. The state exists not solely for our protection and contentment, but also to enable us to live up to our moral obligations and our aspirations to be humans who live with the vision of equality. If the state is solely defending the rights of property as they exist today, then it is hardening a set of distributions of wealth and resources that came about unfairly and through violence. So too, if it simply taxes to protect and make better the lives of its members, it does not go far enough in contesting the formations of the past. It simply perpetuates the violence of the past. Part of letting us live human lives, in contrast to the lives of animals that live more by instinct, is to let us live out and attempt to fulfill our moral sensibilities.

Part of the state's purpose, I am arguing, should be cultural and moral, not just economic. This moral commitment is one that we posit as a foundation of the liberal state. It is one of the commitments that the liberal state should make and through which it should understand itself. While any set of values can be contested from some religious and political perspective, this commitment should be constitutional. It should be as deep in our foundation as free speech and the protection of lives and property. It should be one that we put in our founding constitutions and on which we erect our liberal states, were we to do it again or revise the one we have.

To return to the point I was making, if we have a different notion of property and of the obligations that come with being human and living in the state, then it stands to reason that we can and should reconceptualize what it is that taxes are and should be. I have argued that the property that individuals have in their possession cannot be thought to be strictly their own anyway and that at least a portion of what we have is in trust or on loan from those who invested in us. This means that some benefits of our labor, which stands on the human platform bequeathed to us, belong to human beings in common.

What this amount should be is difficult to say. Ideally, this "equity" repayment on our human debt would be most fair if it were a percentage of gross domestic product. As a percentage of GDP, the larger a country's

GDP, the more it is consuming resources, the more wealth it produces, and therefore the more wealth it should pay back. The dollars raised in this payback should be paid to those countries who have lower GDP and who embrace a similar political philosophy in their constitutions. States themselves should not be the recipient of this repayment or equity payment. It should be distributed to nonprofit organizations that work locally in states to help those who need the most help.

To summarize, we have seen that the traditional definition of the state as an institution that serves to protect the lives, liberties, and properties of its citizens is too limited. That notion of the state assumed that properties came about rightfully and fairly in history and ignored the fact that conquest and violence have always been in the history of the human species and that where individuals labor they do so on the backs of thousands before them. For these reasons, the distribution of properties by individuals and states cannot be thought to be fair. Since individuals are born into a state with a set of obligations to pay back their debt to the past, the state shares in that obligation to history. What we have in part has always been on loan from our ancestors and the human capitalists who invested in us from the past. We have an obligation to pay back their heirs, who are our contemporaries. This means that we each carry a debt that we must fulfill and that the state in which we live carries our collective debts as citizens. We labor to support ourselves and create lives of enjoyment. But we labor too to pay off a debt, and because we are beings with moral aspirations.

Chapter 9
Beyond Economists as
the Priests of Liberty

It is a common refrain today among some that governments should not overregulate economies or markets, just as they should not overregulate people's lives. Both forms of intervention infringe on liberty, and both undermine the economic well-being of the world. This argument is often presented as an argument for protecting individual liberty and has two different flavors or variations, which are interrelated in various ways and are often used to justify each other. One argument says that free markets are a right like other rights of life, liberty, and property. We have a right to sell to whom we want and at what price we want, just as we have a right to our lives, liberty, and properties. Regulation of markets interferes with one of our key liberties, related to our liberty to do what we want with our property and to our liberty in general.[1]

The other argument holds that free markets create economic prosperity and are right and good for a liberal society because they help create and perpetuate liberty and justice. In this version of the argument, the consequence of free markets and an absence of regulation has consequences that are critical to the flourishing of liberty. Economic prosperity is an end in itself, and it also supports a life that embraces liberty.

Sometimes both of these positions are used together, sometimes one or the other. Both use the language of liberty but come at liberty from different perspectives. As we shall now see, however, both have misleading ideas of liberty and distort the liberty tradition in critical ways. Let us dive into these positions in more detail.

Take the first variation of the free market argument, which claims that economic liberty is part and parcel of liberty itself. To protect liberty requires enabling markets and economies to function as freely as possible. You can't have liberty without market liberty. Some of the people who hold this view refer to themselves as "market liberals."[2] In this view, economic freedom is a right just like other kinds of freedoms. Liberty, in other words, by definition includes economic freedom, just as it includes the right to life, liberty, and property. Economic liberty is thus part of the definition of what liberty is and means. It is part of the rights of "liberty" and "property." Milton Friedman, one of the most well-known proponents of this position, put it this way: "underlying most arguments against the free market is a lack of belief in freedom itself," and "freedom in economic arrangements is itself a component of freedom broadly understood, so economic freedom is an end in itself."[3] As we shall see below, this position is wrong in several critical respects. To say liberty by definition includes free markets is not to defend liberty but to become dictatorial by mandating a single position on markets and imposing a set of values by fiat. By contrast, liberty should be understood as giving the right for liberal societies to decide how much freedom to give markets, understanding that that decision is a moral one and that efficiency is not the only value in town.

The second flavor of the argument contends that the liberty of markets is critical for the growth of the economy, wealth, and human prosperity. This argument is utilitarian or "consequentialist" in nature, and it makes the assumption that the material benefits of free markets are superior to the benefits of a regulated economy. Furthermore, because human flourishing is critical to liberty, the freedom of markets is important for the achievement of liberty.

This view traces its history back to the economic insights of Adam Smith's *Wealth of Nations*, in which Smith argued that an "invisible hand" guides the exchanges of the market. By "invisible hand," Smith identified how markets efficiently set prices by the level of demand for goods and services through the thousands of minute exchanges between individuals as they pursued their own individual self-interests. There were several key notions in Smith's work that set the foundation for modern economics, which was built upon Smith's insights. The first was that markets could efficiently regulate the prices of goods and labor without help. Second, the idea that individuals each pursuing their own interests generated not something bad, but a fair exchange of value in the market contrasted with earlier religious views that goods had fixed fair prices based on intrinsic value and that setting too high a price was "usury." On Smith's economic model, the implication was that individuals could pursue their own economic interests wholeheartedly without acting immorally. On the contrary, by pursuing their individual personal interests, they were helping everyone and doing good.

In calling the market mechanisms an "invisible hand," Smith perhaps somewhat unknowingly put the market itself symbolically in the place previously occupied by "God." The market took the omniscient position, or "God's-eye" view, above the fray of thousands of transactions and ultimately set the fair price of a good. For devotees of Smith, since the market is thought to be "omniscient," or at least smarter than governments, it is right for governments to let markets manage themselves. Governments that intervene in markets destroy a market's equilibrium and their ability to adjust and maximize productivity, innovation, and wealth, and such interventions therefore unintentionally undermine the prosperity and happiness of individuals. Philosophers and writers such as Friedrich Hayek, Ayn Rand, and more recently Richard Epstein are among those who have articulated this kind of utilitarian justification of economic liberty. They argue that to limit markets is to undermine human motivation, stultify economic growth, and thereby curtail general human prosperity and happiness. The way to deal with the uneven distribution of resources and wealth is to let the markets operate freely, for by growing markets, more knowledge and benefits will be produced, raising all boats on the rising tide of human advancement. By contrast, redistributing wealth destroys productivity and motivation and ultimately harms everyone by denying growth, opportunity, and future knowledge.

In this approach, the justification of free markets is that the overall benefits to the majority outweigh any individual costs. More overall satisfaction and happiness are produced than would be the case otherwise. More medicines, scientific advances, technological breakthroughs, and overall growth are achieved, leading to more enjoyment, health, and longevity. While the assumption is that individuals who work hard will improve their situations, the end game is not to worry about individuals per se, nor even their rights. The end game is to let things improve overall and for individuals to fend for themselves in this growing pie of more opportunity and better conditions of life.

There are thus two very different philosophical justifications for why governments should stay out of the business of regulating markets. Both link themselves to the concept of liberty in different ways. Those who lean on one do not always buy the arguments of the other. Those who argue from the utility of markets do not always think the concepts of rights make sense.[4] However, because both positions agree that markets should be unregulated as much as possible, there is a political coalition among those who otherwise disagree on a more fundamental assumption. Indeed, market liberals disagree among themselves on whether governments should get involved in other nonmarket matters such as forbidding abortion, defining marriage, and so forth. Libertarian-leaning market liberals tend to want government to get out of the business of enforcing any kinds of moral values and leave such decisions to individuals, though even some of them think government should regulate and forbid abortion. Market liberals who lean on rights arguments often speak with a social and religious conservatism that wants government to stay out of economic markets but to get involved in a set of moral restrictions (such as making it illegal to burn a flag or refuse to say the Pledge to Allegiance, or to have an abortion or a gay marriage).

Rethinking Liberty and Free Markets

In what follows, we see that both of these arguments about market freedom are confused and conflate the question of liberty inappropriately with the question of markets. To begin with, liberty and markets intersect and touch each other but are not the same matter. One can fiercely defend the concept of liberty but still advocate for various kinds of interventions in markets. This is not a contradiction in terms. Indeed, various kinds of interventions in the market are necessary for liberty, and the decision of whether and in what ways to regulate markets is itself part of what it means to live in a liberal society. This is not a position that free market proponents recognize, for they tend to see any intervention in the market as incompatible with liberty. In framing the relationship of liberty and markets in this alternative way, we have turned the free market story on its head. *We believe liberty itself includes the right to decide how much latitude or freedom to allow the market.* Indeed, to take away that freedom by trying to mandate and prescribe a set relationship between government and markets is to deny liberty itself. In other words, to impose free markets and to insist they are not a choice, but a mandate of liberty, is as much an imposition as the imposition of socialism would be. Insisting that governments cannot intervene in markets is tantamount to saying that we cannot try to live our lives by deeply held values and morals.

There are three different pillars on which this alternative understanding of markets and liberty rests. The first pillar is to dethrone economists as the priests of modernity and the source of truth about morality. Economists are good at economics, though they don't all agree on economic theory either. More important, they are not superior to the rest of us at morality and values and, by extension, how to define liberty. Indeed, they risk having moral blinders on precisely because they filter everything through an economist's lens. Economics is only one way of seeing moral questions. It is therefore important to separate economic questions from the questions of morality and see them as two different but intersecting sets of inquiries and knowledge.

The second pillar of our alternative position is to realize that for markets to exist and function well in the first place, they require law and regulation. It is a stable society with a government and laws that makes markets and liberty possible. When there is war or panic, markets don't function well or at all. In other words, governments and intervention help to create stable and prosperous markets. This is a point that often our opponents overlook as they try to insist that regulations are against liberty.

The third related pillar involves understanding how values do and should enter into decisions about the market. To take a position on market intervention is to take a position on a set of values. We don't believe everything should be for sale, such as human lives, for example. Nor do we think people should be sold into slavery. We believe markets should have limits based on values that are themselves part of what we understand liberty to be. And if we recognize limits on selling some things, then we recognize the relevance of values to limiting markets in general. The question is thus when and why to invoke values to set limits on markets. All of these points show us that ultimately liberty gives us the freedom to decide how much we want markets to be free and in what ways and for what reasons. Let us take these points up in turn.

Beyond the Economist as Priest

It is one symptom of our moral decay in the modern world that the economist is often treated like a priest in the medieval Catholic Church. I say this partly tongue-in-cheek but also partly in seriousness too. The professional economist has emerged as the source of values and truth by which we should run our liberal societies. Indeed, economists are often the very favorite spokespersons and authorities of those who hold the liberty-first position, although progressives pay way too much attention to them as well.[5] The notion that free markets are best for prosperity or equivalent to liberty is really a political and moral position that rests on economic models of well-being, human nature, and truth. In putting our modern faith in professors of economics as the source of truth and wisdom, we have abandoned much of our own individual moral judgments and intuitions about what's right, and left them in the hands of a class of professionals who argue from abstract mathematical models that are a mumbo jumbo few of us noneconomists can understand. This "arithomania," as one economist calls it, is just as inaccessible to the average person as the Catholic Latin mass was to the early modern Catholic laity before the Reformation.[6]

I use the analogy of the economists and priests intentionally as more than simply an interesting metaphor. Among our proponents, professors of economics are playing a role similar to priests in the medieval church. The economist is to the market as the priest was to God. Only economists are thought capable of discerning the true inner workings of the omniscient market, which laity cannot possibly understand. People like you and me have nothing meaningful to contribute and should abandon our own individual intuitions and listen to the professional class. We are told to 1) trust the economists who are the source of truth, even though 2) we can't understand their abstract mathematical models, and even though 3) there is evidence that contradicts their claims. We are told too to 4) ignore our own moral intuitions and judgments in favor of their rendition of truth. All of this of course fell apart for the Catholic Church when Luther and the Reformation came along and said that 1) the church is corrupt and serves its own interests, and 2) the relationship between religious and moral life is between an individual and God; a professional class should not dictate our consciences and moral insights.

Economists are not the first type of scientists to have this near-religious status accorded to them in the modern period, though they are perhaps the last to be dethroned from the position. After the Reformation questioned the Catholic Church's monopoly on knowledge, thinkers in the modern tradition turned to science and rationalism as an alternative source of truth. As discussed earlier, philosophers thought they could discern moral truths through the methodologies of science. Modern natural rights thinkers were among those trying to found a human morality on reason and the science of the human being, a project that ultimately failed by nearly all accounts.

There is general agreement among university academics, for example, that the social sciences and humanities have been unable to achieve the same level of certainty that was theoretically possible in the natural sciences, though even the certainty of natural sciences is questioned among some historians as well. Most sociologists, anthropologists, and psychologists would say that the social and human sciences have been unable to discover and likely will never discover laws of human behavior. Instead these disciplines provide insights into the factors shaping human behavior and ways of seeing ourselves and our societies that change and deepen our self-understanding. Economists, however, still pretend to be more like natural scientists than social scientists and put on the air of discovering laws of economic behavior that are as true as laws governing the natural world. For this reason, many people listen to the pronouncements of economists as gospel truth and discount their own moral intuitions that tell us that matters are not right the way they are. In the meantime, we mistake economic theories for moral blueprints about the nature of human beings and our moral obligations.

What is needed for us is a new reformation that dethrones the economists as the priests of our generation. We should see economists as having one interesting angle on truth, but not the only or necessarily best one. Let economists pronounce insights on the economy, but let us *not* turn to economics for insights on morality, justice, and liberty. Our ethicists, historians, psychologists, sociologists, and religious leaders all represent other voices and perspectives on how we should see ourselves and the societies we live in. Those voices emphasize other values and responsibilities that we humans have, based on our moral and religious traditions and based on other analyses of human society and human character.

The first step is to realize that economics has the capacity to harden the heart of the human being precisely in its inclination to view all issues in numbers only and to flatten the complexity of the human being. At the core of traditional economic models are mathematical models and ideal types of the "rational man" (or at times the "rational person"), who is said to act from his personal self-interest, or what economics summarize under the term "utility." The man or person behind the economic models is "half a man" or half a person who acts out of rational self-interest but is not motivated by other dimensions of the person or soul, such as altruism, love, compassion, or duty.[7] If these other dimensions of the person are acknowledged by economic theory, they are reduced to utility as well.

A person is said to be altruistic only because he or she gets benefits or pleasure from it. But the reasoning is circular, for it assumes that anything I do is from my self-interest, and thus it cannot explain why one person's self-interest is in helping others and in selfless behavior whereas another's is in dominating others or building wealth. The rational person model may work as an ideal type for economic models, though it has been criticized from various quarters for portraying a one-dimensional person who pursues only utility. The economic model also fails to grasp the complexity of the psyche and the ways that people's behaviors are shaped by complex nonrational currents in the human personality or "soul," an insight from psychologists for which economic models cannot account.[8] Even if this image of the rational person seeking utility works as a heuristic and predictive basis for economic models, it does not necessarily provide a blueprint for morality and human relations. Economic models provide insights only for economic facts, but not for understanding what human obligation and duty should be. The move from facts to obligations and duties is the business of other human disciplines, such as ethics, religion, and political philosophy. Economic facts are not recipes for human behavior. They are maps of the landscape, perhaps, but not driving directions for a destination.

Even the father of economics, Adam Smith, author of *The Wealth of Nations*, seemed to intuit such a bifurcation between economics and morality, a fact noted by some economists who see the limitations of economic theory.[9] It is not widely known outside academic circles that before writing *The Wealth of Nations*, Smith wrote a completely separate treatise on morality called *A Theory of Moral Sentiments*. In that context, Smith's conclusions about moral inclinations and obligation were not derived from his economic theories of self-interest but from the concept of sympathy, a concept that plays little role in his later economic analysis. In the start of that book, he wrote: "How selfish soever man may be supposed, there are evidently some principles in his nature, which interest him in the fortunes of others, and render their happiness necessary to him, though he derives nothing from it, except the pleasure of seeing it."[10] This attempt to characterize the instinctual nature of care in the human character suggests that even the father of modern economics glimpsed the limits of economic theory for understanding human character. A similar point is being made here. Economics can generate facts that moralists, ethicists, and philosophers should consider and weigh. But it cannot and should not tell us what our obligations and responsibilities are with respect to those facts. For our moral duties and responsibilities arise from our deeply held convictions about what we understand human beings to be and how we weigh different choices about what matter. It is debatable whether any theory can prove that these deeply held convictions are true in some natural and absolute sense.

There are several reasons that economists have no special standing on the question of morality. The first reason is that their theories can only produce facts that are relevant to moral theories, but they are not moral theories themselves. Moral theories are claims about what values matter and why. Moral theories postulate a position about what humans are and should be, based on a set of founding assumptions. These founding assumptions may include ideas about human nature, God, duty, obligation, and so on. For example, the claim that we are all created equal in value is a moral theory that has been, and I believe should be, at the foundation of our understanding of liberty. How that founding assumption should be interpreted and what it means is still up for debate. Economists can't tell us whether we should treat humans equally or not, nor can they tell us how we should interpret that modern position. They can only give us guidance about the consequences of various kinds of economic decisions. But they have no special expertise or standing in helping us draw moral conclusions because their expertise is in economics, not morality.

To make matters worse, economists as a class do not seem able to predict economic outcomes nor to even come to agreement on the causes of economic phenomena. Events such as the Great Depression, as an example, are subject to conflicting interpretations of their primary causes. One perspective, put forward by John Maynard Keynes, interprets the Great Depression as resulting from the instabilities inherent in modern capitalist economies and a failure of government response. In this view, there are many reasons why the self-correcting mechanisms that many economists claim should work during a downturn may not work. From this position arose the view that government should intervene to stimulate the economy and to counter market failures. The other position, put forward most forcibly by Milton Friedman and Ann Schwartz, interprets the Great Depression as a crisis that was deepened by the monetary policy mistakes of the inept Federal Reserve.[11] In this view, it was not primarily the failure of markets that was the cause of the crisis, but the way government responded to markets. As is evident, there are economists on both sides of the story, and alternative explanations as well, showing that a neutral science of economics is not ultimately likely to solve our political disagreements. Each political perspective has economists in support. In some ways, this failure to agree among economists should come as no surprise. Like other human sciences, there seems to be a fundamental inability to discover laws and predict outcomes with consistency or to agree on policies.[12] To rely on economists because they are economists, and not just people like you and me, would be a double mistake. It would be a mistake first because they have no special moral insight, and second because they wear particular moral blinders in looking at decisions through an economic lens only, a lens that posits only a one-dimensional person who acts only out of rational self-interest.

A critique of the traditional abstract economic models has come from a subset of economists themselves as well as from other disciplines of the human sciences. While traditional economic models may be useful for predicting economic outcomes, dubious though that may be, humans are more complex beings than economists posit, with other layers of their psychologies, needs, and souls. Self-interest is only one motivator of human behavior. Sometimes humans do things destructive of their self-interest, an insight understood by premodern religions and rediscovered by modern depth psychology, after Adam Smith. Humans are also altruistic in various kinds of contexts, such as the family and the household and even sometimes at work.[13] Altruism, care, and empathy have not traditionally been lenses built into economic models. In fact, economic analysis has been built on abstract mathematical models of analysis. However, just because an idea is couched in math and is incomprehensible to the average person does not mean it is right. Indeed, mathematical reasoning has the weakness of abstracting away from the concrete nuances of real-life situations. "Nature, childhood, bodily needs, and human connectedness" are cut off and remain safely out of sight.[14] The whole economy of "care" involving women in the household, teachers, nurses, caretakers, providers, and other "feminine" labeled roles, has until recently been ignored for this reason by economists. The point is that the economic models themselves are open to criticism for being one-dimensional, underplaying the complexity of human beings, and using tools of analysis that may not tell the whole or correct story. One has to be an academic and mathematician to even engage in the debate at this level. That tendency is a problem too, for economics tries to sideline the average person's normal moral intuitions as individuals and tell us not to worry about our stirrings of compassion, care, altruism, and responsibility in favor of abstract models we cannot understand or critique. It is the message of our economic priests.

Since there are conflicting interpretations of economic events in the past, the predictive and explanatory ability of economics as a science is in doubt, and we must take the conclusions of economists with a grain of salt. For the reasons described above, economists should be seen as offering a set of insights that should be weighed in the process of deciding what kinds of regulations to make in the market. But they should not have a veto, and their guidance should be set alongside our own moral values and judgments that sometimes must trump those that pretend to be science. This leads us to the second pillar of our argument: prosperous markets invariably rest on regulation and intervention by definition.

Markets by Definition Rest on Regulation

Those who espouse free markets either forget or hide the fact that markets themselves thrive on a foundation of law and regulation and a decently strong and liberal government. Markets of course can exist without any government or regulation at all. People can barter with each other as well as buy and sell even if there is no government present. But what makes more complex markets work well and flourish are the security of a population and the predictability of laws and contracts that bind them in their transactions. Well-functioning markets require and presuppose a government that protects a population from threats from outside and enforces contracts and laws on those on the inside. This seems so self-evident that it is almost embarrassing to have to say it. But often the stability provided by a government, by laws and regulations, and by a judicial system that is enforced fades into the background and is forgotten by those who now take it for granted. Only then can people say "the market should be left alone and free." Yet that position appears plausible only to those who have forgotten how much government and regulation have made the peaceful functioning of a society and its markets possible in the first place. All of this becomes terribly apparent if a people or country sinks into war. War devastates commerce and markets. The lack of a stable society prevents investment from businesses and undermines the security of contracts. The lack of predictable and enforceable laws has the same effect, which is why countries that are lawless cannot sustain economic prosperity.

Indeed, except in a simple barter economy, markets depend on the predictability of contracts. This is because we make all kinds of exchanges where the delivery of payments or goods is delayed beyond an immediate exchange. Such "delayed gratification" is the key to the foundation of more complex and prosperous capitalist economies. We would not make such exchanges if we could not be relatively certain that the payment or the promised goods will be delivered. Without trust or enforceable contracts, we would need markets where delivery and payment occurred at the same time. Even when money is in use in an economy, commerce relies on a dependable currency that requires a stable and peaceful existence and sufficient economic reliability to trust in the currency itself. This is why some theorists see the institution of a contract as the very basis of social life itself.[15] While trust can be the foundation of exchanges between those we know and are intimate with, such as friends and family members, contracts that are governed by law and enforceable by courts and ultimately police powers are required to enable secure exchange between those who are otherwise anonymous to each other.[16] The contract is thus the extension and replacement of either "immediate exchange" or "trust." It allows people to feel protected in their commercial activities without knowing the person with whom they do business. Law and contract are the substitute for trust among people who do not know each other.

In this sense, the market is like liberty itself in having two sides or dimensions. There is a side of liberty that is defined by my privileges and protections of my rights. This side of liberty gives me moral entitlements to do things without interference and imposes a legally enforced boundary, backed up by power, on what others can do to me or my things. The second side of liberty is what I have to give up or sacrifice so that other people can have their rights protected as well. We talked about this paradox of liberty at the start of this book. My liberty implies your restriction, and your liberty implies my restriction. Liberty cuts both ways. My liberties are protected only because you have restrictions in those same areas. Markets are the same way. What appears as the freedom of exchange in markets is only made possible by a set of restrictions that defines and enforces contracts and prevents their violations. Markets come into being through the set of laws and powers that make contracts predictable and secure. The presence of a stable set of predictable laws, a judicial system, and a police power to enforce them are required to make commerce secure and prosperous.

We thus get the benefits of free markets only because there are very serious limitations on what is permitted and not permitted. Markets have a whole host of contract law behind them that specifies rules for selling and buying and doing business. Without contract law, the market could not function with confidence. The point is that good markets are made possible by good governments, both in the peaceful life that government can provide as well as through the sets of enforceable rules that replace trust among people who do not know each other well. What is often forgotten or buried in the claim that "liberty implies free markets" is the fact that both liberty itself and free markets themselves rest on a foundation of restrictions that make them possible in the first place. Government intervention is thus the mother of economic prosperity. Contract law is the foundation of free commerce.

When we understand government's presence as an enabler of fair markets, we see how misleading or simplistic it is to say that that "governments should stay out of markets" in order to protect liberty.[17] Well-functioning markets sit on top of government laws and enforcement by their very nature. These enabling regulations that make fair and free commerce possible are constrictions of economic exchange and thus limitations on liberty, just as the very laws that make societies possible limit liberty even as they make it possible. Both achieve their objective by forbidding certain behaviors and by using law backed up by force to achieve predictability. It is the confidence and trust born of the foundations that allow both liberty and markets to function at all.

The open question before us, therefore, is what kinds of regulations are best to produce the best kinds of markets and the best moral life possible. Reframing the issue this way shows that the issue is one of degree, not of kind. Regulation is necessary for markets to be prosperous and function well. But which regulations are best and why depends ultimately on what the goals are. As soon as we are in the question of degree, and not of kind, we are in the domain of values and judgment. In other words, the question at hand is not whether government should regulate markets, but by what criteria it should regulate them. Those economists such as Milton Friedman who claim that economic liberty is a right are missing the point and really saying nothing very meaningful. As with liberty itself, what we understand to be a right comes into being through restrictions on both ourselves and others that make that right possible. A right is nothing more than a protection or privilege made predictable by law. Without government intervention, there would not be the foundation for prosperous markets, and thus economic liberty is itself born out of regulation. Regulation can be said to produce liberty as much as limit it.

The claim that governments should not interfere in or regulate markets is thus exposed as a rhetorical smokescreen used to criticize certain specific types of governmental interventions that are disliked from within a particular political and philosophical perspective. The government interventions that are preferred or believed in are ignored and treated as background foundations, as if the intervention did not exist. By contrast, those interventions that are not liked are grouped under the category of intrusions and violations of liberty. The problem is that markets have no conscience, and when left on their own they violate our sense of justice and morality in various kinds of ways, as discussed next.

Markets Have No Conscience

Markets may have an omniscient view of economic transactions, but they are not God, for they lack a set of intrinsic values and a conscience. Markets are neither alive nor are they people, but instead represent abstractions of the outcomes of people's choices, which may be based on thousands of individuals transactions motivated by equally many motivations. But markets do have consequences and thus embody a set of values when left alone on their own. Thus, to not act on markets is to act. Or, to put it less cryptically, to not regulate markets is to endorse the consequences of markets and thus implicitly endorse a set of conditions that markets produce. To intervene in markets, by contrast, is to attempt to bring other human values and moral concerns into a process in which they are not present by default.

What values should determine which interventions are deemed acceptable and which are not? It is precisely this question that is at issue, and not the question of liberty itself, as proponents of free markets like to argue. In saying this, I am arguing that there is no neutral definition of liberty that exists above political interests and that does not already serve some group or groups' interests more than another. In other words, the very idea of liberty itself is a political concept whose very definition will ultimately serve to benefit certain people and interest groups more than others. This is an important point that is worth pausing to think about. The concept of "liberty" that is often presented as a "metapolitical" or "nonpolitical" commitment is in fact shot through with political implications. And the question of who benefits from which definition of liberty is precisely what is being debated, not the question of liberty itself. The liberty-first proponents and free market liberals try to position any definition of liberty but their own as "nonliberty" or "socialism." They position their definition of liberty as the only definition and the one embraced by the American founders. At stake is the very question of whose version of liberty shall prevail.

There is no escaping the politicization of the liberty concept. What liberty means is caught up with the question of what interests the concept serves. And the very question of who is served or helped by which conception of liberty is itself contested and part of the debate of what liberty should mean. In other words, part of the question of liberty itself is how much freedom to give markets and why. To have the opportunity as a society to debate and decide how much freedom to give markets is itself part of the right of liberty. This turns on its head the claim of Milton Friedman that economic freedom is part of liberty. On the contrary, liberty includes the right to regulate markets.

The question at hand, therefore, is which interest groups will ultimately own the definition of liberty and the moral meaning of that definition. Many market liberals and liberty-first proponents claim that unfettered markets benefit everyone, that all boats are lifted on a rising tide. This is an argument from the consequences and utility of free markets. Those of us who have a responsibility-first view of liberty and see reasons for government to intervene in key ways in the economy see the free market argument as serving best the well-being of those who already hold wealth and belong to the capitalist class. In other words, the "free market" definition of liberty is a concept of liberty that promotes those who already are economically well to do at the expense of those who have fewer resources.

This alignment of the "liberty-first" or free market philosophy with the interests of the economically well-off explains in part how and why the philosophy has such strong appeal. It resonates with the institutions of late capitalist society and those who occupy positions of power in our systems. This philosophy of liberty fits snugly with the interests of business leaders, financial leaders, and other individuals who comprise the capitalist elites and work in business and financial institutions. It is a theory that endorses minimal government intervention in the economy and in the practices of business. But this explanation alone cannot be sufficient, for this theory of liberty also appeals to many people who lack resources and are not part of the capitalist elites. How do we make sense of this?

There may be many reasons. To begin with, one cannot discount the sheer power and success of the ideology itself, and the failure of liberals to successfully articulate an alternative theory of liberty that is progressive and resonates with the vision of America's founding. The Right and libertarians have built a propaganda machine over the last thirty years that places this view of liberty at its foundation and presents the theory as aligning with evangelical Christian morality and with the founding values of the American republic, which are viewed as compatible. The failure of progressives to successfully articulate an alternative view of liberty that aligns with an understanding of the founding and of Western religions and their willingness to relinquish the concept to conservatives explains in part why this theory of liberty has become so hard to contest. There simply are not many voices articulating a different way of understanding liberty itself.

But there may be other, deeper reasons that are harder to pry loose and render visible. The ideologies in late capitalism often act not only to represent the interests of capital but also to help stabilize and ameliorate the tensions in late capitalism itself. The conservative theory of liberty helps build ideological commitment to the capitalist system and gives laborers reason to overlook and downplay the very discrepancies of wealth that grow increasingly worse. The free market theory of liberty diverts their anger from the issues in free markets that are the source of the problem toward government, which is portrayed as the source of the problem. Ironically, the idea of liberty that justifies free markets is partly responsible for exacerbating the economic inequalities.[18]

The alternative perspective on liberty put forward in this work and by others who move along a similar path holds that certain human values must be brought into the market because in markets there are no values except efficiency and utility. Human values are for the most part "supra" market. Markets do not care about people or the environment. Markets do not care at all really. And thus, when markets are allowed to operate as they would in an unconstrained manner, they do not inherently respect many of the values that we cherish.[19] What markets do very well is push efficiencies in the system. Markets figure out how much demand there is for a product or service and signal, through prices going up or down, that more or less of a product is needed. Markets help with competition that benefits consumers and helps spawn innovation. These are among the results that markets achieve well and for which they should be and have been appreciated. But there are many ways in which markets behave poorly, and if markets were children they would be disciplined for bad behavior.

The Markets in Human Beings

There are countless examples of how markets couldn't care less about certain human values and how laws, which impose values, must be brought to bear on markets. The most telling example, of course, is the market in slavery that existed (and still exists underground) until humans came to discern that protections of life, liberty, and property mattered and that humans should not sell each other nor treat each other as commodities. Markets themselves did not by themselves end slavery. In fact, markets were just as effective in setting prices and demand for slaves as they were with other commodities. It was the idea of liberty itself that gave birth over time to the value that humans should not be slaves. In other words, the interpretation of liberty and the values embedded in an understanding of liberty led to perhaps the most important limitation on markets that we now have. One may not trade in human beings, even if, paradoxically, those human beings wish to sell themselves.

Free market liberals who invoke a rights argument have no way to explain why human beings should not be sold as commodities unless they invoke values as superseding and trumping the idea of free markets.[20] The market system itself, apart from the humans who comprise it, has no way of discriminating between selling an apple, a boat, and a human being. These things all look like commodities if people see them as objects to sell. It is thus certain values that we bring to a market that determine what is a legitimate transaction and what is not acceptable. Most (though unfortunately not all) people today condemn slavery, thus acknowledging a consensus on a case where human moral commitments should trump the liberty of the market. In this case, we have an example where most people who endorse liberty today would agree that the market should be limited by human values, and in so doing we exercise our belief in liberty.

In recognizing the triumph of values over markets in one situation, the question naturally arises as to why and when values should trump market efficiencies in general. On what grounds do we say here that the efficiencies of the market don't matter and that other values triumph? This is really the issue at stake in the debate between the responsibility-led liberals and the free market or liberty-first liberals. The debate is not about liberty per se but about when and why to invoke values other than efficiency.

The answer among those like us who hold the "responsibility-first" position is that values should play a role in the regulation of markets to 1) minimize the suffering of those who cannot outwait the market, 2) protect the interest of those whom the market treats unfairly, 3) represent the interests of the species and thus future generations long term, and 4) pay back the debt to the human ancestors in general.[21]

The key idea here is that markets do not act fairly all by themselves. They do recognize and reward effort, talent, and ingenuity, to some extent. But they hurt people unevenly based on their differential impact on those with fewer resources. Markets need regulation to serve rather than trample on certain key human values. The ability and right to protect our values is part of what it means to live in a liberal society. Market liberals, of course, see regulation as trampling our liberties. But they have it all backward. It is the market that has the potential to trample our liberties, at least those who do not have enough wealth and resources to defend themselves against its mechanisms.

In this responsible view, government interventions are needed 1) to balance out the short-term tendencies of markets to ignore individuals who a) lack resources and power and are b) disproportionally affected by downward market change, 2) to ensure benefits from the labor of past generations are shared across their descendants, and 3) to protect the rights of those who live in the future. In these situations, the interventions in the market are needed to introduce certain human values and to represent the rights and thus the liberties of those who have no market power. The core assumption here is that liberty is a power that can be exercised most when one has resources and wealth at one's disposal.[22] Since markets can trample individual liberty as much as governments, government intervention in markets is about protecting the life, liberty, and health of individuals from markets. Let us take up these ideas in more detail.

If a dictator comes along and says, "I will make everything better in the long run for everyone, but it will require us to reduce your income, take away your housing and job, or affect your health," we would scream that "our liberties are infringed." And we would scream both because we would not be confident in the result and because we might not agree the short-term costs are worth the long-term investment. Yet when markets do the same thing, they are treated as if they are protecting our liberties. The claim that free market advocates make about the beneficial consequences of markets depends on the consequences overall and in the long run. The claim is that markets provide the overall maximization of benefit or utility for the most people overall.

But this is wrongheaded in several different ways. First, it says the short-term negative impact on some individuals is acceptable for the long-term benefit of more people overall. But surely not everyone would agree with that trade-off, and especially those who are affected the worst in the short term or who may lack the resources or wealth to protect themselves from the short-term impact.[23] Indeed, those with less wealth and fewer resources are more negatively affected by downward market shifts in the short run than those with more wealth and resources. The obvious example is the loss of jobs in a down economy such as the "Great Recession" we just recently witnessed, which was the worst since the Great Depression. Those who are in lower-paying positions are more likely to be laid off and have less of a cushion to survive if they do lose their jobs. And because race and gender biases affect which groups have the lowest-paying positions, often the most damaging consequences of a downturn fall on women and minorities.

So suppose for a moment that the market is being efficient, though producing ups and downs in the short term, though over the long run prices will be better, there will be the right number of products on the market, and the production and invention of new products will have been stimulated. Does that long-term outcome justify the short-term pain of those who are hit the hardest short term? By what right is the longer-term benefit to the "all" more important than the shorter-term right of the poor and disadvantaged? Even if the poor will be better off down the road at some point, what if they would make a different decision because the short-term impact is far more painful than their long-term benefit? By what criteria and by whom can the decision be made that long-term outcomes trump short-term pain? Who has that right? Is that right simply the right of a majority? And what is the basis of that right to decide?

Similarly, those with fewer resources are often hurt disproportionately by environmental and health impacts when markets are not regulated. Companies are more likely to spill pollutants into areas that affect low-income or poor individuals than those with money because those with money tend to live farther from industry by nature of where property values are highest. Pollutants' negative effects on the health and properties will be worse for those with less wealth. The same is true among countries as well. Poorer countries get and take disproportionate amounts of trash, e-waste, and pollutants than wealthier developed countries, partly because they have more lax regulations, but also because they do not have sufficient resources to refuse the incentives to take the waste of wealthier neighbors. Wealthier countries ship or smuggle such waste to poorer countries.[24]

Consumer protection attempts to address similar kinds of issues, though in this case harmful effects of products can at times fall more evenly across economic lines, though not necessarily. Businesses have some built-in incentives to protect consumers in the sense that if harm to consumers becomes known, it can produce a negative backlash that undermines a company's brand and future profitability. For example, if it became known that a product, such as cigarettes, the brakes of a car, some medication, or a medical device kills or harms customers, then the market itself has some built-in corrective mechanisms. People will stop buying the product and may reduce what they buy from that company in general. The halo around the brand is damaged, and the company's profits will fall. The company's reputation is tied to its profits. But that built-in punishment occurs over the long term only if the harm becomes visible.

There are thus two critical problems in the way markets regulate harm by themselves: First, the negative consequences of a product on human health, life, or the natural environment may not be known or visible immediately, with many individuals suffering in the meantime irreparable harm, with loss of health, life, or the value of their property. A long-term correction and punishment of a company comes too late for individuals who died or suffered irreversible consequences to their health or fortunes. Second, the short-term harm may very likely fall more painfully on those with fewer resources to deal with the consequence of harm (such as hospitalization, damage from the product, and so forth). Of course, loss of life caused by products cannot be completely ameliorated by wealth, and its harm is more equalized across economic lines. Still, those with more resources may be able to avoid harm and loss of life more easily because they can "purchase safety" by buying quality products that are better made, as, for example, in more expensive and newer automobiles with better and more extensive safety features, or living in areas farther away from damaging pollutants.

Since companies are measured on the short-term profitability on a quarterly basis, they are also not properly incentivized in the short term to invest in discovering the potential harm or remediating it, hence the many documented cases where companies put faulty products into the market, such as faulty automobiles or harmful cigarettes, and hide the faults knowingly.[25] In the well-known Pinto case in the 1960s, for example, Ford chose not to implement an eleven-dollar-per-car safety correction to prevent the Pinto gas tank from catching fire in a rear collision, a problem that caused multiple deaths.[26] Ford's decision was based on a cost-benefit analysis that valued the cost of death at $200,000. Ford was held not guilty, because the company met federal safety standards at the time, though it had itself lobbied to keep the government from implementing tighter standards. Other examples include Dow Corning's possible awareness of the potential harm that silicone breast implants could cause women, and the company A. H. Robins's suppression of evidence that the Dalkon shield could cause pelvic inflammatory disease.[27] These are just a few of many examples where the short-term business incentives are perverse, which is why regulations are needed to set standards to protect people whom the market cannot protect. The market cannot act quickly enough to prevent harm in the short term, and the long-term efficiency gains and expansion of wealth do not always justify accepting the shorter-term consequence.

The tensions described here are well-known, classic issues in the debate between those who favor a "rights" view and those who favor a utilitarian or "consequentialist" view.[28] The two perspectives pull in different directions. A rights view focuses on protecting individuals, whereas a utilitarian or consequentialist view protects the maximum persons over time. The point is that any decision will have consequences for some group of people, whether short term or long term. As a result, it is a complicated moral decision about how to balance those short-term harmful consequences on individuals against longer-term gains that may accrue to the many. If one lets markets work things out for themselves, then one is favoring those with resources who can insure themselves against short-term consequences. While the end game could look better for more people overall, the effects of getting to the end game are not evenly distributed, nor necessarily fair.

To be sure, it is true that one cannot prevent every short-term harm possible. For example, imagine the cost to produce an automobile that does not permit any loss of life at all? The cost would potentially be so astronomically high that only a few people would be able to buy such vehicles, and the automotive dealer would go out of business or be incented to leave the market. This is why we allow automobile driving even though there are thirty thousand to forty thousand deaths a year through accidents.[29] Why don't we claim that automobiles violate our collective rights to life? Of course, it is possible to mandate certain safety features, such as seat belts and bumpers, the cost of which are relatively low but whose safety impact is high. There will always be some trade-off between the end game of overall benefits and the short-term protections of individuals. There will always be a trade-off of safety and cost. Who gets to make the decision and why? There is no general rule that can tell us what costs or which safety features are worthwhile, and which are not. That moral question is at the heart of what a liberal society must debate, and it informs every decision that we potentially make. As discussed above, that trade-off is at the heart of how much consumer protection to provide. The ultimate decision has to be based on some detailed understanding of the cost to life and health, the cost to avoid those harms, and the overall industry in which the decisions are made. No one can legislate that answer in the abstract without the details. And the market by itself places few incentives on short-term protections.

Labor and Safety in Markets

The rules regulating labor and safety in the workplace provide another obvious area where markets and businesses do not build in sufficient protections by themselves. Businesses may have some incentives over time to care for workers, since to do so may lead to higher productivity and profits, as has been demonstrated in some case studies.[30] Yet we know from the history of industrialization and labor practices, and examples that still exist both inside and outside the United States, such as in the garment industry in Bangladesh, that in fact such incentives do not necessarily protect workers or their safety.[31] Businesses will work individuals more than eight-hour workdays if they can and will put very young children to work, and in some cases, even in this country, there is still what amounts to slave labor.[32] The global number of children involved in child labor is 168 million. More than 85 million are involved in hazardous work. Many businesses will not invest properly or suffi-ciently in the safety of the workplace if they have their choice.[33] They may force individuals to do incredibly repetitive tasks that can harm their bodies. They may work them in buildings that are not safe, as became so evident once again recently in Bangladesh's garment industry. We know that many businesses will not pay attention to such issues unless they have to, because when such regulations are reduced or removed, as when US businesses move outside the United States, they can be more lax, as in the example of the company H. B. Fuller selling an adhesive called Resistol that became the dominant source of glue sniffing among chil-dren in Honduras.[34] The H. B. Fuller case study shows the complexity of the ethical issues involved. Some states in the United States require that glue, such as Resistol, containing addictive narcotics must contain oil of mustard, which makes sniffing the glue so painful it is impossible to breathe. But there are debates on the health impact of the mustard oil as well, and the Fuller subsidiary actively lobbied to prevent the mustard oil solution in Honduras. Instead, Fuller focused on the causes of increased abuse in Honduras stemming from difficult economic problems and pov-erty. Ethical situations such as these are complex, multidimensional, and not simple to solve. Of course, businesses act this way only because some individuals who manage the business are willing to cause harm for their own gains and because the incentives of the market encourage those who would otherwise build responsible businesses to ignore their inclinations for care. And there are many individuals who, because of their poor finan-cial situation, are willing to risk their lives and their health; they need to work even in conditions that are not safe.

Businesses, after all, represent the activities of individuals. To be sure, there are of course some business leaders who bring an ethical or moral vision to caring for their business, and there is some evidence that such a moral vision can have a positive impact on profits, as in successful businesses such as Ben and Jerry's and others that have operated with a moral vision or customer-centric philosophy.[35] But numerous examples of businesses that ignore such worries illustrate the fact that shorter-term pressures on profits frequently override moral concerns and the possible long-term consequences of public opinion. Future punishment by public opinion seems too far away to help businesses act morally in the short run if profits are at serious risk. Incentives in the business often motivate individuals to suppress their own moral inclinations that might otherwise lead them to act differently. The system itself with its focus on short-term profits incentivizes business leaders to overlook their moral concerns and even the long-term profitability of the business. Indeed, the board and business leaders who make the decisions may not be present in the company in three to five years and thus worry less about how the company will be punished in the future than about the short-term gains they will achieve in the here and now. The market itself does not have built-in short-term incentives to act justly and with care.

Since markets can behave in unpredictable ways or have consequences that are damaging to human life or health, or to the species as a whole, we should try to harness and channel markets in ways that are less damaging and destructive. Bringing values into the market is a form of protecting the liberty of individuals, not compromising liberty. Or, to put it another way, like any part of liberty, rights are protected through limitations on others.

Human Values are Externalities to Markets

Many human moral values are "externalities" to the business goal. When values are brought into a business, they are attached to or added to the core goal but are usually not intrinsic to it. It is not natural to business, at least as business is currently defined, to pay attention to these issues. Milton Friedman summarizes this position in his well-known argument that "the social responsibility of business is to increase its profits" and that "to focus on anything beyond profits for the owners is to levy a tax and not to act in the best interest of the owners."[36] Indeed, he goes so far as to say a person who promotes concern over social issues is "preaching pure unadulterated socialism." He also insists that "insofar as his action in accord with his 'social responsibility' reduces returns to stockholders, he is spending their money."

Businesses in general tend to care about human values only in situations where by doing so they affect the bottom line or because the business founders or executives bring a social vision or particular care to the business.[37] There have been encouraging developments in this regard with the social entrepreneur movement, which specifically creates businesses with a core social vision. In addition, there has been a strong academic argument in the last couple of decades about businesses being obligated to "stakeholders," which is defined more broadly than simply shareholders.[38] In broadening the obligation of businesses to stakeholders, the business itself is understood to have responsibility not just to shareholders, but to citizens, neighbors, and the larger human community.

The problem with stakeholder theory, unfortunately, is that unless it is backed up by a visionary CEO, government regulation, or market punishment by consumers, it is an ideal that just doesn't have that much impact because incentives are not reinforced in the markets themselves. Markets care about stakeholders only in the long run, but they care about *shareholders* in the short term. This is because it is usually the case that the mechanisms to impose the stakeholders' perspectives are less direct and immediate and appear only over time unless stakeholders organize and leverage their clout via purchasing power, publicity, or their investment strategies.

Apart from these examples, businesses take account of human values in contexts where to do otherwise becomes problematic for the core constituents of the business. Businesses today have corporate social responsibility programs in which they make investments in local and global communities. These programs are understood to be good for business, helping to present the business as a good communal citizen and to give employees pride in their company. These social responsibility programs, however, are not core to the business mission. Most businesses are focused by their mission and by the structure of our economic and social systems to focus on the drive to profit. While other benefits may be core to the product's vision, businesses have a fiduciary obligation to their shareholders and board of directors, who are focused on return on investment. The drive to profit, which defines the core of the business mission, is the amplification and institutionalization of many individuals' economic self-interest. The business is executing the collective goals of the individuals who comprise the board, the executive team, and the shareholders, and ultimately the social and economic interests embodied in the system in which the business operates.[39]

It is fair to say that businesses are focused on satisfying human desires by making products or providing services that meet some human need. Otherwise no one would buy the product in the first place. In this sense, businesses do inherently care about human beings' needs and desires. But in the execution of that goal and vision, businesses don't care inherently about how they get to those results. And thus they will trample certain human beings and certain human needs in the goal of satisfying other broader human desires in the market. Businesses, like markets, do not care intrinsically, for example, about how many hours a person works, the age of the person working, the minimum wage, the safety of employees, or the pollution that they emit. There are thus a host of government restrictions that have come from values, rather than from the goal of growing business or capital. Limitations on the number of hours in the working day, workplace discrimination, minimum wage floors, workplace safety, limitations on pollution, and so forth are all rules that stem from values that the markets do not develop on their own.[40]

It is not widely known, for example, that the great market liberal Milton Friedman went so far as to argue that business owners should have the liberty not to sell to certain types of people, such as blacks and Jews.[41] It was not that Friedman was a racist or anti-Semite (in fact he was born Jewish). It was rather that Friedman believed the marketplace would punish those who discriminated against people and government should stay out of the business of intervening in the matter. In other words, Friedman was willing to leave the question of values and the question of markets as separate domains. He assumed people would be punished in the long run by the market for their discriminatory values. It seems clear, however, that markets are not very good at stamping out bias and discrimination by themselves, as evident by the need for a civil war to end slavery in this country and then ultimately a civil rights movement. If markets can get to the right values, why is there a need for any kind of civil legislation at all? For those who take a responsibility-first position, by contrast, liberty means that we can bring our values to bear on market conditions because we don't trust the market to care about the impact on human lives.

In fact, to argue that markets or businesses should be left alone is really to argue that the lives, liberties, and properties of the lower class or marginalized individuals do not matter as much as others, for the unpredictable and uncontrollable consequences of markets damage those with less the most. Consider two people on the ocean in two different boats. One is a white male who has the means to buy a boat with many different bulkheads. The other is a poor woman of color who has only a raft. When a storm comes along, and the ocean is rocking and rolling, who is most likely to stay afloat, not capsize, and survive? This analogy is apropos. The ocean is the market, and its waves are not always predictable. One can't always anticipate when a storm will come along, and the more bulkheads one has, the more likely one is to weather the storm. Free market advocates argue that a rising market lifts all boats. But they ignore the fact that storms in the ocean can also turn over and destroy boats that are not equipped very well for the ups and downs.

We can now see how the failure to intervene in markets in critical ways can actually be a violation of human liberty. By letting a market act as it will and seek equilibrium, wealth becomes a critical if not primary determination of an individual's life, liberty, and the pursuit of happiness. Markets can be as or more abusive than monarchies from whom liberty was originally intended to protect individuals. Markets have tremendous power and the ability to punish individuals for not having made it financially. While the tyranny of *governments* was the object of the liberty advocates in the seventeenth century and the American founders, the *tyranny of markets* can be as damaging to lives as governments. Both can equally be foes of liberty if not controlled and channeled. The dichotomy between government and free markets is thus a false one. Absolute government and unrestrained markets can both be destructive to liberty. If used widely, government intervention and regulation are the foundation of human liberty.

Environment, Regulation, and Future Generations

Human beings have operated until quite recently as if the oceans, the air, and much of the water in the world were free. The oceans have been free to fish, and the air has been free to breathe. No one owned the oceans or the air or the water in rivers that passed through their nations. The idea that the ocean and the air are still "in common" reaches back to the natural rights thinkers on property, such as Grotius.[42] These natural resources were thought to be in common and thus free, because they were viewed as limitless and also impossible to divvy up into private property. Unlike land, they had no obvious boundaries, and therefore labor could not establish private property on the air or sea.

Similar attitudes toward air, oceans, and water carried over into the business world, with some obvious problems that are now devastating in their clarity. Up until relatively recently in the United States, businesses could ingest air and dispense output into it at no cost. Until recently businesses could do the same with water. Such practices continue in countries that lack regulations, including rapidly developing nations. We now know that such activities do have a cost, and what some businesses put back out into the land, water, and air, and into what has been common, degrades what is left for the rest of us and causes irreparable harm to the environment, as well as health problems and even death. These outputs to the environment have been termed "externalities" by economists, because the costs were not included in a business's profit and loss statement but were born by others in the community in costs of taxes to clean up and in costs to pay for health care and hospitals bills, costs not born by business itself but by individuals and government.[43]

This insight into the harmful impact of externalities is incredibly important and actually exposes some of the deepest flaws in traditional economic and business theory. The discovery of externalities shows that neither markets nor businesses are actually capable of seeing or taking account of all the real costs that go into making a product. There is a large set of hidden costs through use of the environment and through impact on health and welfare that never get incorporated into the profit and loss statements of a company. There is no motivation built into the system for business to try to see these externalities either. *The obvious conclusion is that businesses and therefore the market itself are not really "omniscient" about the actual costs involved in making a product.*

This is a startling discovery that goes against the fundamental assumption of modern economics, for economic theory rests on the assumption that the market is all seeing and can discern what quantities of products to produce by seeing the costs and understanding the demands and the trade-offs individuals will make. If the market cannot see all these costs or cannot associate all these costs to a specific product's production, then the market has a flawed mechanism by which to decide how much of a product to produce and even what kind of product the market produces.

Think about what this means. It means that what the market's invisible hand leads us to produce is flawed, for we end up producing products that, had the real costs been known, would never have been produced or would have been produced in much smaller amounts. Had these hidden costs been borne by the businesses that produced the products over the last three hundred to four hundred years and not by the rest of us in what was owned in common, our business landscape would have been fundamentally different. The very nature of manufacturing would have changed, as businesses incorporated the environmental and health externalities into the cost of doing business.

As an example, imagine if the costs of automobiles to the environment had been anticipated and incorporated into the cost of manufacturing automobiles. Not only would fewer cars have been affordable, but the other ancillary infrastructure that grew up around them, such as highways and gas stations, may have been different too. We would have seen more environmentally friendly cars earlier. We may have seen more rail and public transportation develop too, and less urban sprawl. We have no specific idea really what would have happened had the market been able to see and calculate the whole cost of the product early on. But we do know that it would have changed the shape of manufacturing and put the costs that would be discovered downstream in the future, upstream into the cost of the product.

There are several key insights and conclusions that spring from the understanding of externalities. The first is that the market is not omniscient and does not anticipate all the ways in which products may affect either the environment or human life. The market can't see these impacts until it is too late. By "too late," we mean that time has lapsed between when the costs were invested in the product's manufacture and its harmful consequences. The market can try to correct for this mistake by punishing the company for creating products with negative externalities. But this is after the fact, and therefore we cannot be sure either the company itself or the owners at the time the products were produced end up paying for the costs of the product they shipped and from which they made money. Perhaps the company can be made to pay, but the owners, employees, and shareholders who are paying are not those who necessarily benefitted from the profits of the product. Thus there is a gap between the discovery and the punishment, and the financial punishment falls on the wrong people.

The only way to try to collapse this time lag between the consequences and the original production of a product is through regulation. Regulation thus emerges as one of the principal ways that externalities can be internalized in a product's manufacture. By externalities here we mean not only the external impacts on the environment, traditionally called externalities, but also the negative impacts on human life, as defined by the set of moral values a society brings to the table, some of which have been discussed above. What emerges is a picture of regulation as not a negative, but a positive. Regulation seeks to make the market better by taking external costs that otherwise will occur after the fact and too late and moving them earlier into the production process, closer to when the product is made. It is true that regulators cannot always foresee externalities that are at this moment in time. But regulations attempt to hold companies accountable once externalities are discovered, and they try to enforce testing so that some negative externalities are discovered earlier (as in the production of medicines and testing of automotive safety). Regulators also can move faster than the market in holding companies accountable for externalities that are discovered. When this happens, the result is that those who profit from a product are much more likely to bear the real costs. In this view, it is wrong to see regulation as simply interference in the perfect functioning of a market. On the contrary, regulation becomes the only means by which the market can work effectively, by restoring actual costs upstream to the manufacturing process. To be sure, not all regulations have such a positive impact. There can be good and bad regulation. And because business interests influence regulation, it is difficult to get approval of regulations of this nature. But the point is that it is only through good regulation that the true costs of a product can be discovered in time to hold those who produce the product responsible for its true costs. Without regulation, the discovery of externalities is after the fact, and the clear winners are the owners of the company and the shareholders at the time that the externalities are hidden, for when externalities are hidden, society is subsidizing the cost of the product so that companies can take more profit, with the result that others down the road may be penalized by the hidden costs. And in putting externalities into the environment, companies are using resources that belong to us in common but not paying back for that use. The profit is made on the backs of what we share in common, but the benefits go only to those who are defined as the private owners of the capital. The discovery of externalities, both in welfare costs and cost to the environment, make plain how wrong is traditional economic theory that places all its faith in an unregulated market.

Those who potentially suffer most from undiscovered externalities are younger people and future generations. Nowhere is this clearer than in impacts to the environment. As we have noticed in our earlier discussion of property, if there are not unlimited land and resources, then the first movers and earlier generations can harm the slower movers and later generations. There is less abundance of land to go around. The same is true of the environment itself. The harm done to the air, the ground, and the water profits those who run the companies and businesses in the short term, but it harms future generations, who will have fewer resources and resources at higher cost. While it is impossible to see what life will be like many generations into the future, and while technological advances may solve the problems of shortages that we are beginning to see today, we cannot know that that is the case.[44] Therefore we have to act as if there is a diminishing supply of resources until it is proven otherwise.

The way to address this problem is to seriously treat the ocean, water, air, and wildlife as property in common, in the sense that we are all tenants in common. Tenants in common does not mean it is a free-for-all, which is the supposition of the so-called "tragedy of the commons."[45] There can be ownership in common and regulations about the use of the commons. The use of these resources should cost businesses in proportion to their use, costs that will be passed on in the product itself to those of us who consume those products. Regulations are not unnecessary costs to the business, but costs just like any other cost of sale that a business has. In addition, there should be stricter limits on use until we discover a means of achieving equilibrium. The model for these commonly held properties should be the national parks, which have been successful in preserving beauty, making that beauty shareable among a much wider population than otherwise would have occurred. The only way to preserve nature is by forcing the actual costs of a product, which includes the use of what is in common to us all, to be embedded in the cost of doing business.[46] Cap and trade of carbon is one example of how we can force businesses to pay for their impact on the environment.

The Liberty to Be Moral

The claim that liberty is synonymous with free market capitalism should now be discarded. It should be replaced with our contrasting claim that liberty includes the right to have and pursue responsible and just markets. To be moral means not permitting markets to act as they will in all situations, for markets have no morality and no conscience. To allow markets to be completely free is to renounce the right that liberty gives us to bring our heart and soul, which tune into responsibilities, into social life and try to help those who need help. Liberty, as we have seen in earlier discussions, implies that we have responsibilities that we bring into the societies in which we live. These responsibilities are the other side of the freedom that liberty provides. And these responsibilities teach us that markets that are unregulated can be vicious, unethical, and ultimately destructive as much as they can be efficient, innovative, and beneficial.

Chapter 10
On Truth and Liberty in Political Democracies

One of the reasons we need liberal societies is because one person's truth is not another's, and one religion's view of the world is not another's. Were we all to agree on what truth is, then we would have a much better chance of agreeing on how to organize life in society. Even when religions agree that there is a God, they do not all agree on whether Jesus was a man or the Son of God, whether the pope is the best source of God's wisdom, or what God wants in particular. And even varieties of Christianity that believe Jesus was Christ were unable to agree on how people should live after the Reformation and still disagree today on what Christ wants of us. The political to and fro between Catholics and Protestants after the Reformation, and the religiously inspired wars that followed, were symptoms of the inability of those in the same religion to agree on how life should be lived or what morals and religious practices should govern civil life. This problem is all the more difficult when more than one religion is represented in a commonwealth.

The inability of religions to come to common truths is part of the background to the birth of liberal societies. There was a growing recognition that somehow we had to live together even when we couldn't agree on the fundamental truths, at least with respect to religion and God. The differences of faith would be set aside for the afterlife and God (if there was one), and this life would focus on practical approaches to living together without killing one another.

The natural rights thinkers believed and hoped that an appeal to reason could produce agreement on key moral commitments in a liberal society that were not dependent on the traditional revelation from God. Reason was thought to transcend religious differences and provide a means by which all people, regardless of religion, culture, and historical epoch, could reach agreement on basic human morality. The appeal to natural rights was originally an attempt to find a truth that all could agree on regardless of their religion, though some still argued Christianity was the most reasonable religion of all. The early moderns had a belief—an erroneous one—that all reasonable men would arrive at the same reasonable conclusions through the light of reason. (Women were not originally thought to be as reasonable as men.) The conclusions from reason were thought to result in a core set of moral insights that could guide people in how to live with one another, regardless of their differences in religion.

What we have found instead, in this book and from others who have earlier passed down this same road, is that reason fails to produce unanimity on all the core substantive moral commitments that should underlie a liberal society. While the language of rights held promise as a foundation for a universal set of commitments and is still a powerful language for talking about what we care most deeply about, it turns out in fact that there is no substantive agreement on what those rights should mean, even if we are able to agree on what those rights are.

The first point is that reason does not lead all people to the conclusion that societies should be organized around the rights of life, liberty, and property. Indeed, even the variation "pursuit of happiness" points to the fact that the core definition of rights itself is somewhat variable. Some people would urge that health and work be included in natural rights too, as an example. And in some societies, slavery was permitted and thought of as reasonable and natural up until relatively recently in Western history. It has been "natural" and "reasonable" at various points in time to convert heathens to Christianity, kill Jews, enslave blacks, prevent women from voting, and so on. Even where there is agreement on which rights should be protected, there is no agreement on what substantive commitments fall under those protections. Those who agree on a right to life do not all agree on whether abortion, the death penalty, or euthanasia should or should not be permitted; indeed, what counts as a right to life is still a matter up for grabs. Those who agree on a right to self-preservation do not all agree on the right to carry and bear arms and how far those rights should extend.

Furthermore, the framework of rights and "rights language" that we invoke seems to be most meaningful and intelligible in Western capitalist societies and not necessarily intelligible to all peoples who have not lived in and been acculturated to this tradition of life in capitalist societies. In other words, the very appeal of a rights framework, in the way we think of it in the West, seems to have some of its persuasiveness in part because it fits with the life-forms we are familiar with in postindustrial capitalist societies. What counts as reason itself seems to some extent variable across societies, because what counts as "reasonable" relies on a set of substantive conceptions of what makes sense, and because even what counts as reasonable is to some extent variable.[1] Even if all societies use some language that looks like "rights language," which is possible, there is no unanimity across peoples on what substantive rights should be included in what are thought to be rights.[2]

As we have seen, the fact that reason does not lead to a common set of moral conclusions was evident already among the modern rights thinkers themselves, who wanted reason to provide a universal foundation for human morality. Hobbes's view of reason, for example, led him to assume there was no moral law discernible in nature and that everyone had a right to everything, including each other's body. Hobbes thus came to the conclusion that reason would lead those who contract together in society to realize they need an all-powerful, absolute sovereign to put an end to the disagreements in practice and in belief among those who live together. Hobbes thought reason alone couldn't end substantive human disagreements. He was right in that realization.

Locke's understanding of reason, by contrast, relied on the idea of a Creator who established a law of nature that could be discerned even in a state of nature prior to life in a political commonwealth. Even in nature one had rights to life, liberty, and property (and Locke mentions "health," by the way) that were protected. Locke's view of reason led him to conclude that society should be governed by an elected majority, which represented the consent of individuals who comprised that commonwealth. Locke too recognized that reason would not lead to unanimity on everything all on its own, and he solved that problem by letting the majority decide the rules that govern societies. There was disagreement too, among those who turned to reason, about whether or not property was a natural right and how property was originally created, whether by labor or convention. The upshot is that reason did not by itself lead to a universal consensus about what human beings are or how they should live. And it is likely that the natural rights thinkers such as Locke had already begun to discern the limitations of reason to reach a consensus on human morality, as discussed earlier.[3]

The point I wish to make here is that the very foundation of a society is not completely stabilized by an agreement to appeal to the rights of "life, liberty, and property" or "life, liberty, and the pursuit of happiness." While those commitments rule out others, such as an absolute monarchy, the very meaning of those terms and what they include is debatable in a liberal society. What this means is that the very meaning and interpretation of liberty itself is uncertain and open to debate in a society that embraces liberal principles. Contrary to what liberty-first proponents say, there is no single, stabilized meaning of liberty defined by reason. For the truth is that liberty itself can have many different meanings, and those meanings rest on conceptions of reason, truth, God, and a host of other background assumptions about what it means to be human and to live a good and moral life.

This view and insight have several consequences. First, we should by no means accept as self-evident that liberty always does and always must mean small government, low taxes, free markets, or the host of other claims made by liberty-first interpreters. That is only one interpretation of liberty, and it should have no privileged position because of the claim by some that that is what the American founders or the modern interpreters of liberty meant. Even if that were what the American founders believed, which is doubtful, as I have discussed elsewhere, the founders' vision of liberty need not necessarily constrain our understanding of liberty.[4] For the meaning of liberty in a liberal society is itself at least partially in question and dependent on the values of those who define it and make it so. That is part of what it means to live in a liberal society. And the founders' decision that the Constitution itself could be changed, as documented in Article V of the Constitution, points to their recognition that the very nature of what rights are protected and what they mean were not thought to be completely stable. Liberty is entirely consistent with large taxes, regulated markets, and a large government, should a population deem those to make sense. Those outcomes are consistent with a liberal society, because liberal societies have the right and duty to grapple with the question of who owns property and what responsibilities the citizens have to each other, to the human species, and to subsequent generations. Citizens have the right, and the duty in fact, to hold themselves morally responsible for each other and the species as a whole. They have the right and duty to express that moral value in political laws that bind a body of people with commitments beyond their own narrow self-interests.

This means that liberal societies must invariably grapple with the very meaning of liberty itself in deciding what their societies and their moral commitments are. It is the very essence of what liberal societies do. This is disturbing to many people who would like certainty about what is the proper and moral life to lead. They would like to believe that there is a stable meaning of liberty that was already assumed in the founding of the country and in modernity itself. But in fact there is never unanimity on this question, and this is part of the reason that we need law and a means to enforce some set of laws by which we agree to abide by when we cannot reach that agreement through reasoned discourse only. Power steps in when reasoned discourse fails to achieve consensus. The majority or supermajority ultimately ends up enforcing its view of the world on the minority. And what does and does not achieve consensus through reasoned discourse may change over time as the norms and mores of a society change. Thus, what the liberal state does when it is working is provide a framework, backed up by law and power, to try to peaceably resolve debates about truth and morality. Inevitably someone's truth and someone's morality may not be represented. What the separation of church and state did was try to ensure that what a particular religion said about the right way to live would not be backed up by power of the state but left to individual choice. But other decisions about morality had to be addressed by the state, particularly around what liberty in a liberal state should mean. It is here that the state has to take a stance. It has to decide all sorts of things. What types of protections to offer for life, liberty, and property? How much tax to raise and by what means? What privileges to offer and to whom? What kinds of help to offer citizens in need? What restrictions, if any, should it put on businesses? What kinds of topics can the state and federal government rule on? How many bodies and of what type should govern the country? What rules should be adopted for interacting with other nations? What the liberal state attempts to provide is a framework that tries to be fair and through which debates over the fundamental moral laws get resolved, even if there remains fundamental disagreement about the foundation of those moral commitments.

Having realized this fact, we then are brought to the question of which vision of liberty we Americans, as a particular society, want to embrace and why. Embracing liberty does not by itself mean we embrace morality. Since there are multiple visions of liberty, there can be liberal societies that are immoral. Being a liberal society does not necessarily mean it is a moral society. So which vision of liberty is moral?

It has been the contention of this book that the answer to this question is one that ultimately matters a great deal. It is the question of which vision of liberty we after all want to implement in our society and what is best for the world and future generations. Not all liberal societies are great by definition. As I have been arguing, there is an alternative vision of liberty that is better than the one that has been put forth and become dominant during the last forty years by those on the Right and among libertarians. This progressive vision of liberty that I have outlined in this book argues that responsibility is as natural as rights, and thus it places human responsibility at the core of what liberty means. By this definition of natural responsibility, liberty involves much more than a protection of my rights and property. It involves, just as much, my sacrifices and obligations as a human being, which arise from our vision of what being human means.

The notion that we have responsibilities and obligations arises in several different ways from our understanding of what liberty means and what human beings are and should be. We have seen first of all that liberty by its very definition implies restriction. We can only have liberty in the first place by making sacrifices and curtailing our freedoms. Your protection of rights implies restrictions on me, and my protection of rights implies restrictions on you. You have a right to life only if I have a restriction on killing you. And I have a right to property only if you may not take mine. Sacrifice and limitation are the foundations of liberty itself. Without restriction, there could be no rights at all. The very conception of liberty depends on a restriction of what I can and cannot do.

What defines this mutuality of right and restriction is ultimately the sense of and conviction of human equality. It is the value of human equality that gives the notion of rights their intelligibility. Since we are equal against some moral standard, your life is no more valuable inherently than mine and vice versa. Both Locke and Hobbes were saying this in different ways. Locke said we are all property of God, and therefore we have no rights to harm each other. Hobbes said we were all equal in our mortality and vulnerability to death. The notion of equal value is not self-evident in nature. Humans are not equal in talents, intelligence, strength, artistic abilities, and so on. The claim instead is that humans are equal in terms of some absolute value, however that value is defined. This is a modern conviction, perhaps a key founding assumption of modernity in the West, as I have argued. The equal value of human beings is not self-evident in nature but is constructed and imagined by human beings as they reflect upon themselves and their values. One could argue that this conception of equality is part of what breaks us out of our natural state.

If we do not agree with the proposition that humans all have equal value, then we might argue that we could abandon the concept of liberty and return to the view of a natural hierarchy that treats individuals differently based on their inborn characteristics or their accomplishments only. Were we not equal to each other, your life or property might be worth more than mine. Were we not equal to each other, we might return to slavery and monarchy.

If we accept the fact that the equal value of human beings is our point of departure for our conception of liberty, then we come to the realization that we have come to the place where we are now, in this time and place, through a human and American history that did not live up to this aspiration. On the contrary, history suggests that the human species has had a very difficult time embracing the equal value of human beings. In fact, history suggests that the notion of equal value of human beings may be an impossible ideal.

We have talked about this discrepancy between the ideal and actual history in several ways. Human violence, conquest, and theft have played a prominent role in the distribution of property, wealth, and resources and in the formation of the national entities in which we live. Contrary to the ideal vision of property articulated by Locke, people did not simply spread out across the world and fairly acquire their property through labor. All sorts of violence, conquests, power, and thefts affected the distribution of property and resources over human history. In the founding of America, which is closest to home, there is ample evidence that the rights were themselves founded on a conquest of American land, a view that even the founders articulated and that some found disturbing. The history of conquest and violence of course reaches back as far in time as we can see. Furthermore, accidents of history, such as where the Industrial Revolution began, determined which peoples have benefited the most from human advancement.

The vision of liberty and rights by the "liberty-first" proponents assumes that the history of the past does not matter. Indeed, that view makes the assumption that the effort of my individual labors is strictly my own. This concept, which grounds the notion of property and supposedly sets the limits on what government can take from me, is the keystone of the liberty-first conception. We have seen, however, that this understanding of labor and property is problematic, for it ignores all the efforts of those who came before me, on which I build. My labor does not take place in a vacuum. I take advantage of all sorts of prior inventions and discoveries that make both my labor and its outcomes possible. On the foundation of our human ability to think, speak, use language, and invent tools, our ancestors discovered fire, learned to hunt, domesticated animals, and invented agriculture and medicines, not to mention paper, the printing press, computers, electricity, the network and Internet, and a countless series of inventions that provide a platform on which I labor. The creators of those inventions did not hold patents and reap the benefits forever, or even at all, of what they gave to humankind. If we assume that individuals own the output of their labor, then they should hold all the benefits that accrue to them from those inventions. Each of us who has benefited from them owes back to those inventors and their heirs. The heirs of these earlier inventors and predecessors of course are the human species itself, since we cannot trace either these earlier inventors or their specific lines of descent. This notion that we owe something back to the past, and to the species as a whole, differentiates the conception of property, labor, and liberty in a progressive view from its alternative. For now, we look at our own labor differently and understand that nothing that we create is ours alone. Investments have been made in us. Our labor stands on top of the achievements of countless other people who have come before us. This view of labor and invention sees our predecessors as having made a "capital" investment in us. They passed on to us a human platform on which we could labor and make advances. Thus, any labor that I perform already leverages and takes advantage of the labor that others have done before it. Just as a manufacturer must obtain the materials and parts needed to produce a product, so too our labor is already operating on outcomes of earlier labors before us. This understanding suggests that we do not labor on a blank page, and that we therefore owe back to the investors who contributed to us. In this view, our labor is not strictly our own. It already contains within it an investment from our predecessors. And while I make my own unique contributions through my labor, I do so with all the knowledge and investment of others before me. I owe my investors a payment back, just as an entrepreneur must pay back a loan or a homeowner pays back a mortgage. This view helps us to chisel away at that view that sees everything I accomplish as strictly my own. My labor is only partly my own. Part of it belongs to the human species as a whole. And thus we enter life with a debt back to the people who preceded us, for the work they did on our behalf and the platform they bequeathed to us on which to build.

There is another way too in which the original ideas behind labor and property were clearly mistaken. The notion that labor should create property assumed that there was an unlimited abundance of land and that one person's labor or acquisition of property would not hurt another's. Even though the world was thought to be given in common and to belong to everyone equally, by the theory of original equality, it could be removed from common property, it was thought, because no one would be harmed, since there was unlimited abundance. We now know that this assumption of unlimited abundance was mistaken. Natural resources and land can be exhausted. Where there is not an everexpanding pie, the piece that one person takes means there is less for others. For this reason, arguing that property derives from labor is in tension with the ideal of original human equality and resources shared in common. Historically speaking, to be sure, early humans likely did not hold the view that the world was given in common. Humans spread out over the earth, formed communities, settled lands, and conquered and murdered each other without having envisioned that they were all equal or that the resources were given in common. History is at odds with the ideal that we cherish, and the question becomes what, if anything, we must or should do about it. The view that our labor creates property therefore hides the fact that history was not fair and that labor was not the mechanism by which property was allocated across the human population and species. In other words, human communities developed without any of the ideals about liberty that we have been discussing.

The argument here is that as individuals we can't reasonably say that everything in our possession was fairly earned by our ancestors or ourselves as individuals. It is much more complicated, and behind every piece of property and land ownership is a history of the human species, both its contributions and its violence. Locke perceptively discerned how even a loaf of bread depends on the contributions of many dozens or even thousands of other peoples to get it to my dining-room table. It is not just the farmer who planted the wheat, but the manufacturer who made the tractor, the person who harvested latex from trees or petroleum from the ground for the tires, the manufacturer of the ship or truck that transported the bread to market, and so on and so forth. There are countless hands, an entire supply chain, that potentially are involved in the creation and delivery of any one product. The same is true from a historical perspective, where countless contributors made possible the developments of each of these inventions that are taken for granted in the making of my bread. This is why some of the natural rights thinkers thought property was a human convention and not a law of nature. The notion that everything that we own is ours rests on the assumption that history does not matter or we cannot correct the past.

While we cannot possibly fathom how to correct all the unfairness of the past, we have the opportunity to allow the idea of fairness to enter into our actions in the future. What we are talking about here is a different conception of liberty than the one that we are being offered by the liberty-first proponents.

Let us imagine some of the principles that could guide us and by which ultimately we could interpret our Constitution. This could be thought to be a new kind of Declaration of Independence or vision by which we reinterpret our commitments to liberty.

> When in the course of human events, it becomes necessary for a people to dissolve or reconfigure the government that they have previously made and refound those institutions in better accordance with the liberties and values by which they and humans should be entitled to live, a decent respect to the opinions of

humankind requires that they should declare the causes which impel them to do so.

We hold these truths to be self-evident, that all people are born equal in value, and they are endowed in their birth with certain inalienable rights and responsibilities, among them life, liberty, the pursuit of responsibility, and the duty to care for each other. To secure and operationalize these rights and duties, governments are instituted among people, deriving their just powers and obligations from those of the governed and from the human species. Whenever any form of government becomes destructive of these ends, it is the right of the people to alter or abolish it and to institute a new government, laying its foundation on such principles and organizing its powers in such form as to them shall seem most likely to effect their safety and happiness and fulfill their duties as human beings and citizens of the world. Prudence, indeed, will dictate that governments long established should not be changed for light and transient causes; and accordingly all experience has shown that humankind are more disposed to suffer while evils are sufferable than to right themselves by abolishing the forms to which they are accustomed.

But when a long train of abuses and usurpations pursuing invariably the same object evinces a design to destroy either the liberties of its citizens or the moral foundation in equality from which their liberties derive, it is their right, it is their duty, to try to alter such government and to provide new guards for their future security and that of their children and human beings everywhere. Such has been the patient sufferance of these United States; and such is now the necessity that constrains them to alter their former systems of government.

The history of the present United States is a history of repeated injuries and usurpations, all having in direct object the establishment of an immoral order and intolerable consequences over these states and their citizens. To prove this, let facts be submitted to a candid world.

The United States, under the banner of liberty, has increased inequality dramatically, justifying the rich getting richer and the poor getting poorer.

The United States, under the banner of liberty, has squandered and destroyed natural resources, both at home and abroad, that belong in common to all, as founded on our vision of equality.

The United States, under the banner of liberty, has reduced the moral obligations on the management of businesses and markets, letting them operate without sufficient regard to the impact on the environment, on the lives of peoples in other countries, and on our own citizens.

The United States, under the banner of liberty, has reified markets and economists, letting efficiency and the invisible immoral hand replace our conscience and determine what moral values, if any, infuse our commerce.

The United States, under the banner of liberty, has forgotten history and the obligations we carry from the past and the reparations we owe to the descendants of those who came before us and on whose backs our efforts started.

The United States, under the banner of liberty, has at times protected inequality and allowed racism, sexism, and other forms of discrimination to fester and become acceptable.

The United States, under the banner of liberty, has allowed businesses, which are not persons, to have rights, but not responsibilities, thereby undermining the representation that citizens have in their government and offering profit more protection than values.

We, therefore, the people of the United States of America, though not hereby assembled, appealing to our conscience for the rectitude of our intentions, do, in the name and by the authority of the good people of these United States, solemnly publish and declare that these United States are and of right ought to be not only a free but a moral state, that individuals who live herein are held morally responsible for their allegiance to a government that uses liberty to cloak misdeeds and are accountable for a view and practice of liberty that is and ought to be totally dissolved; and that as a free and independent people, we have the power and duty to limit war, conclude peace, contract alliances, establish moral commerce, protect common resources, repay debts to the past and the people who preceded us, and do all other acts and things that independent moral states may and should of right do. And for the support of this declaration, with a firm reliance on the protection of the ultimate commitments and values to which we aspire, we mutually pledge to each other our lives, our fortunes, and our sacred honor.

Notes

Preface

1.   Tuck, "Introduction" to *The Rights of War and Peace*, 6. For a deeper discussion of the influences on Jefferson, see my own Schwartz, *Liberty in America's Founding*.

2.   The other book I wrote on this topic is *Liberty in America's Founding*. I have also published a number of essays on my website: www.freedomandcapitalism.com.

3.   One can peruse the bibliography to see the hundreds of other voices who have influenced and shaped my own views.

4.   See, for example, Boyd, *Declaration*, 16; Becker, *Declaration*, 25; Ford, *Works*, vol. 10:343; Malone, *Jefferson*, 220; Schwartz, *Liberty in America's Founding*, 18–21.

INTRODUCTION

1.   Friedman, *Freedom and Capitalism*, 15, 8.

2.   See Hayek, *Road to Serfdom*, xxxv, and his essay called "Why I am not a Conservative" in *Constitution of Liberty*, 397–411. Contrast this with my essay, Schwartz, "Why 'Market Liberals' Are Not 'the True Liberals.'"

3.   I take this impulse as also behind the writing of others in the progressive or justice tradition, including but not limited to John Rawls, Amartya Sen, Ronald Dworkin, Cass Sunstein, Paul Hawken, Robert Kuttner, and many others who inspired me and whose names appear in the endnotes and bibliography.

4.   Libertarians tend to be more consistent in their use of liberty than Republicans or Tea Party advocates. They tend to invoke the notion of individual rights more consistently regardless of the issue. Republicans and Tea Party advocates tend to use the concept when it suits their purposes. For the discussion of the Pledge of Allegiance, see, for example, Hannity, *Let Freedom Ring*, 113–142. On the abortion issue, see, for example, Ron Paul, *Liberty Defined*, 1–9; he argues against the right to abortion, but otherwise holds a fairly strict adherence to a proliberty position. Of course, he gives reasons for holding this view. But that is precisely the point, that when there are reasons to limit liberty, he will choose other values over liberty itself.

5.   For a further discussion, see also my discussion, Schwartz, "Why Can't My Daughter Drive a Tank?"

6.   I am not alone in my concern with this broad range of issues and instead wish to see myself building on and synthesizing discontent expressed by a number of people with various parts of the "liberty-first" platform. I see my own work as attacking one key root of the liberty-first position often ignored by others. Among those who are asking similar questions but from different perspectives are the following: Hawken, *Ecology of Commerce*, and Hawken et al., *Natural Capitalism;* Sunstein, *Free Markets and Social Justice* and *Second Bill of Rights*; Breyer, *Active Liberty;* Stiglitz, *Price of Inequality*; Dworkin, *Taking Rights Seriously*; Rawls, *Theory of Justice*; Sen, *Ethics and Economics* and *Development as Freedom*; Kuttner, *Economic Illusion* and *Everything for Sale*; Glendon, *Rights Talk*.

7.   See my thinking in Schwartz, *Liberty in America's Founding*

Chapter 1

1.   The early modern natural right philosophers drew attention to this paradoxical side of liberty. In *Leviathan* (14:5, 87), for example, Hobbes says the second law of nature implies "*that a man be willing, when others are so too, as far-forth, as for peace, and defense of himself he shall think it necessary, to lay down this right to all things; and be contented with so much liberty against other men, as he would allow other men against himself.* For as long as every man holdeth this right, of doing any thing he liketh; so long are all men in the condition of war. But if other men will not lay down their right, as well as he; then there is no reason or any one, to divest himself of his: for that were to expose himself to prey, (which no man is bound to) rather than to dipose himself to peace. This is that law of the Gospel; *whatsoever you require that others should do to you, that do ye to them.*" [italics in original]

Locke has a similar perspective contrasting natural liberty with liberty in society. "The *Natural Liberty* of Man is to be free from any Superior Power on Earth, and not to be under the Will or Legislative Authority of Man, but to have only the Law of Nature for his Rule. The *Liberty of Man, in Society*, is to be under no other Legislative Power, but that established, by consent, in the Common-wealth, nor under the Dominion of any Will, or Restraint of any Law, but what the Legislative shall enact, according to the Trust put in it." Disagreeing with one of the popular royalists at the time, Locke writes, "*Freedom* then is not what Sir *Robert Filmer* tells us….*A Liberty for everyone to do what he lists, to live as he pleases, and not to be tyed by any laws.*" On the contrary, "*Freedom of Men under Government*, is, to have a standing Rule to live by, common to every one of that Society, and made by the Legislative Power erected in it; A Liberty to follow my own Will in all things, where the Rule prescribes not; and not to be subject to the inconstant, uncertain, unknown, Arbitrary Will of another Man. As *Freedom of Nature* is to be under no other restraint but the Law of Nature" (II § 22, Laslett, 283–284) [italics in original]. For Locke, liberty in society meant not freedom, but the right to have a standing law to live by. Liberty means the right to follow my will where the rule is silent.

Again Locke: "For in all the states of created beings capable of laws, w*here there is no Law, there is no Freedom.* For *Liberty* is, to be free from restraint and violence from others which cannot be, where there is no Law: but Freedom is not, as we are told, *A Liberty for every man to do what he lists:* (For who could be free, when every other Man's humour might domineer over him?) But a *Liberty* to dispose, and order, as he lists, his Person, Actions, Possessions, and his whole Property, within the allowance of those Laws under which he is; and therein not to be subject to the arbitrary will of another, but freely follow his own" (Locke II § 58; Laslett, 306). [italics in original]

2.   For discussions of the varying definition of rights and liberty and their histories, see, for example, Tierney, *Idea of Natural Rights*, 43–89; Munzer, *A Theory of Property*, 15–56; Tuck, *Natural Rights Theories*.

3.   See note 1 on the foundation of this view in modern natural rights thinkers. We shall see below that some modern thinkers see rights, and thus liberty, as the opposite of law (law meaning restriction), whereas others think of rights, and thus liberty, as including restrictions of the law.

4.   See, for example, Locke, II § 62–71.

5.   In some sense this was Thomas Hobbes's question in *Leviathan*, which arguably is about why people can't live with unlimited desires in the state of nature.

6.   On this definition of economics, see, for example, Flynn, *Economics for Dummies*, which states that "Economics is all about how people deal with scarcity." Or Okun, *Equality and Efficiency*, which says that "Tradeoffs are the central study of the economist."

7.   In particular, the focus on natural rights has all but eclipsed the great moral insight that individuals have responsibilities to each other as members of the human species, in addition to each other as neighbors or members of the same communities, nations, or religious communities.

8.   One of the interesting questions is whether our responsibilities devolve to those with whom we share a commonwealth or political society or whether we have broader obligations to the human species itself and, if so, what is the ground of that obligation. The natural rights philosophers do not all agree on this point. Hobbes, for example, sees rights and obligations emerging only with society, and thus the core of one's obligations are to fellow citizens. Locke, by contrast, sees right emerging as creatures of God and thus being implicit in nature even before the existence of a commonwealth. Thus Locke is also willing to speak about an obligation to "mankind" and not just to the citizen. As we shall see, I derive this obligation to the species in a different way, without needing to resort to the concept of God, which may be a stumbling block for some people who do not believe in God or who conceive of God in other ways.

9.   See, for example, Epstein, *Principles*, 133–157, which argues that charity and altruism are private matters.

10.   We shall see below that the "social contract" assumed by the natural rights tradition has also a "natural responsibility" dimension. By entering into society, one takes on more responsibilities than one had in nature.

11. See, for example, Epstein, *Principles*, for a liberty-first position that rejects the concepts of rights. If rights are neither "self-evident" nor "natural," then how we go about constructing the focus of government is an entirely different matter and requires an entirely different set of arguments. In that case, we can't rely on "self-evident" truths and must devise other ways of determining what our political entities focus on. I shall turn to the question of rights' self-evidence in the following discussion.

Chapter 2

1. The idea had its predecessors in the natural law tradition and the Greek philosophical traditions from antiquity. The relationship of modern natural rights thinking to those of late antiquity and premodern Christianity and the Renaissance is complex. See, for example, discussions by Tuck, *Natural Rights Theories* and *Philosophy and Government;* Tierney, *The Idea of Natural Rights*; Strauss, *Natural Right and History*; Skinner, *Foundations of Modern Political Thought*, 2 vols., and Skinner, *Liberty Before Liberalism*. See also Zuckert, *Natural Rights*, for a contrasting view of Locke and Locke's relationship to Jefferson.

2. Many have written on this topic of Jefferson's intellectual influence. For a review, see my discussion of the influences on Jefferson in Schwartz, *Liberty in America's Founding*, 18–50, 273–306.

3. Both Jewish and Christian thinkers synthesized Greek philosophical ideas about God, nature, and reason with the biblical traditions. In the Jewish tradition, Philo, the first-century Jewish thinker in Egypt, and Maimonides, the twelfth-century Spanish Jewish philosopher, were among the most famous synthesizers of the two traditions. In the Christian tradition, thirteenth-century philosopher Thomas Aquinas is the most well-respected premodern synthesizer of both traditions.

4. See, for example, Hobbes, *Leviathan*, 14.3, where he distinguishes law from right and defines right as the ability to choose to do or not to do whereas law is the duty not to do something. See the early Locke, *Essays*, 111, where he makes a similar distinction in very Hobbesian language.

5. In his *Two Treatises*, Locke tends to see natural law as providing the foundation for natural rights which are implied by natural law. Natural law exists in nature and is discernible when reason perceives the existence of a moral creator. That recognition that we are all God's property and creation leads to the corollary that we cannot harm the life, liberty, or health of another and that we have the right to punish an offender and get reparations for injury. See Locke II § 6; Laslett, *Two Treatises*, 271.

6. See Grotius, *Rights of War and Peace*, Preliminary Discourse, 10:1, 54, where he defines right as a dictate of right reason and sections III to X, where he discusses multiple meanings of the term "right."

7. In the synthesis between Greek philosophy and both Christian and Jewish views of revelation, illustrated by Philo, Maimonides, and Aquinas, among others, reason was thought to align perfectly with insights from revelation. One of the ways in which

the modern view differed was in seeing that insights from reason and revelation were not necessarily identical. This emerging tension between reason and revelation would occupy the deists who come after Locke and in fact set the stage for the modern discussion that continues today. For discussions of this topic, see Manuel, *The Eighteenth Century Confronts the Gods* and *Changing of the Gods*; and my discussion, Eilberg-Schwartz, *Savage in Judaism*, 31–48.

8.   In Christian thought, Jews had been examples of peoples who rejected God's revelation. With the Reformation, Protestants and Catholics argued that each had misinterpreted God's word and the will of Christ. For a similar perspective, see, for example, Wolterstorff, "Locke's philosophy."

9.   Grotius, *Rights of War and Peace, Preliminary Discourse*, 24:42.

10.   The diversity of human belief and practice would be one of key problems that European intellectuals would ponder in the sixteenth and seventeenth centuries. From the beginning of Columbus's discovery in the late fifteenth century throughout much of the sixteenth and seventeenth centuries, Europeans were fascinated and horrified by the description of cultures and practices in the Americas. The bewildering diversity of human beliefs and practices among the native peoples discovered by Europeans further amplified the problem caused by the breakdown of a single view of truth among European Christians themselves. The turn to reason and the law of nature in the seventeenth century was in part an attempt to find a common foundation for truth across human populations in the common consent of nations, a position held, for example, by Grotius. At the same time, however, this diversity of belief and practice among peoples of the world posed a difficult challenge for the new emerging intellectual view that reason could discern a universal law among nations. For example, John Locke, in his early *Essays* on the natural law, would name diversity as one of the key challenges to the view that reason could be the universal basis for morality. "The only thing, perhaps, about which all mortals think alike is that men's opinions about the law of nature and the ground of their duty are diverse and manifold—a fact which, even if tongues were silent, moral behavior, which differs so widely, would show pretty well. Men are everywhere met with, not only a select few and those in a private stations, but whole nations, in whom no sense of law, no moral rectitude, can be observed. There are also other nations, and they are many, which with no guilty feeling disregard some at least of the precepts of natural law and consider it to be not only customary but also praiseworthy to commit, and to approve of, such crimes as are utterly loathsome to those who think rightly and live according to nature" (Locke, *Essays*, 7:191).

11.   On Galileo's physics influencing Descartes and both influencing Hobbes, see Tuck, *Hobbes*, 19, 20–25. See also Manuel, *Eighteenth Century Confronts the Gods*. All of the writers in the natural rights tradition were seeking to explore and find a foundation of human morality, which seemed shaky. We shall come back to this point later for the quest to find the source of morality in reason and in a natural sciences methodology that ultimately failed and posed a problem that continues to occupy us.

12.   Grotius, *Rights of War and Peace, The Preliminary Discourse*, 11, 38.

13. The rationalist conception of God as a clockmaker was influenced by the growing prestige of science in the wake of Descartes. But it also had roots in the rationalist philosophy of Thomas Aquinas, which had already achieved a synthesis of classical Greek and Christian thought.

14. I associate this stream of thought with both Grotius and Hobbes. By contrast, see Locke, *Essays*, I, 119 where he lists the instinct to preservation as the fourth type of argument for natural law, though it is not the foundation of his own position. He also notes that "all [thinkers] direct perhaps more attention to this point than is necessary" (*Essays*, 4, 159).

15. See, for example, Grotius, *Rights of War and Peace*, Preliminary Discourse, VI and VIII, 36, "this Sociability, we have described in general, or this Care of maintaining Society, in a Manner conformable to the Light of human Understanding, is the Foundation of Right." Locke at times also recognizes this social impulse as well (*Essays*, 4, 157–59).

16. Hobbes, for example, does not see humans as social by nature but as at war and in competition by nature. He instead sees humans becoming social as a means to peace, and thus sociability is achieved through human development rather than inherently part of human nature.

17. This is the position of Hobbes, *Leviathan*, chaps. 13–14.

18. This is how I understand Hobbes's position that in the state of nature a human being has unlimited rights, even to one another's body and life, because there is no moral law in nature. Hobbes calls these "rights" because they are natural and because there is not yet a moral law that declares them "wrongs."

19. Grotius, Hobbes, and Locke all share this view to some extent.

20. From this social nature of the human creature, different thinkers inferred a broader or narrower set of laws. At the very least, social life depended on a set of standards and rules that protect a person's life, liberty, and property. For others, the rules that were inferred by reason were broader than simply life, liberty, and property. As we shall also see, some thought these rights were already evident by reason in nature prior to the existence of social life.

21. For a detailed exposition of this distinction, see Pufendorf, *Law of Nature and Nations*, book 2, chap. 1:4, 98.

22. Locke and Hobbes would both say that humans were animals who curtained their natural liberties or inclinations, though Locke envisioned laws and restrictions in nature and Hobbes did not.

23. Hobbes, *Leviathan*, 14:4, 87.

24. Mt. 7:12 and Lk. 6:31.

25. Hobbes, *Leviathan*, 15:1, 95. See also Grotius, *Rights of War and Peace*, *Preliminary Discourse*, 16, 38.

26. To convert promises into contracts, societies must have a coercive power that makes them enforceable. Thus the very foundation of social life is the contract, which requires a power to enforce it and hence the need for government. See, for example, Hobbes,

Leviathan, 11:3, 95. Contrast Locke, II § 14, and Laslett, *Two Treatises*, 276, which sees promises as binding on people even in a state of nature "for the truth and keeping of faith belongs to men, as men, and not as members of society."

27. Locke, II § 77; Laslett, *Two Treatises*, 318–319.

28. For an example, see James Otis, "Rights," 423.

29. As Grotius, *Rights of War and Peace*, Preliminary Discourse, 11, 38, puts it, "what without the greatest wickedness cannot be granted."

30. Hobbes, *Leviathan*, 15:41, 106, by which Hobbes means that natural law is not really law but "dictates of reason." In his Essays 4, 151, Locke says something similar when he writes that "in order that anyone may understand that he is bound by a law, he must know beforehand there is a law-maker, i.e. some superior power to which he is rightly subject." Thus both agree that you need a Lawgiver to have natural law, but Hobbes therefore concludes natural law is not a law in fact, but only a mistaken idiom, whereas Locke concludes it is law and a lawmaker is discernible. Hobbes thus seems to imply that God, the Lawgiver, either does not exist or that the natural law is not enforced by God. For subtle implications such as this, the accusation of "Hobbism" in the seventeenth century was often associated with "atheism."

31. Grotius, Hobbes, and Locke all had to flee their countries at some point in their careers for political safety. Thus the question of how open these thinkers were with their deeply held convictions is a matter of debate in the academic literature and was most forcefully articulated as an interpretive question by Leo Strauss in *Persecution and the Art of Writing* and taken up by his students.

32. See Locke's rejection of tradition and innate knowledge as sources of moral knowledge in his early *Essays* (2, 131). He carries these themes forward in his magisterial *Essay Concerning Human Understanding*, which develops and further demolishes the idea of innate ideas already articulated in his earlier *Essays*. On the challenge this presented to more traditional religious understandings and understandings of the mind, see Wolterstorff, "Locke's Philosophy of Religion," Jolley, "Locke on Faith and Reason," and Rickless, "Locke's Polemic against Nativism."

33. In his *Essays*, 4, 153, Locke builds on but diverges from Descartes's proof of God in his *Meditation 3*. See the comment of von Leyden, "Introduction," notes, 153. Locke revisits the assumption of a creator in numerous places in passing in his *Two Treatises* and repeatedly in various places in his *Essay Concerning Human Understanding*. As discussed below, it is surprising that Locke did not scrutinize or question the proof of God in more detail given his skeptical theory of knowledge that he ultimately articulates. Below, I suggest that Locke may have had a more skeptical position on God's existence than many interpreters think.

34. Having inferred a creator from the evidence of the senses, Locke argues (*Essays*, IV, 153–155) that "reason lays down that there must be some superior power to which we are rightly subject, namely God who has a just and inevitable command over us and at his pleasure can raise us up or throw us down, and make us by the same commanding power happy or miserable." See also Pufendorf, *Law of Nature and Nations,* 3:10, 56 ff.

35. Locke, *Essays*, 4, 157.

36. Ibid., 159.

37. Ibid., 7, 195.

38. See Locke, II § 6 and 7, and Laslett, *Two Treatises*, 270–271.

39. See Hobbes, *Leviathan*, 15, 35, 104.

40. Locke's words "free, equal, and independent" (II § 95) are similar to the words used by Jefferson in the first draft of the Declaration of Independence and in the Virginia Declaration of Rights, authored by George Mason and a document that may have influenced Jefferson in writing the Declaration. I return to this point in a subsequent discussion. For discussions of these and related points see, for example, Schwartz, *Liberty in America's Founding*, 72–82; Boyd, *Declaration;* Boyd, *Papers*, 345; Ganter, "Pursuit of Happiness"; Maier, *American Scripture*, 134; Becker, *Declaration;* Dershowitz, *America Declares Independence*, 75; Jayne, *Jefferson's Declaration;* Zuckert, *Natural Rights;* Gerber, *To Secure These Rights;* Carey, "Natural Rights, Equality and the Declaration of Independence."

41. Locke, II § 6, and Laslett, *Two Treatises*, 270–71. [italics in original]

42. I am referring here to Locke's view of property, discussed in more detail below, where we shall have occasion to look at alternative perspectives.

43. There is a seeming tension or contradiction in Locke. On the one hand, he says that humans are God's workmanship or the property of God. On the other hand, he says they own their labor. This has led to an interesting discussion in the secondary literature on what Locke intended and whether it makes sense. Contrast Zuckert, *Natural Rights*, 220ff and 239ff, with Schwartz, *Liberty in America's Founding*, 378, notes 66 and 67, and "Liberty Is Not Freedom"; Tully, *A Discourse on Property*, 105–106; and Waldron, *Right To Private Property*, 177–184, who see no contradiction between these positions, understanding that the human life can belong to God but the will is the possession of the individual.

44. Locke, II § 9, 11; Laslett, *Two Treatises*, 272–273.

45. See, for example, Pufendorf's *Law of Nature and Nations*, book 2, chaps. 1:2, and 2:5–6, discussion of why God did not see fit to give humans "wild liberty."

46. I am anticipated in part by Glendon's wonderful work, *Rights Talk: The Impoverishment of Political Discourse*; she is moving along similar lines although she comes at it from another direction.

Chapter 3

1. See Strauss, *Natural Right*, 182, for example; Strauss partly characterizes one difference between modern and ancient notions of natural rights around the shift from "duties" to "rights."

2. The lengthy discussion by Locke (II § 52–76; Laslett, *Two Treatises*, 303–317) on paternal power and the relationship between parents and children has to do in part with his rejection of Filmer's patriarchalism and Filmer's claim that fathers own their chil-

dren and wives as property. That patriarchal assumption was key in Filmer's argument that Adam was the owner of the whole world and that all property and people that followed were Adam's property and that of his heirs. This was the basis for Filmer's justification of monarchy. The kings were seen as the descendants of Adam and thus inherited his rights to absolute ownership over their children and their people. In addition, there are other impulses at work as well in the discussion of parent/children relationships in the natural rights theorists. The very question of authority over persons, which is at the heart of the discussion of political power, led Locke and others to discuss the relationship of power and rights over all peoples and to the assumptions of the patriarchal family. Grotius, *Rights of War and Peace*, book 2, chap. 5:1–8, 49–51, at the start of the century discusses parents' authority over children and articulates the patriarchal position asserting the father's right to "pawn" his children and the husband's status as head of the household. By contrast, Hobbes, *Leviathan*, 22, 4–9, 133–134, sees the father and mother more equally and also sees the parent's dominion as based on a child's consent. For discussion on the patriarchal family as a context for Locke's thinking, see Schochet, "Family and Origins of State."

3.   This analogy is key to the argument of King James in his *Trew Law of Free Monarchies*, published in 1598, on absolute royal authority. See Zuckert, *New Republicanism*, 30ff.

Chapter 4

1.   Hobbes, in *Leviathan*, 13:13, 44, had argued something similar when he argued that right and wrong emerge with the beginning of society. "The notions of Right and Wrong, Justice and Injustice have there no place. Where there is no common Power, there is no Law: where no Law, no Injustice…They are Qualities, that relate to men in Society, not in Solitude."

2.   Locke in particular questioned "tradition" as a source of knowledge in his *Essays* and his *Essay Concerning Human Understanding*. He argued that tradition was not a sufficient basis for knowing God or morality and that reason instead must be the way to discern the source of truth.

3.   Writers in the seventeenth and eighteenth centuries aspired to emulate the methods of the natural sciences in the study of human beings. Max Weber in the modern period is often credited with developing the "antipositivism" position within sociology, as an example, which denied that the methods of science could be applied to the study of the human phenomenon. The debate in the modern period has been over whether the social or human sciences (anthropology, sociology, psychology, economics, and political science) are sciences in the same way as natural sciences and can use the same methodologies. In all of these disciplines there are those who see the discipline and methodologies as interpretive and humanistic (nonscientific) and those who lean more toward positive, scientific methodologies and ways of characterizing what they do. Each discipline has fought out this battle in its own discipline.

4.   This goal of the seventeenth-century thinkers, such as Hobbes, Pufendorf, and Locke, among many others, was to produce a science of morality. Emulating the natural sciences, Locke, for example, thought that ethics was and could be a demonstrative science like mathematics (von Leyden, "Introduction," 54–55). Here is Locke in his own words, *Essays* 7, 201: "it seems to me to follow just as necessarily from the nature of man that, if he is a man, he is bound to love and worship God and also to fulfill other things appropriate to the rational nature, i.e. to observe the law of nature, as it follows from the nature of a triangle that, if it is a triangle, its three angles are equal to two right angles, although perhaps very many men are so lazy and so thoughtless that for want of attention they are ignorant of both these rules."

Though Locke would ultimately in his more mature work reshape how we understood the mind and human knowledge, he ultimately failed, and he may have realized he had failed, in his quest to found morality on the basis of reason. I take up this point again below.

5.   Locke, like others in the natural law tradition, had a problem explaining why, if reason can lead to the correct foundations of knowledge, all people don't come to the same conclusions about morality and about how to live. As mentioned in the previous note, Locke at one point in his early essay blames lack of agreement on tradition, people's laziness, or thoughtlessness. Sometimes (*Essays* 1, 113) Locke compares those who do not discern the results of reason to a blind person (113) who cannot read a legal notice. And though everyone is endowed with reason, not everyone cultivates reason.

Hobbes (*Leviathan*, 11, 69–70) has a much more pessimistic view of knowledge and argues that the reason people don't dispute "the doctrine of lines, and figures" (i.e., mathematical truths) is because "men care not, in that subject what be truth, as a thing that crosses no man's ambition, profit or lust. For I doubt not, but if it had been a thing contrary to any man's right of dominion, or to the interest of men that have dominion, *That the three angles of a triangle, should be equal to two angles of a square; that doctrine should have been, if not disputed, yet by the burning of all books of geometry, suppressed, as far as he whom it concerned was able.*" While Hobbes still relies on reason to arrive at his laws of nature, he is more likely to see that what counts as truth depends on a human being's interests.

6.   See my essay on this topic in Schwartz, "Why Can't My Daughter Drive a Tank?"

7.   Seventeenth- and eighteenth-century thinkers grappled with the presence of polygamy in other cultures and as an accepted practice in the Hebrew scriptures, among other instances of cultural variations. See Grotius, *Rights of War and Peace*, book 2, chap. 5:9.2 and 9.4, 51–52. The discussion continued into the eighteenth century. See Hume's tongue-in-cheek essay "Of Polygamy and Divorce," discussing whether marriage practices are universal.

8.   Grotius, Hobbes, Locke, and Pufendorf all start with the right to life or instinct to self-preservation and derive the other rights from this more basic right. They disagree, however, on where this primary right comes from. As discussed previously, for Locke, this primary right comes from the discernment of God the Creator. Grotius, *Rights*

of War, book 1, chap. 2:1.1, 62, refers to it as "instinct of every animal" and as "first duty." Hobbes never says where this "right of self-preservation" comes from and thereby suggests it is something like an instinct. Indeed, the word "right" for Hobbes can be understood as what derives from human nature, and thus is "natural."

9.   See, for example, Locke, II § 11 and I § 18, 19. Grotius, *Rights of War and Peace*, book 1, chap. 2:2, 88, also reflects on the thief who may be killed but notes the scriptural passage (Ex. 32:2) that distinguishes a thief killed during the night from a thief killed during daylight. No punishment applies to the first, but it does to the second.

10.   See Hobbes, *Leviathan*, 17:2 and 17:4, 111–112, and Locke, II § 145.

11.   Compare Pufendorf, *Law of Nature and Nations*, book 8, chap. 6:9, 837, with Grotius, *Rights of War and Peace*, book 2, chap. 22:9, 269–70. See Grotius and Pufendorf's disagreement with Francis Bacon about whether violation of the laws of nature constitute grounds for just war. Locke dodges the whole issue and doesn't define the just war at all.

12.   One way to read the rich history of anthropological thought from the twentieth century to the present is about contesting the sharp dichotomies between civilized and savage peoples that were bequeathed by nineteenth-century evolutionary anthropologists such as Edward Burnett Tylor, James George Frazer, Lucien Lévy-Bruhl, and others. Twentieth-century cultural anthropology questioned the dichotomies between savage and civilized cultures, led by the pioneering work of the British anthropologists such as E. E. Evans-Pritchard, and providing the foundation for the work of American cultural anthropologists such as Clifford Geertz and French structural anthropologist Claude Lévi-Strauss. For discussions, see Harris, *Rise of Anthropological Theory*; Wilson, *Rationality*; Eilberg-Schwartz, *The Savage in Judaism*, 1–28.

13.   In every humanistic discipline and social science, there is a fundamental and unresolvable divide over whether unambiguous interpretation of human behavior or writings is possible. Whether in history, literature, anthropology, religious studies, sociology, or the political sciences, there are those who believe it is possible to arrive at a set of unequivocal conclusions or interpretations of history, texts, or human behavior and those who believe you can't, and that interpretation is always ambiguous and open ended. The literature on the subject is vast in each discipline, and the founding assumption fundamentally divides methodology and conclusions.

Among the many important discussions on the subject are those flowing in philosophy from Rorty, *Objectivity, Relativism, and Truth;* in hermeneutics from Gadamer, *Truth and Method*; and in science from Thomas Kuhn, *Structure of Scientific Revolutions*. For a discussion in literature, contrast the position defending authorial intent, by Hirsch, *Aims of Interpretation*, with the positions arguing for the death of the author, by Barthes and Derrida, among others.

For a debate related to the interpretation of the Constitution, contrast, for example, Levy, *Original Intent*, and the view of Scalia, *A Matter of Interpretation*; related to history, contrast, for example, Skinner, *Natural Right and History*, with my own Schwartz, *Liberty in America's Founding*, 309–322.

14. There were several different ways of approaching the question of whether the law of nature and law of nations are the same concept. Some thinkers distinguished the two concepts and others did not. Grotius (*Rights of War and Peace*, Preliminary Discourse 41, 45) distinguishes the law of nature from the law of nations, though he acknowledges that others define the terms differently (see also book 1, chap. 1, 9:1, 55). In his view, the rules that are consented to by "many" people historically and across nations, he calls the "law of nature" and distinguishes it from "laws of nations," which are not generally or widely accepted. (See also book 2, chap. 8:1.2, 93 on this distinction.) But Grotius also distinguishes the law of nations from the civil law, though that distinction is less clear (*Rights of War and Peace*, book 1, chap. 1:14, 57). Indeed, at times Grotius seems to forget his own distinction and calls the laws consented to by most nations the law of nations.

Locke does not use the term law of nations at all in the *Two Treatises* and refers instead only to the law of nature. This is consistent with his rejection of consent among nations as evidence for the law of nature (Locke, *Essays,* 5, 161–179, and Von Leyden, "Introduction," 100). Instead, Locke believes the law of nature is evident through reason even before political society comes into existence and thus available before there is any nation that can consent to it. Hobbes says the law of nations and the law of nature are the same thing (Hobbes, *Leviathan*, 30:30, 235). Pufendorf, for his part, has a whole chapter devoted to the subject and tends to agree with Hobbes (*Law of Nature and Nations*, book 2, chap. 3:23, 149ff).

15. Locke, *Essays* 1, 113.

16. See, for example, Locke (*Essays* I, 113–115). Locke (*Essays* 7, 191) also writes, "There are also other nations, and they are many, which with no guilty feeling disregard some at least of the precepts of natural law and consider it to be not only customary but also praiseworthy to commit, and to approve of, such crimes as are utterly loathsome to those who think rightly and live according to nature."

17. Hobbes, *Leviathan*, 18:9, 118.

18. Hobbes's ideas about natural rights were fundamental in shaping the discussion in the seventeenth century, including the ideas of Locke, whom many regard as fundamental in shaping the American founding. Both Hobbes and Locke, among others, start from the equality of human beings. But Hobbes despairs of humans ever being capable on their own of resolving matters without an all-powerful sovereign.

19. Hobbes did think reason leads people to seek peace, which is the foundation of the law of nature, and this is the foundation for the rational decision to give up control of truth to the sovereign.

20. Gerber, in *To Secure These Rights*, makes this argument most explicit by arguing that we should interpret the American Constitution based on the Declaration and therefore limit our understanding of rights to what John Locke meant. This is a position that has been implied in many accounts that show a direct line from John Locke's *Second Treatise on Government* to Jefferson's Declaration of Independence. For positions holding this view, see, for example, the now classic Becker, *Declaration of Independence*, as well as the

more recent Zuckert, *Natural Rights*; Dworetz, *Unvarnished Doctrine*; Jayne, *Jefferson's Declaration*. Contesting this view, see my own Schwartz, *Liberty in America's Founding*, and Dunn, "The Politics of Locke."

21. The *Essays* were written in the late 1650s and completed after 1660 and before 1664 when Locke was in his late twenties and early thirties (von Leyden, "Introduction," 10–11). His more mature works, such as the *Two Treatises*, were being written in 1679–80, some sixteen years later. On the dating of the *Two Treatises*, see discussions in Laslett, *Two Treatises*, 57–66; Gough, *Political Philosophy*, 143–144; Dunn, *Political Thought*, 47–53.

22. Locke II, § 12; Laslett, *Two Treatises*, 275.

23. In 1687, James Tyrrell, a close friend of Locke and an author on natural law in his own right, wrote a number of letters to Locke encouraging him to take up again the foundation of the law of nature, especially after reading Locke's *Essay* (von Leyden, "Introduction," 9–10 and again 62–63). Tyrrell had been among the group of five or six friends Locke mentions at the start of the *Essay* (*Epistle to the Reader*, xiv) whose conversation with Locke about the basis of morality and its relation to natural and revealed law had set Locke off in the first place to write on the underlying themes that led to *An Essay Concerning Human Understanding* (see von Leyden, "Introduction," 61, and Milton, "Locke's Life," 11).

Tyrrell was aware that Locke had already written earlier essays on the subject of natural law and was encouraging Locke to develop them, especially when critics of Locke's *Essay* challenged and questioned his position on the law of nature. Tyrrell was also suspicious that Locke was the author of the *Two Treatises*, which Locke published anonymously, and pressed Locke to acknowledge he was the author, which Locke refused to do. In any case, it is an interesting question how the Locke who wrote the *Essay*, which challenged the foundation of knowledge and the basis of knowledge in tradition or innate ideas, could also have been the Locke who wrote the *Second Treatise*, which takes for granted the law of nature (Gough, *Political Philosophy*, 12).

24. This view of Locke is held by many of his interpreters. In this line of thinking, Locke assumed reason could discern a moral lawgiver and from that assumption flowed certainty about the natural law. See, for example, Gough, *Political Philosophy*, 10, which describes this as part of Locke's unquestioned faith in a Christian God that is never subjected to the same scrutiny to which he subjects other sources of knowledge. See also Aarslett, "The State of Nature," 99–136, for a similar theological understanding of Locke. Dunn, in *Political Thought*, 21–26, 198–199, tends to also see Locke this way and minimizes the tension between the *Two Treatises* and the *Essay*.

See von Leyden, 68ff and 72, for example, which offers several possibilities on why Locke doesn't work out the tension between the *Two Treatises* and the *Essay*. One is that Locke's theory of God as the foundation of morality was coming into conflict with his emerging theory of hedonism, a conflict that Gough (*Political Philosophy*, 14) thinks von Leyden overstates. But von Leyden also speculates (75), in a position that I find persuasive, that Locke avoided the question of natural law's foundation in God because "he found himself at a loss to give full expression to his view of the demonstrative character of morality."

In considering this issue, we have to bear in mind Locke's refusal to acknowledge his authorship of the *Two Treatises*. This may have been due to his fear of reprisals, to the uncertainty of the political situation in which he wrote, and to his own experience in exile (Laslett, *Two Treatises*, 78). Laslett also questions whether that part of Locke's hesitation about revealing his authorship of the *Two Treatises* was because he was aware of the inconsistencies with the *Essay* and that it was no simple matter to reconcile their doctrines (Laslett, ibid., 66; Gough, *Political Philosophy*, 20). But Laslett and others also suggest that the *Second Treatise* should not be interpreted in the genre of philosophy in the same sense as the *Essay*, and that the *Second Treatise* was more of an "exclusion tract" or political work rather than a philosophical work. Since it is a nonphilosophical genre, it should not be held to the same expectations of philosophical rigor or consistency. In other words, it would be a category mistake to hold the *Second Treatise* to same expectation of philosophical rigor as the *Essay*. To complicate matters further, we know that Locke is not one of the most consistent and methodical thinkers, as Laslett notes, and thus we are at risk of overinterpreting Locke when we make too much of these inconsistencies.

25. Locke deleted a last chapter of the *Essay* called "Of Ethick in General," which was intended to be an essay on the foundation of morality and a culmination of the *Essay* (see MS Locke c 28, printed in Peter King, *The Life of John Locke*, 308–313). For discussions, see von Leyden, "Introduction," 69; Dunn, *Political Thought*, 187; Laslett, *Two Treatises*, 187. According to von Leyden, this deleted essay shows a trend toward "hedonism" (i.e., arguing that morality is based in pleasure and pain rather than reason) in Locke's thinking, which Locke may have realized was inconsistent with his argument for the foundation of morality in a concept of God and the law of nature and may be why he never published it as part of the *Essay*.

26. This is a telling irony in the story of modern natural rights thinking. One of the West's most important natural rights thinkers, John Locke, sometimes called the father of natural rights, may have doubted reason's ability to discern the moral law. The doubt appears in Locke's *An Essay Concerning Human Understanding*, one of the most important European books written to be written about the foundation of human knowledge. It is clear that here Locke is moving toward a much more skeptical understanding of what the mind can know. It is not entirely clear whether this articulated theory of knowledge fully reshaped how Locke thought about the idea of God and the natural law. For a discussion of Locke's view of God and religion in his *Essay*, see Jolley, "Locke on Faith and Reason," and the discussion that follows.

27. Locke, *Essay*, book 4, chap. 3:27, 454.

28. See discussion, for example, in Lowe, *On Human Understanding*, 7–9. Initial hostility to the *Essay* was directed at features thought to be hostile to religion, particularly its skeptical theme and its criticism of innate ideas. Critics such as Edward Stillingfleet,

Bishop of Worcester, saw dangers to their Christian faith in Locke's emphasis on reason and experience. See also Jolley, "Locke on Faith and Reason."

29. Locke, *Essay*, "Introduction," 5, 3.

30. Locke, *Essay*, book 4, chap. 10, 527–536.

31. See note 24.

32. Ibid.

33. I see Laslett, "Introduction," heading in this direction. Dunn, however, draws back from this conclusion.

34. Various thinkers in the seventeenth century had already begun to question whether conclusions derived from reason were entirely consistent with revelation. This was one of the ways in which the Enlightenment thinking would break free from the medieval synthesis of reason and revelation that had been articulated in the Christian and Jewish traditions. Examples of this earlier synthesis, for example, were achieved most notably in writers such as Philo, Aquinas, and Maimonides. In that earlier tradition, reason appeared for the most part consistent with revelation.

With the Enlightenment, this nice alignment begins to break down. This was apparent, for example, already in Hobbes, and part of the reason that "Hobbism" was such a serious charge throughout the century. It was also visible in other thinkers, such as the precursor of deism, Lord Herbert of Cherbury (1583–1648), and his book *De Veritate* (1624), the first major statement of deism. In this work, Herbert begins to distinguish the key innate ideas that are reasonable and evident in Christianity and true religion from accretions and superstitions that must have infiltrated scripture and revelation. While Locke demolished Herbert's theory of innate religious ideas, he nonetheless carried forward and left unresolved the tension between "reason and revelation." Locke himself to some extent allowed reason to shape his interpretation of scripture in his *First Treatise on Government*. But Locke did not take this challenge to revelation by reason to its logical conclusion, and the deeper challenge was developed and carried forward by the deists who followed and saw the more radical implications, including Matthew Tindal, *Christianity as Old as Creation*; Anthony Collins, *Grounds and Reason of the Christian Religion*; Thomas Chubb, *Discourse Concerning Reason*, among others. For discussions of Herbert, see Hutcheson, "Introduction," Gay, *Deism*, Manuel, *Changing of the Gods*, and my Eilberg-Schwartz, *The Savage in Judaism*, 44–66.

35. Hume, "The Original Contract," 199.

36. I discuss the impact of Hume on Dickinson and Jefferson in *Liberty in America's Founding*, 134–135. See also 273ff.

37. Bentham, "Anarchical Fallacies," 914. Others who follow the utilitarian perspective include Epstein, "Principles" and "Simple Rules." For an alternative view arguing the language of rights is still defensible, see Dworkin, *Taking Rights Seriously*. Rawls, *A Theory of Justice*, is also an attempt to rehabilitate the Lockean notions of a social contract and a state of nature.

38.   There is an extremely interesting debate on whether even what counts as rationality is common across cultures, in Wilson, *Rationality*. See discussions as well in Reynolds and Tracy, *Myth and Philosophy*.

39.   See my discussion in Schwartz, *Liberty in America's Founding*.

Chapter 5

1.   See for a similar position, Dworkin, *Taking Rights Seriously*, 192–205, and Schwartz, "Why Can't My Daughter Drive a Tank?"

2.   Schwartz, *Liberty in America's Founding*, 15–82. More on the topic of land below.

3.   See Maier, *Ratification*.

4.   See Maier, *Ratification*, and Bowen, *Miracle*.

5.   See Madison, *Notes*, on the debates during the convention. The very presence of emerging Federalist and Republican interpretations testifies that there was no consensus on either what rights meant or what the Constitution meant. For a discussion of the emerging Federalist and Republican positions, see Elkins and McKitrick, *Age of Federalism*, and Wootton, *Essential Federalist*. For a discussion questioning the notion of the original founding meaning, see Levy, *Original Intent*. For a description of the unfolding debate in the states, see Maier, *Ratification*.

6.   See Levy, *Original Intent*, 284–387, which makes a similar point. On calls for a return to a lost Constitution, see Napolitano, *Constitution in Exile*, and Randy Barnett, *Restoring the Lost Constitution*.

7.   See Levy, *Original Intent*.

8.   See Detweiler, "The Changing Reputation"; Maier, "Strange History"; and Schwartz, *Liberty in America's Founding*.

9.   Differences among branches of various religions (e.g., Protestants versus Catholics, Orthodox Jews versus Conservative and Reform Jews) often come down to arguments over the meaning of the original scriptures (God's word) and who has the rightful authority and interpretation.

Similarly, a key debate in literary theory, and one that has carried over to history and the academic discipline of religious studies as well, is whether texts have specified determinative meanings and whether those meanings can be based on authorial intent, the historical context, or the text itself, or whether the very meaning is produced through a reading. The literature on this topic is vast and spans debates across new criticism, postmodernism, deconstruction, postcolonial theory, and gender studies, just to name a few of the theoretical disciplines that have taken up the topic. Interestingly enough, debates about rights often assume that there are specified rights in nature or in the Constitution, even among jurists. In some ways this theoretical divide is more important than others.

10.   See Hoekstra, "Hobbesian Equality," which argues that the idea of original equality was quite common in the Christian and Greek tradition, apart from Plato and Aristotle, and that Hobbes's use of equality should not be considered new or surprising. A

more thorough examination of this question needs to be done for several reasons. First, the Aristotelian position of natural hierarchy revived in importance in the Renaissance and remained a prominent position against which natural rights theorists defined themselves. Second, interpretations of Genesis in the church saw Eve as a secondary creation after Adam and thus placed women in a secondary role with respect to men. Third, the social form of the family and society was patriarchal in the medieval period, with the father and men having the dominant positions.

11.   For Aristotle's theory of slavery, see *Politics*, book 1, chaps. 3–7, and *Nicomachean Ethics*, book 7. See Hanke, *Aristotle and the American Indians* and *The Spanish Struggle for Justice*, for a discussion of how Aristotle was used to justify the enslavement of Indians in debates related to the Spanish conquest of Latin and South America. We return to this subject below.

12.   The position was implicit as well in the writings of King James I and was developed fully by Sir Robert Filmer in *Patriarcha*. See the discussion in Curran, "Hobbes on Equality," and the critics of Hobbes, such as Clarendon, who argued for natural hierarchy.

13.   Boyd, *Papers*, 317–18, Becker, *Declaration*, 212–13, Ellis, *Founding Brothers*, 81-119.

14.   On the three-fifths rule and the compromise over slavery, see Bowen, *Miracle*, 95; 200–204. Bowen notes that in exchange for the "three-fifths" rule and the agreement to limit the import tax on slaves to ten dollars a head, Southern states agreed that importation of slaves would cease in the year 1808. For discussions in the convention on those days, see Madison, *Notes*, 103, 409–411, 503–508. The slavery question flared up regularly around the question of representation, power among the states, and taxes on imports and exports of goods, among other contentious subjects of discussion.

15.   Madison, *Notes*, 411.

16.   I understand Dworkin, *Taking Rights Seriously*, 179–183, to be moving in this same direction in his analysis of Rawls's work, as when he points out that a commitment to equality is assumed already by Rawls's "original position." In Dworkin's reading, Rawls's original position is not empty of all commitments. Instead "equality" is one of the key commitments already granted but never justified in Rawls's concept of the original position. Further, Dworkin, 269–275, carves out equality as the real meaning or dimension of rights, interpreting what rights mean to be identical with equality. By contrast, I see rights as a concept that pulls in different directions than equality. Ultimately this is a language issue and not necessarily a disagreement in substance.

17.   Schwartz, *Liberty in America's Founding*.

18.   See, for example, Springborg, "Introduction," Hobbes's *Leviathan*, 1. See also Skinner, *Hobbes*, and Tuck, *Hobbes*.

19.   On the dating of *Leviathan*, see Tuck, *Hobbes*, 34; Skinner, *Hobbes*, 127.

20.   Hobbes, *Leviathan*, 13:1, 82.

21.   Hobbes was not the only royalist to start with human equality. John Locke, for example, notes that other royalists had started with the same assumption. For a

discussion on this surprising use of equality by Hobbes, see the contrasting discussions by Hoekstra "Hobbesian Equality," and Curran, "Hobbes on Equality."

There is an interesting debate in the secondary academic literature on whether Hobbes really endorsed and believed in equality or whether he considered it an instrumental or pragmatic concept that people should acknowledge for the creation of peace. While notions of equality had existed since antiquity, some royalists, such as Robert Filmer and Clarendon, attacked equality as a threatening doctrine and instead justified hierarchy and absolutism by identifying inequality embedded in nature.

Some interpreters argue that Hobbes was beginning with the assumption of his adversaries, such as the Levellers, and showing that even from those starting assumptions one ends in a view of absolutism. Hoekstra offers a similar instrumental view. He argues that Hobbes treated equality as a pragmatic idea that was necessary to achieve peace but did not really think of humans as equal and that his philosophy in fact presupposed that they were not equal either in nature or after they left nature. Curran questions this assumption, arguing that Hobbes really did embrace the idea of equality and was not just using the concept for instrumental purposes.

Understanding exactly what Hobbes meant by equality is not simple. In my view, Hobbes is not saying that humans are equal in nature in general, though he does note that experience and training tend to level differences in nature. Instead, Hobbes is saying that mortality is the great equalizer of human beings and that from the equal vulnerability to death, humans eventually discover through their reason the first law of nature, which is to seek peace, and thus to join a commonwealth. This realization that they are all equally vulnerable before death drives them to seek protection, to overcome their sense that they are better than one another, and to relinquish their rights in nature, which is the foundation of human society and ultimately morality. As Hobbes notes, in reality individuals think of themselves as superior to each other in many ways. But because they are mortal, they are led to understand that they must overlook their confidence in their own superiority and be willing to treat each other as equals to achieve peace.

In other words, it is *fear of death* that makes us the same and trivializes the other differences between us, such as strength, wit, and so forth. I thus understand Hobbes to be saying that it is our mortality that leads us to live in fear (i.e., we know we can die at the hands of anyone). From this fear of death, reason leads us to realize that we have to leave the state of nature. We trade our rights to everything in nature for more limited rights in political society to reduce or escape this fear of death. On that reading, I do not see Hobbes as using equality as simply a pragmatic concept (we need to acknowledge each other for peace), but as saying that it is our actual equality in mortality and our resulting fear of death that lead us to follow reason into a society in which we lose some of our freedoms and rights held in nature. Humans come to understand that they have a better chance of life and protection with loss of liberty (under the commonwealth) than fear of death, unlimited rights, and total liberty in the condition of mere nature.

22. Hobbes, *Leviathan*, 8:1, 45.

23. This kind of statement by Hobbes is interpreted by some as proving that Hobbes thought equality was a pragmatic or instrumental concept critical for peace, even though he recognized that people were not equal in all sorts of ways. See Hoekstra, "Hobbesian Equality."

24. Interpreting Hobbes as saying that death is an equalizer, I think, comes closer than the way that Hoekstra, "Hobbesian Equality," 76, which characterizes it as "they are equal because of their natural ability to kill one another."

25. Hobbes, *Leviathan*, 13:1, 82–83.

26. Hobbes treats the concept of "prudence" as "experience" and thus like skills that are developed. Elsewhere he says that animals have prudence, by which he means the kind of knowledge developed through experience and contrasted with knowledge developed by reasoning. He also sees no difference between the "prudence" of husband and wife that should justify the man having dominion over the children.

27. Hobbes does make an interesting exception in the case of science (i.e., philosophy), for which few have the capacity, in his view. Thus when he says there is a basic equality in faculties of mind, Hobbes seems to be referring to general adult capabilities, not those of the scientist or philosopher. But, unlike Aristotle, Hobbes does not make this difference a basis for one's role or status in society. The scientist deserves no special consideration for their differences in cognitive abilities.

28. Hobbes, *Leviathan*, 15:21, 102, in his comments on the ninth law of nature. [italics in original]

29. Ibid.

30. Ibid., 15:24, 103. [italics in original]

31. Ibid., 15:25, 103. [italics in original]

32. Ibid., 15:26, 103.

33. Hobbes, *Leviathan*, chap. 13:3, 83.

34. Locke, II § 2; Laslett, *Two Treatises*, 269. [italics in original]

35. Filmer, *Patriarcha*, 53; Laslett, *Filmer*, 11–20. Filmer's book was published during the Exclusion Crisis in the reign of King Charles II, in which the party led by Locke's patron, Lord Ashley, 1st Earl of Shaftesbury, tried to exclude King Charles's son from taking the throne. On the publication of *Patriarcha* in the midst of the Exclusion Crisis, see Laslett, *Filmer,* 33–35, and discussions also in Laslett, *Locke,* 46–66, and Dunn, *Political Thought,* 58–76.

36. Filmer, *Patriarcha*, 54.

37. Ibid.

38. As a contrast, see the view of Pufendorf, *Law of Nature and Nations*, book 4, chap. 4:4, 320, which said it is in vain to argue about the original ownership of Adam.

39. Gen. 1:28.

40. There is some evidence that Locke wrote his *First Treatise on Government*, which is a refutation of Filmer, after he had already written most of his *Second Treatise on Government*. For a discussion on the relationship of Locke's *Two Treatises* to the publication of

Filmer's *Patriarcha*, and to the argument of Filmer, see Laslett, *Locke*, 46–66 and 67–78, and Dunn, *Political Thought*, 58–76.

41.   As discussed previously in chapter 4, there is a fascinating debate in the secondary scholarly literature on Locke, trying to understand why he does not provide a philosophical foundation for his idea of natural law and, of course, the idea of liberty and equal rights that comes with it. For discussion of this point, see chap. 4, note 23.

42.   Locke's *Second Treatise* was written during what became known as the Exclusion Crisis, when there was fear that King Charles II would be succeeded by his Catholic brother, James Duke of York, who was also an advocate of the divine right of kings. Whigs led by Lord Shaftesbury, the patron of Locke, feared that a Catholic "popish" monarch would impose absolute rule, including control of religious freedom.

43.   See Locke, I § 4, § 67 ; and Laslett, *Two Treatises*, 150–190 [italics in original]. Locke is quoting Filmer, who mentions the same three individuals as vindicators of the divine right of kings but starting from the assumption of natural liberty and equality (Filmer, *Patriarcha*, 54). It is possible to read Locke's *First Treatise* as focused in large part on proving that revelation accepts the natural liberty and equality of humankind in opposition to Filmer's reading, whereas the *Second Treatise* assumes the equality is self-evident from reason.

44.   There is a complicated academic debate on why Locke does not refer to Hobbes and whether Hobbes is everywhere, always hovering in the background but unmentioned, or whether Locke simply had not read his work. The issue is complicated by the fact that Filmer and Pufendorf, both of whom Locke read and engaged with, both were reflecting on Hobbes. For discussions, contrast Laslett, *Two Treatises*, 67–79; Dunn, *Political Thought*, 77–83; Zuckert, *Natural Rights*, 218–220; Gough, *Political Philosophy*, 119–120. See Strauss, *Natural Right*, 221–251; Strauss sees Locke as more consistent with a position of Hobbes than do others.

45.   Locke, II § 6.

46.   See Zuckert, *Natural Rights*, 188, drawing the contrast between Locke and Grotius.

47.   Locke, II § 54. [italics in original]

48.   For versions and discussion, see Becker, *Declaration*, 198, and Maier, *American Scripture*, 132. See also Schwartz, *Liberty in America's Founding*, 66–82.

49.   Schwartz, *Liberty in America's Founding*.

50.   As noted earlier (this chapter, note 16), Dworkin, *Taking Rights Seriously*, argues that equality is assumed in the "original position" of Rawls's theory of justice. On that reading, Rawls's theory of justice is both assuming and trying to create equality as a foundation for the moral life by moving people into the original position where they do not know their future quality of life. In this way, Rawls attempts to rule out biases that arise from knowing who an individual will be or his or her own personal life histories.

51.   For discussion of what the state of nature meant to these writers, see, for example, Tuck, *Rights of War and Peace*, and Laslett, 98. See Locke II §§ 14–15, 100–105, where he explicitly takes up the objection whether there ever was a natural state of

humankind. Locke hedges his bets in all sorts of ways. On the one hand, he argues there is historical evidence of people starting new societies from the state of nature and also leaving societies and starting new ones (II §§ 102–103). He argues too that the origins of government in early societies are often buried in history and not always discoverable, and thus many political commonwealths may have started in a social contract out of the state of nature, though that history is lost (II § 101). While Locke thus wants to anchor his state of nature in real historical examples, Locke also dismisses those who argue from history (i.e., Filmer) and claims that "though at best an argument from what has been, to what should of right be, has no great force" (II § 103). Here Locke seems to be saying that the argument of natural rights does not need to rest on an actual historical account of how societies did come together but instead on how they should come together. Other modern thinkers such as Laslett, 93, and Rawls, *Theory of Liberty*, have followed this impulse and interpreted the social contract as a kind of ideal thought experiment rather than as a historical reality. Rawls's concept of an "original position," in fact, is an attempt to put people into a thought experiment where they imagine themselves in a kind of state of nature. Similarly, Hobbes, *Leviathan*, 13:11–12, 85, anticipates Locke, arguing that while there was never a time when everyone was in a state of nature, there are still "savage people in many places of America…[who] have no government at all; and live at this day in that brutish manner." He also notes that sovereign governments are in a state of nature or posture of "gladiators" toward one another, since they have no power to enforce a set of standards across more than their own national boundaries.

52.   My thinking here aligns with the insights of Dworkin and Rawls. As noted earlier, the concept of the "original position" in Rawls's *Theory of Justice* is analogous to an idealized state of nature. As noted earlier, Dworkin argues that Rawls's "original position" is not empty of all content and is already presupposing a commitment to the idea of equality through this thought experiment.

53.   Among the many ironies of history is the fact that early arguments that the monarch's power derived from the people, rather than from God, came from the representatives of the Catholic Church seeking to undermine the power of the secular authority and restore the prestige and power of the Church (McIlwain, "Introduction" to *Political Works of James I*, xvii–xix).

54.   I take this to be one of the central conclusions of Williams, "Idea of Equality."

55.   These assumptions are implicit in the work of Ayn Rand, Hayek, Friedman, Epstein, and others.

56.   See, for example, the essays in Ferber and Nelson, *Feminist Economics,* as well as the various theoretical challenges to this core economic assumption.

Chapter 6

1.   For example, see, Hobbes, *Leviathan*, 15:3, 96: "And therefore where there is no *own* [i.e., "mine"], that is, no propriety, there is no injustice; and where there is no coercive power erected, that is where there is no commonwealth, there is no propriety;

all men having right to all things [italics in original]." Pufendorf, *Law of Nature and Nations*, book 4, chap. 4:4.3, 364, for example, writes that "From what has been offer'd, "tis evident that as well positive Communion, as Propritey, does imply the Exclusion of others from the Thing thus said to be either common, or proper, and consequently doth presuppose more persons in the World than one." See, for example, Locke II § 36, "I dare boldly affirm, that the same *Rule of Propriety*, (*viz.*) that every man should have as much as he could make use of, would hold still in the World without straitning any body; since there is Land enough in the world to suffice double the inhabitants [italics in original]." Similarly Locke, I § 41, writes "that by this donation of God, *Adam* was made sole proprietor of the whole Earth, what will this be to his sovereignty? and how will it appear, that *propriety* in land gives a man power over the life of another [italics in original]?" I am quoting the Hollis edition here; the Laslett edition has "property" instead of "propriety."

2.   Richard Epstein, for example, a legal and political philosopher who embraces the "liberty-first" position, abandoned the notion of rights in favor of a utilitarian approach. A utilitarian or consequentialist position argues on the basis not of individual rights, but on the basis of the general impact and consequences of a policy or decision on the general welfare.

3.   Locke, II § 49. On the history of humankind in Locke's political philosophy, see Schochet, "Family and the Origins of State," 81–136. See also Strauss, *Natural Right*, 215ff. For a similar quote by Hobbes, see his comments on the state of nature and the brutish manner in which the savages of American live (Hobbes, *Leviathan*, 13:11–12, 85).

4.   Pufendorf, *Law of Nature and Nations*, book 4, chap. 3:2, 356. "It is therefore beyond Dispute, that Almighty God, inasmuch as he is the Maker and Preserver of all Things, doth likewise hold, as it were, an Originary and super-eminent Property over all, and they belong so strictly to Him, as that no one can pretend to the least Right in them, without his permission and consent."

5.   There are many important books making this argument including, among others, Hawken et al., *Natural Capitalism*, and Hawken, *Ecology of Commerce*.

6.   See, for example, Locke, I § 86 and II § 25 and more below.

7.   Throughout my book, I generally follow the translation of the King James Version (KJV), but in this case it has a wording that is difficult to understand or is a mistake. The KJV reads: "And God blessed them, and God said unto them, Be fruitful, and multiply, and replenish the earth, and subdue it: and have dominion over the fish of the sea, and over the fowl of the air, and over every living thing that moveth upon the earth." And God said, Behold, I have given you every herb bearing seed, which *is* upon the face of all the earth, and every tree, in the which *is* [sic] the fruit of a tree yielding seed; to you it shall be for meat. (Gen. 1:.28–29). See http://www.kingjamesbibleonline. org/Genesis-Chapter-1/. Most seventeenth-century philosophers such as Locke could read the original Hebrew.

8.   See Strauss, *Natural Right*, 215–217, for an insightful and interesting discussion of the challenge of linking Locke's state of nature with the biblical account. Strauss notes that Locke assumes people can eat meat in the state of nature, but the biblical account assumes people can eat meat only after the dispensation to Noah. Therefore, Strauss argues, Locke's state of nature cannot be identical with the pre-Fall biblical state. By contrast, Waldron, *Right to Private Property*, 165, sees Locke as embracing the conception of a fall in his theory of property and the fall from a natural state.

9.   Locke, II § 25. See also Locke, I § 86, 87. [italics in original]

10.   See Daly, "Absolute Monarchy," for a discussion on how the claim of divine right of kings did not always entail claims of absolutism for the kings who understood themselves to be subject to the laws of the kingdom.

11.   See Locke, I §§ 86–87, where he explains his position with respect to Adam and Adam's children. Hobbes, *Leviathan*, 13:3, 83, makes a similar assumption when he claims that all people have a right to everything in the state of nature, but never justifies this position with respect to scripture.

12.   See Tully, *A Discourse*, 61, quoting Macpherson, *Democratic Theory*, 123–5, who calls these "inclusive rights." Pufendorf, *Law of Nature and Nations*, book 4, chap. 4:2, 362, originally differentiated between what he called "negative" or "positive" communion. Positive communion was his term for "tenants in common."

13.   See, for example, Pufendorf, *Law of Nature and Nations*, book 4, chap. 4:2, 362 where he calls this "negative" communion. For a discussion, see also Tully, *A Discourse on Property*, 61ff, and Waldron, *Right to Private Property*, 153ff.

14.   The Hebrew "Adam" has all the same ambiguities and possible masculine biases as "Man." It is also possible in fact to read Genesis 1 as speaking about the creation of a human being who is "pregender" and that the distinction of male and female is created only when the being is split in half in Genesis 2. For a discussion, see Phyllis Trible, *God and the Rhetoric of Sexuality*, 72–143.

15.   The Hebrew verbs in the "Be fruitful and multiply" passage are also conjugated in the plural and agree with the plural pronoun "them."

16.   See Trible, *God and the Rhetoric of Sexuality*, 72–143. There is an extensive academic and popular literature on the meaning of Genesis 1:26–28, including what it means to be made in the image of God, whether God had a human form, or whether the passage is metaphorical. I have discussed some of this literature in *God's Phallus and Other Problems for Men and Monotheism*.

17.   The injunction to be fruitful and multiply suggests that the writer assumed the differentiation of the sexes had already taken place and that Adam was understood as "humankind," inclusive of male and female.

18.   Locke, II § 25; Laslett, *Two Treatises*, 286. [italics in original]

19.   See Pufendorf, *Law of Nature and Nations*, book 4, chap. 4:1, 362 which argues it ""tis an Idle Question, Whether the Property of Things arise from Nature, or from Institution? Since we have plain evidence that it proceeds from the Imposition of Men; and that the Natural Substance of Things suffers no alteration, whether Property be

added to them or taken from them." See also book 4, chap 4:4, 364. See also Grotius, *Rights of War and Peace*, book 1, chap. 2:2.2, 63, which argues that "what we call *Property* had never been introduced" in nature and that anyone could "have made use of Things that were then in common, and to have consumed them, as far as Nature required, had been the Right of the first Possessor [italics in original]." Similarly, Hobbes, *Leviathan*, Chap 15:3, 96, "And therefore where there is no *own*, that is, no propriety, there is no injustice; and where there is no coercive power erected, that is, where there is no commonwealth, there is no propriety; all men having right to all things: therefore where there is no commonwealth, there nothing is unjust."

20.   Grotius, *The Rights of War and Peace*, book 1, chap. 1:10.4 and 10.7, 54–55 and chap. 2:3, 63, makes this explicit, indicating that in nature people had a right to protect their "lives, limbs, and liberties" as part of the right to self-preservation but not a right to property. By contrast, for Hobbes, *Leviathan*, 14:4, 86–87, life, liberty, and property have the same status in nature. Every person has a right to everything, and there are no laws protecting life, liberty, or property in nature.

21.   See, for example, Grotius, *Rights of War and Peace*, book 2, chap. 2:2 and 2:4, 19–20. See also Hobbes, *Leviathan*, 13:11, 85, "It may peradventure be thought, there was never such a time, nor condition of war as this;* and I believe it was never generally so, over all the world: but there are many places, where they live so now. For the savage people in many places of America, except [accept] the government of small families, the concord whereof dependeth on natural lust, have no government of all; and live at this day in that brutish manner, as I said before." [asterisk represents footnote in original]

22.   See Grotius, ibid. See also Hobbes, *Leviathan*, 13:13, 85, and 15:3, 95–6.

23.   See Pufendorf, *Law of Nature and Nations*, book 4, chap. 4:5, 366, quoting from the writings of Lambert van Velthuysen, "But forasmuch as all Human Institutions and Ordinances are made with exception of extreme Necessity, therefore when so desperate a Case happens, the primitive Right to all things revives: Because, in the Common Agreement for the Divisions of Things, every one is suppos'd to have renounc'd his Right to those Things which were alloted to other with this Reserve and Restriction, Unless I am unable otherwise to compass my own Preservation. My Calamity doth not give me a Right to those things, to which I had none before; but the extremity of my Danger makes that Condition cease, under which I gave up my first Right."

24.   Lambert van Velthuysen (1622–1685) quoted in Pufendorf, *Law of Nature and Nations*, book IV, chap. 4:5, 366. On the significance of Velthuysen, see discussion in Blom, *Rise of Naturalism*, 104ff.

25.   Pufendorf, *Law of Nature and Nations*, book 4, chap. 4:6, 367.

26.   Hobbes, *Leviathan*, 13:3, 83, emphasizes equality as the source of fear of death, which leads to war in nature. Contrast with Grotius, *Rights of War and Peace*, book 2, chap. 2:3, 20, who emphasizes humans leaving a primitive state and weaves it closely into the biblical story of the Fall of Adam and Eve and the inclination for pleasure and vice among their descendants, thus associating this development with the development

of culture and the arts. Pufendorf, *Law of Nature and Nations*, book 4, chap. 4:6, 332, focuses on property as reducing human conflict.

27.   On gradual agreement to property, Pufendorf, *Law of Nature and Nations*, book 4, chap. 4:6, 367.

28.   See, for example, Pufendorf, ibid., book 4, chap. 6, 367.

29.   See, for example, Grotius, *Rights of War and Peace*, book 2, chap. 2:2.5, 21, on the tacit agreement to treat seizure or first possession as the mechanism of ownership. See Pufendorf, *Law of Nature and Nations*, book 4, chap. 4:6, 367, for a longer discussion of "first occupancy," in which he also emphasizes enclosing and developing the land through labor as one "tills and manuers it." As we shall see later, this emphasis on ownership being associated with "improving the land" becomes one of the justifications for taking the lands of American Indians, whom Europeans mistakenly characterized as being strictly nomadic and lacking agricultural techniques and any notions of property.

30.   Pufendorf, *Law of Nature and Nations*, book 4, chap. 4:4, 364.

31.   Hobbes, *Leviathan*, 15:3, 96: "And therefore where there is no *own*, that is, no propriety, there is no injustice; and where there is no coercive power erected, that is where there is no commonwealth, there is no propriety; all men having right to all things."

32.   See, for example, Pufendorf, *Law of Nature and Nations*, book 4, chap 4:6, 322.

33.   Pufendorf, ibid., book 4, chap. 4:7, 367–368, notes that the proposition "that the settling distinct properties turn'd to the real Benefit and Advantage for men" when people had grown numerous is illustrated by the arguments of Aristotle: "But now upon the introducing of Property, all these Complaints are silenc'd; every one grows more Industrious in improving his peculiar Portion; and Matter and Occasion is supplied for the Exercise of Liberality and Beneficence towards others." Hegel would take up a similar line of thinking and develop it. See Waldman, *Right to Private Property*, 343–389, for a discussion.

34.   I am in agreement with the general reading of Waldron, *Right to Private Property*, 153, that Locke's intent is to make property a natural right, and I disagree with the view of Tully, *A Discourse on Property*, 98, which sees Locke taking a conventionalist view similar to Pufendorf.

It is important to distinguish the view that property is a right self-evident in nature itself from the view that it is in accord with reason and natural law but implemented by human beings as part of creating human society itself. The view that property was part of natural law was not new with Locke. Pufendorf, *Law of Nature and Nations*, book 4, chap. 4:4, 365, for example, discusses the view of other authors who believe property rights were given in nature by God and that the prohibition of stealing in the Decalogue shows that property was already given by God, and thus a law of nature.

35.   Gough, *Political Philosophy*, 92–93, sees Locke's "labor theory" of property becoming a commonplace of economic theory and being taken up and assumed by Adam Smith.

36.   Locke, II § 25 and I § 86.

37.   Locke, II § 26. [italics in original]

38.   See Locke, I § 29, where he interprets Gen. 1:28 as meaning the natural world was given in common to all mankind, and II § 26, 287, where he calls the first humans "Tenants in common." I here agree with the reading of Waldron, *Right to Private Property*, 153. Gough, *Political Philosophy*, 80, misunderstands Locke, assuming Locke thought humans had no common ownership in the beginning (i.e., "negative rights"). Gough, ibid., writes, "not that there was any positive communism or common ownership of property, but simply that nothing belonged to anyone in particular (just as nobody today owns the air or the sea)."

But if no one had any rights in anything in nature, there would be no issue in Locke's mind in appropriating something like acorns from nature. If no one had any rights, anyone could take what he or she wanted. Yet Locke specifically says that there must be a mechanism to make acorns "mine." Locke would not see this as a problem unless everyone was "tenants in common" and each had rights in everything. It is being tenants in common that generates the Lockean puzzle of how something can become mine out of something that is ours. Since everyone has rights in everything, I have no right to take it out of nature without their approval. Gough, 86, seems to miss this point again even when he quotes Locke as saying that if a person takes more than he can use, "it is more than his share, and belongs to others" (II § 31 and 37). Here Gough sees the predominant focus of Locke on the "common right of all...to preservation," meaning that taking more than I can use undermines the welfare of the species in general. But what Locke seems to mean is that I can't take more than I need from what is common, because then it is stealing from what belongs to all, and I am violating the rights of others.

39.   Grotius, *Rights of War and Peace*, book 2, chap. 3: 7–11, 33–35, was innovative early in the century in arguing that the seas belonged to no country. This partly justified the expansion of the East Indian Trading Company, to whom Grotius was an adviser. For a discussion of this idea and its development in Grotius, see Tuck, "Introduction," in *Rights of War and Peace*, 17.

40.   Gough, *Political Philosophy*, 92. For a longer discussion and analysis of what Locke meant, see Waldman, *Right to Private Property*, 137–251, and Tully, *Discourse on Property*, 108ff.

41.   Locke, II § 27. [italics in original]

42.   Locke, II § 47.

43.   Locke, II § 6. In his *Essay*, Locke spends a great deal of time arguing that the idea of God is not innate, and that we can derive a divine law from the idea of God that is discovered by reason, but he does not link natural rights to the idea that humans are God's workmanship. For examples, see Locke, *Essay*, book 2, chap. 28:8, 308. This is another of the reasons why the Locke of the *Essay* and the Locke of the *Two Treatises* seem inconsistent.

44.   Locke, II § 23.

45.   See Waldman, *Right to Private Property*, 158–161, for a thorough analysis of what Locke may have meant and who sees this as one possible interpretation, though he rejects it on philosophical grounds. For a contrasting interpretation, see Zuckert, *Natural Rights*, 220ff and 239ff.

46.   Locke, II § 35.

47.   Locke, I § 86.

48.   There are some interesting discussions in the secondary literature that discuss this view of property that Locke puts forward. It may seem that the appeal to the "strong desire" or instinct here contradicts his view in his *Essay* that there are no innate ideas. But see Laslett, *Two Treatises*, 205, and notes to 19–20. As I read him, Locke in his *Two Treatises* still sees reason as the means of discovering the right of property when humans reflect on their instinct to preservation. Thus reason intervenes as the means by which humans come to understand and interpret their instinct to survive. There is also an interesting interpretive question of how Locke understood God's decision in Genesis to forbid eating animals until after the flood. The right to eat creatures as opposed to have dominion over them was a significant topic of discussion for Pufendorf that Locke passes over in a couple of sentences. It is not clear here how Locke would explain why the first humans were forbidden to eat animals and how his thinking about reason discovering the right to own animals can be meshed with the biblical account. Stauss, *Natural Right and History*, 215ff, discusses the tension between Locke's view and the biblical story.

49.   Locke, II § 25, 26, 30; I § 86.

50.   Hobbes and others did not see the implication of equality this way. But Filmer saw how the concept of natural liberty and equality could be used to undermine royal authority and the natural hierarchy in patriarchal traditions. The Levellers in the English Civil Wars were among those who took the idea of natural liberty and equality to its furthest conclusions. Hobbes may in fact have been using the argument of the Levellers against them in adopting equality as the foundation of his system that ended in authoritarian rule. Locke comes closest to adopting the Leveller position, though he limits the conclusions when it comes to property.

51.   There are many fine deep philosophical analyses and critiques of Locke's conception of property and its limitations as well as the notion of property itself. I have benefited from Tully, *Discourse on Property*, Waldman, *Right to Private Property*, Gough, *Political Philosophy*, among others.

52.   See Pufendorf, *Law of Nature and Nations*, book 4, chap. 5:2–3, 379, which in a somewhat convoluted set of paragraphs distinguishes the earth from air, light, water. Air, light, water, and wind are inexhaustible and thus should not be subdivided. Pufendorf argues that the earth is treated differently as an exemption even though it is like these other natural phenomena. "But that a thing lying in common to Mankind, and sufficient for the promiscuous Use of all, should be shared out into distinct Parts, is certainly repugnant to Reason. The Earth is of such a magnitude, as to serve the Occasions of all People in all Uses to which they can apply it; yet it would not thus serve them,

were it possess'd, without Division, by so vast Bodies of Inhabitants as it now contains: Because it could never afford them Sustenance, unless manur'd and improv'd. Therefore there is plainly this particular Reason, why the extent of the Earth should not hinder its being divided; and yet the same Reason would make the division of the Ocean appear a ridiculous Absurdity."

53.   Locke, II § 33 [italics in original]. See also II § 36 and I § 33.

54.   E. A. Wrigley, et al., *The Population History of England*, and Hatcher, *Plague, Population*.

55.   Locke, II § 36.

56.   Locke, II § 40, Laslett, *Two Treatises*, 296.

57.   Locke, II § 41. [italics in original]

58.   Ibid.

59.   Locke, II § 32, Laslett, *Two Treatises*, 291.

60.   This point is discussed below in chapters 7 and 8.

61.   See, similarly, Nozick, *Anarchy*, 174–177, and also Waldron, *Right to Property*, on this point.

62.   Locke, II §§ 30–31.

63.   See Waldron, *Right to Private Property*, 190, which raises a similar question.

64.   Locke, II § 43, Laslett, *Two Treatises*, 298. [italics in original]

65.   See chapter 9 for a discussion of the assumptions of modern economic theory. On Locke's role in the development of early modern economic theory and his impulse to see economics as functioning by natural value and natural principles, and not inherent value, see Letwin, *Origins*, 158–195, particularly on the British controversy over lessening interest rates to 4 percent and the recoinage controversy. On Locke's labor theory anticipating Adam Smith's, see Gough, *Political Philosophy*, 93.

66.   Nozick, 175, quoted in Waldron, *Right to Private Property*, 190, asks something similar when he poses the question, "should one's entitlement extend to the whole object rather than just to the added value?" Nozick draws different conclusions from this question than do I.

67.   I see Nozick, *Anarchy*, 174ff, posing the same line of critique here against Locke's theory of labor, though coming to very different conclusions ultimately.

68.   Locke (I § 92) says property by definition includes the right to "destroy the thing, that he has property in by his use of it, where need requires." See Gough, *Political Philosophy*, 86, which discusses this position of Locke and sees it as evidence of the "communal" or "social" tendency of this thought.

69.   Locke, II § 31 [italics in original] and again in II § 51.

70.   This position differentiates Locke from the view of Hobbes in which people in the state of nature competed for the same goods and thus were led to seek peace in part out of the competition for goods.

71.   See Locke, II § 36, and Laslett, 293 [italics in original]. See also II § 47. See also II §§ 107–108, where Locke talks about the early history of mankind and early forms of government and the Indians. "The equality of a simple poor way of liveing confineing their desires within the narrow bounds of each mans smal propertie made few

controversies and so no need of many laws to decide them." For a discussion of Locke's underlying understanding of the transition from simple to more complex societies, and the corresponding complexity in social structure, see Schochet, "Family and Origins of State."

72.   See Locke, I § 86 and II § 25.

73.   Locke does see some basic inequality arising directly from the nature of labor itself, but these inequalities are amplified by money. "And as different degrees of Industry were apt to give Men Possessions in different Proportions, so this *Invention of Money* gave them the opportunity to continue and enlarge them" (Locke, II § 47, Laslett, *Two Treatises*, 301).

74.   Why humans desire more than they need is not a question that Locke reflected upon, though earlier rights thinkers such as Pufendorf spend a great deal of time discussing God's intention in making humans the way they are. Locke simply takes for granted that this is how people are without asking the theological question of why God made humans this way or whether this was related to a "fall from grace." In this sense, Locke, like Hobbes (but in contrast to Pufendorf), sidesteps the theological questions that occupied the theological tradition and simply started with assumptions about human nature itself.

75.   Macpherson, *Possessive Individualism*, 194–257.

76.   Waldron, *Right to Private Property*, 165, also arrives at a similar conclusion.

77.   I take it that this is in part the purpose of Rawls's conception of the "original position." As noted earlier, Dworkin, *Taking Rights Seriously*, 179–183 argues that Rawls's concept of the original position begins already by assuming the principle of equality, which is what makes the original position intelligible. It is beyond the present essay, but one can argue that Rawls gives in too easily to the arguments that market efficiency overrides the impulse to equality.

78.   Locke, II § 7, § 8, and § 11 [italics in original]. See also II § 135 for mention of preservation of humankind in general. On this "social" dimension of Locke's theory, see Gough, *Political Philosophy*, 22–25, and Kendall, *Majority Rule*, which carried this interpretation to its logical interpretation.

Chapter 7

1.   Locke, II § 124 and § 134. [italics in original]

2.   Ibid., II § 123. [italics in original]

3.   Ibid., II § 138. [italics in original]

4.   See Hobbes, *Leviathan*, 13:3-4, 83; Locke (II § 123) describes enjoyment of property as unsafe and the state of nature as full of fears and continual dangers, and he (ibid., 137) emphasizes the purpose of government as the protection of property as well as peace and quiet. See also II § 127. Locke (II § 21) also says in very Hobbes-like language that "To avoid this State of War…is one great reason *of Mens putting themselves into Society and quitting the State of Nature.*" See also II § 94, where Locke refers to leaving the

state of nature for safety and security, and II § 101, where he refers to "inconveniences of that condition [state of nature], and the love, and want of Society" that drove people together. For an interesting discussion and summary of Locke's understanding of the state of nature and the tensions in his view, see Simmons, "Locke's State of Nature."

5.   Locke, II § 137. For Hobbes, there was no law in nature anyway and therefore no justice prior to society.

6.   Locke, II § 77. For accounts of what Locke meant by the state of nature, see for example, Simmons, "Locke's State of Nature," and Ashcraft, "Political Philosophy."

7.   See Locke, II §§ 123, 127, 137, where he assumes the development of political societies out of earlier human social groupings is almost inevitable.

8.   If asked why humans were created by God to live in a fearful state of nature, the more theologically oriented, such as Pufendorf, would have said that humans were a distinctive animal just below the angels and thus given free will. And it was the ability to choose good versus evil that distinguished humans from animals. This theological question is one that neither Hobbes nor Locke takes up, in contrast to Pufendorf, who still operates in a more theological mode of thinking.

9.   The boundaries of the states, according to Locke, would thus be worked out in similar ways to the boundaries of property between individuals. See, for example, Locke, II § 45, in his discussion of property, where he reflects on how early commonwealths and political groupings were extensions of individual property. Locke envisions it as a two-step contract, where individuals first contract together to form a political entity that now has rights to regulate the territory defined by their individual properties, and then the national entities contract with each other to define and recognize their boundaries. Here is Locke: "The several *Communities* settled the Bounds of their distinct Territories, and by Laws within themselves, regulated the Properties of the private Men of their Society, and so, *by Compact* and Agreement, *settled the Property* which Labour and Industry began; and the Leagues that have been made between several States and Kingdoms, either expressly or tacitly disowning all Claim and Right to the Land in the others Possession, have, by common Consent, given up their Pretences to their natural common Right, which originally they had to those Countries, and so have, by *positive agreement*, *settled a Property* amongst themselves, in distinct parts and parcels of the Earth." [italics in original]

Locke seems to be saying here that states or kingdoms first arise around individuals who acquired property through labor. They then go through a process of consenting to the boundaries of each other's territory. He thus envisions the agreements of states about what territories they oversee to follow after individuals already have their own properties. The dispute over boundaries of states is thus independent from a prior right of individuals to land for which they labored.

10.   See, for example, Grotius, *Rights of War and Peace*, book 2, chap. 2:4, 22.

11.   See Locke, II §§ 106–107 and §§ 71–76, and discussion in Schochet, "Family and Origins of State."

12.   Locke, II § 121. "But since the Government has a direct Jurisdiction only over the land, and reaches the Possessor of it (before he has actually incorporated himself in the society) only as he dwells upon, and enjoys that: *The Obligation* any one is under, by virtue of such Enjoyment, to *submit to the government, begins and ends with the Enjoyment* [of the land]; so that whenever the Owner, who has given nothing but a *tacit Consent* to the government, will, by Donation, Sale or otherwise, quit the said Possession, he is at liberty to go and incorporate himself into any other Commonwealth; or to agree with others to begin a new one, in *vacuis locis*, in any part of the World, they can find free and unpossessed." [italics in original]

13.   Locke, II §§ 8, 121, and 119. For discussion, see Schwartz, *Liberty in American Founding*, 141.

14.   This was a standard critique of Locke by, for example, Hume, "The Original Contract," and others. For Locke's reflections on the question whether there ever was a state of nature and a contract that created a nation, see Locke, II §§ 14–15, 100–105. See Hobbes, *Leviathan*, 13:11, 85 where he asks the same question. Hobbes takes for granted a war in the state of nature until hostilities cease through a social contract. Thus he does not have the same dilemma in his theory as does Locke, since he never assumes there is a right to property until the commonwealth comes into existence.

15.   Rawls argues that in the original position, people would agree to the principle of fairness, namely, that laws must work to the absolute benefit of the worst-off members of society. But what if the people in the original position could know or become suspicious that natural resources might be depleted? If they asked that question and concluded that it was feasible resources could be depleted, and they did not know in what time period they would live or in what country, they reasonably would not have agreed to rules of private property at all, at least in the form we now know them.

16.   Locke, II § 175, feels this contradiction and tries to resolve it in his last chapter. He writes, "Though Governments can originally have no other Rise than that before mentioned [i.e., consent], nor *Polities* be *founded* on any thing but *the Consent of the People*; yet such has been the Disorders Ambition has fill'd the World with, that in the noise of War, which makes so great a part of the History of Mankind, this *Consent* is little taken notice of: And therefore many have mistaken the force of Arms, for the consent of the People; and reckon Conquest as one of the Originals of Government. But *Conquest* is as far from setting up any Government, as demolishing an House is from building a new one in the place. Indeed it often makes way for a new Frame of a Common-wealth, by destroying the former; but, without the Consent of the people, can never erect a new one [italics in original]." In this passage, Locke tries to reconcile his theory of consent with the actual historical nature of conquest and war. He argues that it is always consent that is the legitimate, rightful basis of government, even if it is not the historical basis of government. But Locke does not take up the question that if war and conquest undermine or disturb the rightful relationships of individuals to their property, then consent after the fact can't be based on a prior rightful allocation of property by the labor theory of property. Property is no longer matched rightfully to individuals, and

therefore individuals who consent to the state bring with them properties that they do not completely own.

17.   See note 4 above.

18.   See Locke, who makes this argument. Locke reflects on the modern just-war tradition that grew out of earlier Catholic arguments about what constitutes a just war. In the modern period, the concept of just war was developed by Grotius, who argued that some wars between nations were just. Locke's position diverges dramatically from Grotius. Grotius (*Rights of War and Peace*, book 1, chap. 2:4, 189, and book 3, chap. 2:8) had argued that a just war would entitle the conqueror to enslave the population, take their lands and property, and institute government or sovereignty.

Locke, by contrast, in one of the most difficult and convoluted parts of his *Second Treatise*, argues that if a people are conquered, whether in a just or unjust war, the state becomes legitimate only if the people who are conquered consent to the new entity. Thus consent in Locke's view remains the criterion of a rightful state, whether or not the war is just. Locke distinguishes a just from an unjust war based on who is the aggressor. The aggressor is always unjust, and if the aggressor wins, then even consent cannot make the state legitimate (II § 176). If the war was just, and those who were attacked won, then the sovereign has absolute authority over those who fought against him and has the right to enslave them. But even in this case the sovereign's power is only over those who fought and not their properties, wives, or children (II § 180). For a discussion of Locke's position, see Moseley, "Political Philosophy of John Locke."

19.   Locke tries to make this argument about consent throughout II §§ 175–196. While Locke denies the right of conquest, he doesn't deal with or recognize the deeper problem with "consent." A postwar situation still involves the distortion of property rights from the way they should have been aligned based on the natural right of labor. There is no way to reconstruct the right alignment of property rights and labor. But Locke does not reflect on this problem. Hobbes, for his part, doesn't have this conceptual problem that faces Locke because he assumes that people have unlimited rights in nature, and thus stealing and conquest are right and just in some sense in nature. There is no "unjust" distribution of property caused by war and theft, at least in nature. The political state is the end of that state of war. And political states are still in a state of war with each other until they too conclude a treaty. The equality in nature as conceptualized by Hobbes does not expect a fair allocation of property, but fairness and equity arise only after the state is formed.

20.   Nozick, *Anarchy*.

21.   I see this question as intersecting with the interesting thinking in what has come to be called "postcolonial" theorizing.

22.   Locke, II § 192. [italics in original]

23.   In this sense, Hobbes's theory, in contrast to Locke's, seems to recognize more fully the actual messiness of history and the fact that the human species always had the

tendency to violence. In Hobbes's view, there was no just distribution of property until the state was created. Justice is thus limited to within the state. The problem, then, is that Hobbes never envisions a solution between states themselves. There is no sovereign power beyond the state and thus no right beyond that of the state, though states may go through the same process as individuals in confronting each other in a state of war and eventually come to the decision to pursue peace.

24.   Schwartz, *Liberty in America's Founding*.

25.   See, for example, Stannard, *American Holocaust*; Williams, *American Indian*; Bergreen, *Columbus*; Banner, *How Indians Lost Land*.

26.   See prior note on discussions of the conquest. I have written about this question from another perspective in Schwartz, *Liberty in America's Founding*.

27.   Though Locke does not come to see the significance of this conclusion, it is implied by his very claim that conquest of an aggressor never justifies new government or the taking of property.

28.   On Jefferson's views, see Schwartz, *Liberty in America's Founding*, 163–233.

29.   See Stannard, *American Holocaust*, and Williams, *American Indian*, 119–125. On the comparison of British and Spanish conquests, see also Elliot, *Empires of the Atlantic*.

30.   In my earlier work, Schwartz, *Liberty in America's Founding*, 166–67, I discuss the relationship of Jefferson's natural rights understanding to Locke's. On this point, Jefferson can be seen to be moving away from Locke, who argued that people cannot leave a state once they explicitly consent to become citizens.

31.   Jefferson, *A Summary View*, in Boyd, *Papers*, 1, 122. See my discussion in Schwartz, *Liberty in America's Founding*, 39, and a review of the literature there.

32.   Jefferson, ibid., 133.

33.   See my discussion in *Liberty in America's Founding*, 237–307. While in many other ways Jefferson seems to rely on or align with Locke's view of rights, he passes over in silence in this context Locke's argument (II § 175–196) that conquest does not entitle conquerors, even in a just war, to the property of the vanquished. Jefferson would have known, however, that other political philosophers did think conquest was a foundation of right. As we shall see, Jefferson later will express the view that the Indians' land was purchased from them, though he suppressed his reservations about the legitimacy of that position (Banner, *How the Indians*, 50).

34.   James Wilson, "*Considerations*," 34, and discussion in Schwartz, *Liberty in America's Founding*, 40–41.

35.   Taylor, *Papers of John Adams*, 317.

36.   This view had been voiced earlier by some settlers throughout the colonial period, though it was not universally accepted in the colonies. See Banner, *How the Indians Lost Their Land,* for a discussion of the differing views on this topic and how in practice the colonies often purchased land from the Indians, recognizing native ownership.

37.   Taylor, *Papers of John Adams*, 317.

38.   See Schwartz, *Liberty in America's Founding*, 38–47, 61–65, for a discussion of how the question of the right to lands is essentially unanswered and hidden in the Declaration of Independence.

39.   Others have discussed this paradox in the founding period, including Maier, *American Scripture*, 191–201; Bowen, *Miracle at Philadelphia*, 197–204; and Ellis, *Founding Brothers*, 81–119.

40.   Grotius, *Rights of War and Peace*, book 2, chap. 20:40.4, 239. Jefferson likely would have been familiar with Grotius's theory since he had read Samuel Pufendorf, whose own theory of rights was influenced by and provided a commentary on Grotius. For a discussion of the ideas of conquest in the humanist and scholastic traditions prior to Grotius, see Tuck, *Rights of War*, 47–77, and for a discussion of Grotius's views, see ibid., 78–108.

41.   Grotius, ibid., book 2, chap. 20, 48:1, 246. See Tuck, *Rights of War*, 103.

42.   Ibid., book 2, chap. 20:40.3, 239; Tuck, *Rights of War*, 103.

43.   Ibid., book 2, chapter 3:8, 96. [italics in original]

44.   Ibid., book 3, chap. 8:3, 73; book 2, chap. 2:40.1 and 40.3, 238–9. See also Tuck, "Introduction," *Rights of War and Peace*, 16–17.

45.   Ibid., book 8, chap. 6:6, 227. [italics in original]

46.   Locke, II §§ 14, 36, 37, 41, 43; Grotius, *Rights of War and Peace*, book 2, chap. 2: 2.1, 19.

47.   Grotius, ibid., book 2, chap. 2.7, 29, writes, "And if there be any waste or barren Land within our Dominions, that also is to be given to Strangers, at their Request, or may be lawfully possessed by them, because whatever remains uncultivated, is not to be esteemed a Property, only so far as concerns Jurisdiction, which always continues the Right of the antient People."

48.   See chap. 5, note 70 and related discussion.

49.   Grotius, *Rights of War and Peace*, book 2, chap. 2:2.1, 19. [italics in original]

50.   Locke, II § 49. On Locke's discussion of whether there were ever people in a state of nature, see also II §§ 14, 41, 100–102, and his references to peoples of the Americas and Indians in those contexts. See also his allusion to Indians in his discussions of the origins of property, II § 30.

51.   Locke, II § 36 and my discussion earlier (chapter 6) on Locke's assumption that resources and land are limitless.

52.   Locke, II § 37 and see also II § 37; Laslett, *Two Treatises*, 294.

53.   Locke, II § 34, [italics in original] see also II § 35. For discussion of this theme of taking possession of open wilderness, see Tuck, *Rights of War*, 120–126.

54.   Vattel, *Law of Nations*, book 1, chap. 17 § 209, 100. Originally written in French in 1758, the book was translated into English in 1759. James Otis, for example, mentions Vattel in *The Rights of the British Colonies* (July 1764).

55.   See Stannard, *American Holocaust*, for a lengthy argument on this point. But even if "holocaust" were not used, it is clear that it was a conquest.

56. Williams, *American Indian*, 44.

57. Ibid., 14.

58. Ibid., 79.

59. See Williams, *American Indian*; Stannard, *American Holocaust*.

60. Williams, ibid., 81–85.

61. Eilberg-*Schwartz, The Savage in Judaism*, 32–37.

62. See especially Stannard, *American Holocaust*.

63. Williams, *American Indian*, 99.

64. For discussions of discovery as the means of taking ownership, see Banner, *How the Indians*, chap. 1; Williams, *American Indian*, 78; Stannard, *American Holocaust*, 64–65; Robertson, *Conquest by Law*.

65. Robertson, *Conquest by Law*.

66. See Williams, *American India*n, 96–108, on this point.

67. Ibid., 104.

68. Hanke, *Aristotle and the American Indians*, 17.

69. Ibid., 54.

70. Ibid., 38.

71. Ibid., 74–95.

72. The question of similarities and differences between the Spanish and British conquests is an interesting and complex one and is discussed by Williams, *American Indian*, 119–225, and Elliot, *Empires*.

73. Vespucci, like Columbus, was Italian but was financed by Spain and Portugal. For a discussion of the transmission and translation of earlier Spanish ideas into English translations, see Williams, *American Indian*, 121–191.

74. On the conquest of the Irish being a model for conquest of the Indians, see Williams, *American Indian*, 140ff.

75. Ibid., 211.

76. Ibid. On the Indians' abilities with agriculture in general and the permanence of many of their settlements, see the discussion in Stannard, *American Holocaust*, 3–54, and Banner, *How the Indians*, 10–48.

77. Banner, ibid., 6–9, argues that property and sovereignty are separate concepts. At the level of "sovereignty," England and the settlers viewed the American land as unoccupied, meaning that England could justify its government of the territory, even though it was recognized that the property was owned by Indians. I find Banner's distinction of sovereignty from ownership confusing, since sovereignty of a commonwealth could only be applied to territory rightfully occupied by a people who comprised a society under that sovereign.

78. Banner, *How the Indians*, 13.

79. Ibid., 14.

80. Banner, *How the Indians*, offers a brilliant exposition of this issue.

81. Robertson, *Conquest by Law*.

82.   Jefferson, *Notes on Virginia*, 497; see Banner, *How the Indians*, 50, on Jefferson's deleted note.

Chapter 8

1.   Locke, II § 123.

2.   Hobbes, *Leviathan*, 13:3-4, 83; Locke, II §§ 21, 94, 101, 123, 137, and see the longer summary above in chapter 7, note 4.

3.   Our position on what the state or government should be and how it should act is thus tied deeply into and rests upon prior notions about our rights and property that were articulated in the early modern period. Indeed, in many ways the modern understanding of the state is really nothing more than an extension or expansion of the core ideas of individual rights and property that serve as its conceptual foundation. Since we have already questioned both the self-evidence of natural rights and the modern understanding of property that came with it, it stands to reason that the very conception of the state has to come under some serious scrutiny too.

4.   In "The Original Contract," for example, David Hume calls the notion of a social contract a political myth analogous to the myth of divine right of kings.

5.   The idea that states were founded on conquest, and not on consent, was a persistent theme prior to Locke, was familiar to many of the American founders, and was mentioned by some of the early American colonists. See, for example, the discussion in chapter 7.

6.   See note 2.

7.   I discussed this point in the previous chapter.

8.   As discussed earlier, Locke actually waffles on this point, sometimes arguing that there is an actual state of nature and an actual social contract and at times suggesting it is an ideal state only. For Locke's reflections on the question whether there ever was a state of nature and a contract that created a nation, see Locke, II §§, 14–15, 100–105. See Hobbes, *Leviathan*, 13:11, where he asks the same question. Modern interpreters who still embrace something like a notion of social contract tend to portray it is as an ideal for which liberal states should strive. I take this to be part of the thrust of Rawls's work and also the way that Laslett, 93, makes Locke intelligible.

9.   See doubts among the American founders about the social contract theory in my *Liberty in America's Founding*, 85–128, including summaries by James Otis, 100–101, on typical critiques of the idea of a social contract.

10.   Locke, II § 59, 61, and discussion of how natural freedom and "subjection to parents" can subsist together.

11.   See, for example, Locke, II §§ 75, 87, and Friedman, *Freedom and Capitalism*, 15, on the use of the umpire analogy.

12.   On the view that states are like individuals in a state of nature with respect to each other, see, for example, Locke, II § 183; Hobbes, *Leviathan*, 13.12, 85, and discussion in Tuck, *Rights of War*, 8–9.

13.   According to Alan Krueger, chairman of the Council of Economic Advisers, "Land of Hope and Dreams," "An astonishing 84 percent of total income growth from 1979 to 2011 went to the top 1 percent of families, and more than 100 percent of it from 2000 to 2007 went to the top 1 percent." For additional discussions see also Stiglitz, *Price of Inequality*.

14.   For inequality falling unevenly across races and genders, see Stiglitz, *Price of Inequality*.

15.   This link of property, industriousness, and fairness is evident already; see Pufendorf, *Law of Nature and Nations,* book 4, chap. 4:7, 367–368, as a justification of property. The importance of property to the self was developed most intensely in the modern period by Hegel. See Waldron, *Right to Private Property*, 129, 343–389.

16.   A thoughtful critique of how conceptualizing payments to the disadvantaged as "charity" impacts self-esteem and self-value of recipients is offered by Munzer, *Theory of Property*, 110–119.

17.   Locke, II § 138. [italics in original]

18.   Tuck, *Hobbes*, 30.

19.   See Skinner, *Hobbes and Republican Liberty*, 124; Tuck, *Hobbes*, 30.

20.   Hobbes, *Leviathan*, 30:17, 229.

21.   Ibid.

22.   Ibid., 30:18, 230.

23.   On dating of Locke's *Second Treatise*, see Laslett, *Two Treatises*, 45–66, which dates the *Second Treatise* to the period of 1679–81.

24.   Locke, II § 140. [italics in original]

25.   Ibid., II § 97. [italics in original]

26.   For a more detailed reading of Locke in this way, see Kendall, *Doctrine of Majority Rule*.

27.   Locke, II § 95. [italics in original]

28.   Ibid., II § 42. [italics in original]

29.   Ibid., II § 51, and see also II §46 and 50.

30.   Locke, I § 42 [italics in original]. See also Grotius, *Rights of War and Peace*, book 2, chap. 2:6, 4.

Chapter 9

1.   Friedman, *Freedom and Capitalism*, 15, 8.

2.   See, for example, Boaz and *Crane, Market Liberalism*.

3.   Friedman, *Freedom and Capitalism*, 15, 8.

4.   A notable example is Richard Epstein. See Epstein, *Simple Rules*, 30; *Principles*, 9–39, and "Utilitarian Foundations," 718, where Epstein argues that the original natural rights theorists often used utilitarian arguments and thus in their conclusions converge in many ways with utilitarian conclusions. He suggests that the loss in faith in God has led to a

modern emphasis on those utilitarian reasons but that core concepts developed by the rights tradition make sense and are consistent with a utilitarian perspective.

5.   Milton Friedman, Fredrick Hayek, and Moses Mises are the most famous of those applauded by the Right and libertarians.

6.   See Nelson, "Study of Choice," 31, quoting Georgescue-Roegen, *Analytical Economics*, 341. See also Debreu "Mathematization of Economic Theory."

7.   There are a number of critiques of neoclassical economics for its single-minded narrowing. These come from within and outside economics. Examples of writers in this tradition include Sen, Sunstein, Kuttner, Hawken, England, Mansbridge, Nelson, Sibley, among others.

8.   See the psychoanalytic and psychological traditions emanating from Freud and Jung and more recent commentators on the psyche, such as James Hillman, *Suicide and Soul*.

9.   On this other side of Smith, see, for example, Sen, *On Ethics and Economics*, 22–28. See also Raphael and A. L. Macfie, "Introduction" to *Moral Sentiments*, 29.

10.   Smith, *Moral Sentiments*, 3.

11.   The fundamental disagreement arises from the positions of Keynes, *The General Theory of Employment*, and the monetary understanding was put forward by Friedman and Schwartz, *A Monetary History*. There is a vast second literature on the subject and disagreement. For useful summaries, see, for example, Smiley, "Great Depression," and White, "Boom and Crash."

12.   On this critique specifically to economics, see Kuttner, *Economic Illusion*, and essays in Ferber and Nelson, *Beyond Economic Man*, and R. Nelson, *Economics as Religion*.

13.   See England and Folbre, "Contracting for Care," and Nelson, "Study of Choice" on the way in which families and care pose a fundamental challenge to traditional economist models and the new economic theorizing about care. See also essays in Mansbridge, *Beyond Self-Interest*, and Leibenstein, *Beyond Economic Man*. For a counterpoint that argues that altruism doesn't exist, see Epstein, *Principles*, 133–157, and "Utilitarian Foundations."

14.   Nelson, "Study of Choice," 26.

15.   Hobbes, *Leviathan*, chaps. 14 and 15 are eloquent on this point. For a recent perspective, see Epstein, *Simple Rules*, 71–90.

16.   See, for example, Epstein, *Simple Rules*, 43. In smaller and simpler social situations, pressure through social mechanisms of disapproval can suffice to pressure compliance, though it is doubtful that such mechanisms can work in broader, more anonymous exchanges, thus requiring "law" to enforce compliance.

17.   This is basically the position of Hayek, Friedman, and Epstein, among others.

18.   See, for example, the summary of analyses in Barrow, *Critical Theories of State*, for an understanding of how capitalist class interests may be developed and maintained through roles, institutions, and structures of late capitalist economies.

19.   These views are influenced by many writers, including Kuttner, Sunstein, Hawken, Sen, among others.

20.   Those who favor a utilitarian perspective must try to argue for the end of slavery without invoking the notion of rights. See, for example, Epstein, "Utilitarian Foundations," which tries to derive all the core values of the natural rights tradition from a utilitarian perspective. For my tongue-in-cheek critique of natural rights theory on this point, see my essay on endorsing suicide and slavery as part of a free society in Schwartz, "Liberty and the Public Good."

21.   I am distilling the insights from Kuttner, Hawken, and Sens. I also see Rawls as attempting to ask a similar question but not going far enough.

22.   See Waldon, *Right to Property,* who anticipates this perspective.

23.   This is one of the classic challenges to the utilitarian position in general. For a discussion of objections to utilitarian approaches in general, see, for example, a useful summary and references in Velasquez, *Business Ethics,* 73–87. Rawls tries to mitigate this challenge by arguing everyone would agree with a liberal political system if they were in the original position and had a veil of ignorance about what their position would be. Since they don't know whether they will be poor or rich in the original position, they can come to agreement on how the system is most fair, and thus they can live with it, whatever the results. But as critics have noted, this strips the individuals of all the things they might want to know in the original position and thus undermines the ability of those in the original position to make rational decisions. For a critical discussion of Rawls's thinking, see Daniels, ed., *Reading Rawls.*

24.   See, for example, Rosenthal, "Smuggling Europe's Waste," and NPR staff, "Electronic Waste."

25.   Examples have been documented in Donaldson and Gini, *Case Studies.*

26.   See Hoffman, "The Ford Pinto," 207–214.

27.   Smith, et al., "Dow Corning," 39–42, and Gini and Sullivan, "The Dalkon Shield," 221.

28.   See Velasquez, *Business Ethics,* 73–87.

29.   http://en.wikipedia.org/wiki/List_of_motor_vehicle_deaths_in_U.S._by_year and NHTSA.dot.gov, June 2012.

30.   See Pfeffer, *Human Equation,* and O'Reilly and Pfeffer, *Hidden Value.*

31.   See, for example, the record of safety in the garment industry in Bangladesh, Ali Manik and Yardley, "Gross Negligence in Factory Fire," McCarthy, "Bangladesh Collapse," and Clean Clothes Campaign, "Making Bangladesh Garment Industry Safe." Another example is the treatment of workers in the fast food industry, as documented in Schlosser, *Fast Food Nation.*

32.   See the International Labour Organization report on child labor "Marking Progress against Child Labour."

33.   For documentation in the fast food industry, see Schlosser, *Fast Food Nation*. Recently, labor abuses have been reported in Apple manufacturing plants, Associated Press staff, "China labor watchdog accuses Apple supplier of worker abuse." http://www. nbcnews.com/business/china-labor-watchdog-accuses-apple-supplier-worker-abuse-6C10783106.

34.   Bowie and Lenway, "H. B. Fuller in Honduras."

35.   See case studies documented by Pfeffer.

36.   Friedman, "The Social Responsibility of Business."

37.   See, for example, the various critiques in Ferber and Nelson, eds., *Beyond Economic Man*, and *Feminist Economics Today*.

38.   On stakeholder theory, see Freeman, "Stakeholder Theory," and Goodpaster, "Stakeholder Analysis." See, for example, Benioff, *Compassionate Capitalism*.

39.   In this sense, I take Friedman's argument about the purpose of business to be for the shareholders as a description of how things in reality are, but not as a description of what they morally should be, though Friedman believes this is the way it should be as well. For the complexity of trying to see the relationship between corporate executives, board members, shareholders, and class, see the discussions in Barrow, *Critical Theories of State*.

40.   It is difficult to see how one can get to all of these values from a utilitarian account.

41.   See Friedman, *Freedom and Capitalism*, 108–118.

42.   Grotius, *Rights of War and Peace*, book 2, chap. 3:1–16, 32–39, on the air and sea. For a discussion, see Tuck, "Introduction," *Rights of War and Peace*.

43.   On use of term "externalities" by economists, see, for example, Flynn, *Economics for Dummies*, chap 14. For a sustained alternative perspective, see books by Hawken.

44.   For discussions of how future generations should figure into ethical calculations, see the discussion in Velasquez, *Business Ethics*, 308–312, and references there.

45.   I take this to be one of the original points of Garrett James Hardin in his original essay on "The Tragedy of the Commons," and one point I agree with. In my reading of Hardin's original essay, his point is that the commons becomes a tragedy *only if it is not regulated and that regulation is needed to protect it*. One example he gives is the national parks, which are owned in common (public property) but must be regulated to protect them. His point is that without regulation, things cannot be owned in common successfully. It is beyond the present context to discuss the extensive subsequent scholarship and popular discussion of whether the commons always ends in tragedy or not, and I do not agree with some of Hardin's subsequent moral conclusions, such as his moral conclusions about preventing immigration in his metaphor of "Living on a Lifeboat."

46.   See on this point Hawken, et al., *Natural Capitalism*, and Hawken, *Ecology of Commerce*.

Chapter 10

1.   See Wilson, *Rationality*. This was already noted as a problem by Locke and others as they reflected on why non-Europeans did not all come to the same reasoned assumptions about social life. This remains a key problem that is unresolved by liberal societies.

2.   In other words, even if we argue there is shared rationality in modes of thinking, the substantive conclusions of rational people are not always the same. On the argument that there is a universal understanding of right and wrong, see discussion in Tierney, *Idea of Natural Rights*, 2–3, and Gewirth, *Reason and Morality*.

3.   See my discussion earlier on this point, in chapter 4 and notes to that chapter.

4.   Whether it is possible to discern the founders' intent and whether that should govern or dictate what we believe and do is itself an interesting question that I take up in *Liberty in America's Founding*, 309–323. See also Levy, *Original Intent*.

Bibliography

Aarsleff, Hans. "The State of Nature and the Nature of Man in Locke." In *John Locke: Problems and Perspectives*, edited by John W. Yolton, 99–135.

Ashcraft, Richard. "Locke's Political Philosophy." In *The Cambridge Companion to Locke*, edited by Vere Chappell, 1994, 226–251.

Associated Press staff. "China Labor Watchdog Accuses Apple Supplier of Worker Abuse." NBC News. July 29, 2013. http://www.nbcnews.com/business/china-laborwatchdog-accuses-apple-supplier-worker-abuse-6C10783106.

Bailyn, Bernard, ed. *Pamphlets of the American Revolution*. 1750–1776. Vol. 1. Cambridge, MA: Belknap Press of Harvard University, 1965.

Banner, Stuart. *How the Indians Lost Their Land: Law and Power on the Frontier*. Cambridge, MA: Belknap Press of Harvard University, 2005.

Barnett, Randy E. *Restoring the Lost Constitution: The Presumption of Liberty*. Princeton: Princeton University Press, 2004.

Barrow, Clyde W. *Critical Theories of the State: Marxist, Neo Marxist, Post-Marxist*. Madison: University of Wisconsin, 1993.

Becker, Carl L. *The Declaration of Independence*. New York: Vintage Books, 1922.

Benioff, Mark, and Karen Southwick. *Compassionate Capitalism: How Corporations Can Make Doing Good an Integral Part of Doing Well*. Pompton Plains, NJ: Career Press, 2004.

Bentham, Jeremy. "Anarchical Fallacies: Being an Examination of the Declarations of Rights Issued During the French Revolution." In *The Works of Jeremy Bentham*. Vol. 2, edited by John Browring, 896–971. Edinburgh: William Tait, 1843.

Bergreen, Laurence. *Columbus: The Four Voyages 1492–1504*. New York: Penguin, 2011.

Blom, Hans W. *Causality and Morality in Politics: The Rise of Naturalism in Dutch Seventeenth-Century Political Thought*. Rotterdam, 1999.

Boaz, David, and Edward H. Crane. "Introduction: The Collapse of the Statist Vision." In *Market Liberalism: A Paradigm for the 21st Century*, edited by David Boaz and Edward H. Crane, 1–20. Washington, DC: Cato Institute, 1993.

Bowie, Norman, and Stefanie Ann Lenway. "H. B. Fuller in Honduras: Street Children and Substance Abuse." In *Case Studies in Business Ethics*. 4th ed., edited by Thomas Donaldson and Al Gini, 267–290.

Boyd, Julian, ed. *The Declaration of Independence*. The Library of Congress, 1999.

———. *The Papers of Thomas Jefferson*. Vol. 1. Princeton: Princeton University Press, 1950.

Brenan, Mary C. *Turning Right in the Sixties: The Conservative Capture of the GOP*. Chapel Hill: University of North Carolina, 1995.

Breyer, Stephen. *Active Liberty: Interpreting Our Democratic Constitution*. New York: Alfred A. Knopf, 2006.

Carey, George W. "Natural Rights, Equality, and the Declaration of Independence." *AveMaria Law Review*. 3:1 (2005): 45–67.

Chappell, Vere, ed. *The Cambridge Companion to Locke*. Cambridge: Cambridge University, 1994.

Chubb, Thomas, 1978 [1730]. *The Comparative Excellence and Obligation of Moral and Positive Duties*. New York: Garland.

Clean Clothes Campaign. "Hazardous Workplaces: Making the Bangladesh Garment Industry Safe." *http://www.cleanclothes.org/resources/publications/2012-11-hazardousworkplaces.pdf/view*. 2013.

Collins, Anthony, 1976 [1724]. *A Discourse on the Grounds and Reason of the Christian Religion*. New York: Garland.

Cox, R. H. *Locke on War and Peace*. Oxford: Oxford University Press, 1960.

Curran, Eleanor. "Hobbes on Equality: Context, Rhetoric, Argument." In *Hobbes Studies* 25. (2012):166–187.

Daly, James. "The Idea of the Absolute Monarchy in Seventeenth-Century England." *The Historical Journal* 21, no. 2 (June 1978), 227–250.

Daniels, Norman, ed. *Reading Rawls: Critical Studies on Rawls' "A Theory of Justice."* Stanford, CA: Stanford University Press, 1989.

Debreu, Gerard. "The Mathematization of Economic Theory." *American Economic Review* 81 (1991):1–7.

Detweiler, Philip F. "The Changing Reputation of the Declaration of Independence: The First Fifty Years." *William and Mary Quarterly,* 3rd ser. (1962):557–65.

Donaldson, Thomas, and Al Gini, eds. *Case Studies in Business Ethics*. Upper Saddle River, NJ: Prentice Hall, 1984.

Dunn, John. *The Political Thought of John Locke: An Historical Account of the Argument of the "Two Treatises of Government."* Cambridge: Cambridge University, 1969.

———. "The Politics of Locke in England and America in the Eighteenth Century." In *John Locke: Problems and Perspectives*, edited by John W. Yolton, 45–81.

Dworetz, Steven M. *The Unvarnished Doctrine. Locke, Liberalism, and the American Revolution*. Durham, NC: Duke University, 1990.

Dworkin, Ronald. *Taking Rights Seriously*. Cambridge, MA: Harvard University, 1977.

Eberstadt, Mary, ed. *Why I Turned Right: Leading Baby Boom Conservatives Chronicle Their Political Journey*. New York: Threshold Editions, 2007.

Eilberg-Schwartz, Howard. *The Savage in Judaism: An Anthropology of Israelite Religion and Ancient Judaism*. Bloomington: Indiana University, 1990.

Elkins, Stanley, and Eric McKitrick. *The Age of Federalism: The Early American Republic, 1788–1800*. Oxford: Oxford University Press, 1993.

Elliot, J. H. *Empires of the Atlantic World: Britain and Spain in America, 1492–1830*. New Haven: Yale University Press, 2006.

Ellis, Joseph J. *American Sphinx: The Character of Thomas Jefferson*. New York: Vintage Books, 1996.

———. *Founding Brothers: The Revolutionary Generation*. New York: Vintage, 2000.

England, Paula. "Separable and Soluble Selves: Dichotomous Thinking in Economics." In *Feminist Economics Today: Beyond Economic Man*, edited by Marianne A. Ferber and Julie A. Nelson, 33–59.

England, Paula, and Nancy Folbre. "Contracting for Care." In *Feminist Economics Today: Beyond Economic Man*, edited by Marianne A. Ferber and Julie A. Nelson, 61–79. 2003.

Epstein, Richard A. *Principles for a Free Society: Reconciling Individual Liberty with the Common Good.* Reading, MA: Perseus Books, 1998.

———. *Simple Rules for a Complex World.* Cambridge, MA: Harvard University Press, 1995.

———. "The Utilitarian Foundations of Natural Law," *Harvard Journal of Law and Public Policy* 12 (1989):711–751.

Ferber, Marianne A., and Julie A. Nelson, eds. *Feminist Economics Today: Beyond Economic Man.* Chicago: The University of Chicago Press, 2003.

Feulner, Edwin J., Jr. *The March of Freedom: Modern Classics in Conservative Thought.* Dallas: Spence Publishing, 1998.

Filmer, Sir Robert. *Patriarcha: A Defence of the Natural Power of Kings against the Unnatural Liberty of the People.* In *Robert Filmer: Patriarcha and Other Political Works,* edited by Peter Laslett, 53–126. New Brunswick, NJ: Transaction Publishers, 2009 [1680].

Flynn, Sean Masaki. *Economics for Dummies.* Hoboken, NJ: Wiley Publishing, 2005.

Freeman, R. Edward. "Stakeholder Theory of the Modern Corporation." In *Ethical Issues in Business,* edited by Thomas Donaldson, Patricia Werhane, and Margaret Cording, 38–48.

Friedman, Milton. *Freedom and Capitalism.* Chicago: University of Chicago, 1962.

———. "The Social Responsibility of Business Is to Increase Its Profits." In *Ethical Issues in Business,* edited by Thomas Donaldson, Patricia Werhane, and Margaret Cording, 33–38.

Friedman, Milton, and Anna Schwartz. *A Monetary History of the United States, 1867–1960.* Princeton: Princeton University Press, 1963.

Gadamer, Hans-Georg. *Truth and Method.* New York: Continuum Publishing Group, 1979.

Ganter, Herbert Lawrence. "Jefferson's "Pursuit of Happiness' and Some Forgotten Men." *William and Mary College Quarterly.* Part 1. 2nd ser. 16:3 (July 1936): 422–434; Part 2, 16:4 (Oct. 1936): 558–585.

Gay, Peter. *Deism: An Anthology.* Princeton: D. Van Nostrand, 1968.

Georgescu-Roegen, Nicholas. *Analytical Economics.* Cambridge, MA: Harvard University Press, 1966.

Gerber, Scott. *To Secure These Rights: The Declaration of Independence and Constitutional Interpretation*. New York: New York University, 1995.

Gewirth, A. *Reason and Morality*. Chicago: University of Chicago Press, 1978. Gini, Al, and Terry Sullivan. "A. H. Robins: The Dalkon Shield," In *Case Studies in Business Ethics*. 4th ed., edited by Thomas Donaldson and Al Gini, 215–223.

Glendon, Mary Ann. *Rights Talk: The Impoverishment of Political Discourse*. New York: The Free Press, 1991.

Goodpaster, Kenneth E. "Business Ethics and Stakeholder Analysis." In *Ethical Issues in Business*, edited by Thomas Donaldson, Patricia Werhane, and Margaret Cording, 49–60.

Gough, J. W. *John Locke's Political Philosophy*. Oxford: Clarendon Press, 1973.

Grotius, Hugo. *The Rights of War and Peace [De Iure Belli ac Pacis]*, edited by Richard Tuck, from the edition by Jean Barbeyrac. Liberty Fund: Indianapolis. 2005 [1625]. http://oll.libertyfund.org/title/1425

Hanke, Lewis. *All Mankind Is One: A Study of the Disputation between Bartolomé de Las Casas and Juan Ginés de Sepúlveda on the Religious and Intellectual Capacity of the American Indians*. DeKalb: Northern Illinois, 1974.

———. *Aristotle and the American Indians*. Bloomington: Indiana University, 1975.

———. *The Spanish Struggle for Justice in the Conquest of America*. Dallas: Southern Methodist, 2002.Hannity, Sean. *Let Freedom Ring*. Harper: New York, 2002.

Hardin, Garrett James. "Living on a Lifeboat." *The Social Contract*. Fall 2001: 36–47.

———. "The Tragedy of the Commons." *Science*. Vol. 162 (1968): 1243–1248.

Harris, Marvin. *The Rise of Anthropological Theory*. Lanham, MD: AltaMira Press, 1969.

Hatcher, John. *Plague, Population, and the English Economy, 1348–1530*. New York: Macmillan, 1977.

Hawken, Paul. *The Ecology of Commerce: A Declaration of Sustainability*. New York: HarperBusiness, 1993.

Hawken, Paul, Amory Lovins, and L. Hunter Lovins. *Natural Capitalism: Creating the Next Industrial Revolution*. Boston: Little, Brown and Company, 1999.

Hayek, Friedrich A. The *Constitution of Liberty*. Chicago: University of Chicago Press, 1960.

———. *The Road to Serfdom*. Chicago: University of Chicago Press, 1994.

Herbert of Cherbury. *De Religione Laici*. Trans. Harold L. Hutcheson. New Haven: Yale University, 1944 [1645].

———. *De Veritate*. 3rd ed. Translated by Merick H. Carré. Bristol: J. W. Arrowsmith, 1937 [1624].

Hilman, James. *Suicide and Soul*. Harper & Row, 1965.

Hirsch, E. D. *Validity in Interpretation*. New Haven: Yale University Press, 1967.

Hobbes, Thomas. *Leviathan*. Edited by J. C. A. Gaskin. Clarendon: Oxford University Press, 2005 [1651].

———.Thomas. *Leviathan*. Oxford: Oxford University Press, 1909 [1651 repr.]

Hoekstra, Kinch. "Hobbesian Equality." In *Hobbes Today*, edited by S. A. Lloyd. Cambridge: Cambridge University, 2013.

Hoffman, W. Michael, 1984. "The Ford Pinto." In *Case Studies in Business Ethics*. 4th ed. Edited by Thomas Donaldson and Al Gini, 207–21.

Hume, David. "The Original Contract." In *Essays, Moral, Political, Literary*, edited by Eugene F. Miller, 199–208. Indianapolis: Liberty Fund, 1987 [1777], http://oll.libertyfund.org/Home3/EBook.php?recordID=0059.

Hutcheson, Harold L. "Introduction" to *De Religione Laici*, by Lord Herbert of Cherbury. New Haven: Yale University, 1944.

International Labour Organization. "Marking progress against child labour," 2013. http://www.ilo.org/ipec/Informationresources/WCMS_221513/lang--en/index.htm.

Jayne, Allen. *Jefferson's Declaration of Independence: Origin, Philosophy, and Theology*. Lexington: University of Kentucky Press, 1998.

Jefferson, Thomas. *Notes on the State of Virginia*. In *The Works of Thomas Jefferson*, Vol. 3, edited by Paul Leicester Ford, 494–512. New York: G. P. Putnam's Sons, 1904 [1781].

Jewish Publication Society. *TANAKH: The Holy Scriptures*. The New JPS Translation According to the Traditional Hebrew Text. Philadelphia: The Jewish Publication Society, 1988.

Jolley, Nicholas. "Locke on Faith and Reason." In *The Cambridge Companion to Locke's "Essay Concerning Human Understanding*," edited by Lex Newman, 436–455. Cambridge: Cambridge University. 2007.

Kendall, Willmoore. *John Locke and the Doctrine of Majority Rule*. Urbana: University of Illinois, 1959.

Keynes, John Maynard. *The General Theory of Employment, Interest, and Money*. Amherst, NY: Prometheus Books, 1997 [1936].

King James Bible. http://www.kingjamesbibleonline.org/.

Krueger, Alan B. "Land of Hope and Dreams: Rock and Roll, Economics, and Rebuilding the Middle Class." June 12, 2013, http://www.whitehouse.gov/blog/2013/06/12/rock-and-roll-economics-and-rebuilding-middle-class#fulltext.

Kuhn, Thomas. *The Structure of Scientific Revolutions*. Chicago: The University of Chicago Press, 1962.

Kuttner, Robert. *The Economic Illusion: False Choices between Prosperity and Social Justice*. Philadelphia: University of Pennsylvania, 1984.

———. *Everything for Sale: The Virtues and Limits of Markets*. Chicago: University of Chicago, 1996.

Laslett, Peter, ed. "Introduction" to *Locke: Two Treatises of Government*, 3–127. Cambridge: Cambridge, 1960.

———. "Introduction" to *Robert Filmer: Patriarcha and Other Political Essays*, 1-46. New Brunswick, NJ: Transaction Publishers, 2009.

Leibenstein, Harvey. *Beyond Economic Man: A New Foundation for Microeconomics*. Cambridge, MA: Harvard University, 1976.

Letwin, William. *The Origins of Scientific Economics*. Garden City: Doubleday, 1964.

Levy, Leonard W. *Original Intent*. Chicago: Ivan R. Dee, 1988.

Lewin, Mark R. *Liberty and Tyranny: A Conservative Manifesto*. New York: Threshold Editions, 2009.

Locke, John. *An Essay Concerning Human Understanding*. Amherst, NY: Prometheus, 1995 [1693].

———. *Essays on the Law of Nature*, edited by W. von Leyden. Oxford: Clarendon, 1954 [1660].

————. "Of Ethick in General." In *The Life of John Locke: With Extracts from His Correspondence, Journals, and Common-Place Books,* 308–313. Edited by Lord Peter King. London: H. Colburn and R. Bentley, 1829 edition [1886–87], or vol. 2:122–133, 1830 edition.

————. *Two Treatises of Government*, edited by Peter Laslett. Cambridge: Cambridge. 1960 [between years 1679–1690].

————. *The Works*. Vol. 1. *An Essay Concerning Human Understanding*. 12th ed. Online Library of Liberty. London: Rivington, 1824 [1689].

Macpherson, C. B. *The Political Theory of Possessive Individualism*. Oxford: Oxford University, 1962.

————. *Democratic Theory*. Oxford: Clarendon, 1975.

Madison, James. *Notes of Debates in the Federal Convention of 1787*. New York: W. W. Norton, 1987 [1840].

Maier, Pauline. *American Scripture*. New York: Vintage Books, 1997.

————. *Ratification: The People Debate the Constitution, 1787–1788*. New York: Simon and Schuster. 2010.

————. "The Strange History of "All Men Are Created Equal.' " *Washington and Lee Law Review*. 56:3, (1999): 873–878.

Manik, Julfikar Ali, and Jim Yardley. "Bangladesh Finds Gross Negligence in Factory Fire." *New York Times*. Dec. 17, 2012. http://www.nytimes.com/2012/12/18/world /asia/bangladesh-factory-fire-caused-by-gross-negligence.html?_r=0.

Mansbridge, Jane J. *Beyond Self-Interest*. Chicago: The University of Chicago, 1990.

Manuel, Frank. *The Changing of the Gods*. Hanover: University Press of New England, 1983.

————. *The Eighteenth Century Confronts the Gods*. Cambridge, MA: Harvard University, *1959.*

McCarthy, Julie. "Bangladesh Collapse: The Garment Workers Who Survived." National Public Radio. July 10, 2013. http://www.npr.org/blogs/parallels/2013/07/10/200644781/Bangladesh-Collapse-The-Garment-Workers-Who-Survived.

McIlwain, Charles Howard. "Introduction." *The Political Works of James I*. Cambridge, MA: Harvard University Press, 1918.

Milton, J. R. "Locke's Life and Times." In *The Cambridge Companion to Locke*, edited by Vere Chappell, 1994, 5–25.

Moseley, Alexander. "Political Philosophy of John Locke." In *Internet Encyclopedia of Philosophy*, edited by James Fieser and Bradley Dowden, 2005. http://www.iep.utm.edu/locke-po/#H1.

Munzer, Stephen R. *A Theory of Property*. Cambridge: Cambridge University Press, 1990.

Napolitano, Andrew P. *The Constitution in Exile: How the Federal Government Has Seized Power by Rewriting the Supreme Law of the Land*. Nashville: Nelson, 2006.

National Public Radio Staff. "After Dump, After Dump, What Happens To Electronic Waste?" December 21, 2010. http://www.npr.org/2010/12/21/132204954/after-dump-what-happens-to-electronic-waste.

Nelson, Julie A. "Separative and Soluble Firms: Androcentric Bias and Business Ethics." In *Feminist Economics Today: Beyond Economic Man*, edited by Marianne A. Ferber and Julie A. Nelson, 81–99.

———. "The Study of Choice or the Study of Provisioning? Gender and the Definition of Economics." In *Beyond Economic Man*, edited by Marianne A. Ferber and Julie A. Nelson, 23–36.

Nozick, Robert. *Anarchy, State, and Utopia*. New York: Basic, 1974.

Okun, Arthur. *Equality and Efficiency: The Big Tradeoff*. Washington: The Brookings Institute, 1975.

O'Reilly, Charles A., III. *Hidden Value: How Great Companies Achieve Extraordinary Results with Ordinary People*. Boston: Harvard Business School, 2000.

Otis, James. "The Rights of the British Colonies Asserted and Proved." In *Pamphlets of the American Revolution, 1750–1776*. Vol. 1, edited by Bernard Bailyn. Cambridge, MA: Belknap Press of Harvard University, 1992 [1764].

Paul, Ron. *A Foreign Policy of Freedom*, Lake Johnson, TX: Foundation for Rational Economics and Education, 2007.

———. *Liberty Defined*. New York: Grand Central, 2011.

Peffer, Jeffrey. *The Human Equation: Building Profits by Putting People First*. Boston: Harvard Business School, 1998.

Pufendorf, Samuel. *Of the Law of Nature and Nations*. 8 vols. 4th ed., translated by Basil Kennett. Based on the edition by Jean Barbeyrac. London. 1729 [1672].

Raphael, D. D., and A. L. Macfie, ed. "Introduction." *The Theory of Moral Sentiments*. Vol. 1 of the Glasgow Edition of the Works and Correspondence of Adam Smith. Indianapolis: Liberty Fund, 1982.

Rawls, John. *A Theory of Justice*. Cambridge, MA: Belknap Press of Harvard University Press, 1971.

Reynolds, Frank E., and David Tracy. *Myth and Philosophy*. Albany: State University of New York Press, 1990.

Rickless, Samuel C. "Locke's Polemic against Nativism." In *Locke's "Essay Concerning Human Understanding,"* edited by Lex Newman. 2007. Cambridge: Cambridge University. 2007.

Robertson, Lindsay G. *Conquest by Law: How the Discovery of America Dispossessed Indigenous Peoples of Their Lands*. Oxford: Oxford University, 2005.

Rorty, Richard. *Objectivity, Relativism, and Truth*. Cambridge: Cambridge University, 1991.

Rosenthal, Elisabeth. "Smuggling Europe's Waste to Poorer Countries" *New York Times*. September 27, 2009. http://www.nytimes.com/2009/09/27/science/earth/27waste.html?pagewanted=all&_r=2&#.

Scalia, Antonin. *A Matter of Interpretation: Federal Courts and the Law*. Princeton: Princeton University, 1997.

Schlosser, Eric. *Fast Food Nation: The Dark Side of the All-American Meal*. New York: Houghton Mifflin, 2001.

Schochet, Gordon J. "The Family and the Origins of the State in Locke's Political Philosophy." In *John Locke: Problems and Perspectives*, edited by John W. Yolton, 81–98, 1969.

Schwartz, Howard I. *Liberty in America's Founding Moment: Doubts about Natural Rights in Jefferson's Declaration of Independence*. San Francisco: Other Ideas Press, 2010.

———. "Liberty is Not Freedom," FreedomandCapitalism.com, April 2007.

———. "Liberty and the Public Good: Endorsing Suicide and Slavery as Part of a Free Society." FreedomandCapitalism.com, February 2007.

————. "Why "Market Liberals' Are Not "The True Liberals' or Who Really Inherits the Liberty Tradition?" FreedomandCapitalism.com, March 2007.

————. "Why Can't My Daughter Drive a Tank? Reflections on the Meaning of Liberty and Freedom in a Civil Society." FreedomandCapitalism.com, April 2007.

Sen, Amartya. *Development as Freedom*. Anchor: New York, 1999.

————. *On Ethics and Economics*. Oxford: Blackwell. 1987.

————. *Rationality and Freedom*. Cambridge, MA: The Belknap Press of Harvard University, 2002.

Shain, Barry, ed. *The Nature of Rights at the American Founding and Beyond*. Charlottesville: University of Virginia, 2007.

Sibley, Angus. *The "Poisoned Spring" of Economic Libertarianism*. Paris: Pax Romana, 2011.

Simmons, John. "Locke's State of Nature." In *The Social Contract Theorists*, edited by Christopher W. Morris, 97–120. Lanham, MD: Rowman and Littlefield, 1999.

Skinner, Quentin. *The Foundations of Modern Political Thought*. 2 vols. Cambridge: Cambridge University, 1998.

————. *Hobbes and Republican Liberty*. Cambridge: Cambridge University, 2008.

————. *Liberty before Liberalism*. Cambridge: Cambridge University Press, 1998.

Smiley, Gene. "Great Depression." In *The Concise Encyclopedia of Economics*. 2008. Library of Economics and Liberty, 2013. http://www.econlib.org/library /Enc/ GreatDepression.html.

Smith, Adam. *The Theory of Moral Sentiments*. New York: Prometheus, 2000 [1759].

————. *Wealth of Nations*. Amherst, NY: Prometheus Books, 1991 [1976].

Smith, N. Craig, Andrew D. Dyer, and Todd E. Himstead. "Dow Corning Corporation: Marketing Breast Implant Devices." In *Case Studies in Business Ethics*. 4th ed., edited by Thomas Donaldson and Al Gini, 39–52.

Stannard, David E. *American Holocaust: The Conquest of the New World*. Oxford: Oxford University Press, 1992.

Stiglitz, Joseph E. *The Price of Inequality: How Today's Divided Society Endangers Our Future*. New York: W. W. Norton, 2013.

Strauss, Leo. *Natural Right and History*. Chicago: The University of Chicago, 1950.

Springboard, Patricia, ed. *The Cambridge Companion to Hobbes's Leviathan*. Cambridge: Cambridge University, 2007.

Sunstein, Cass R. *Free Markets and Social Justice*. New York: Oxford University, 1997.

———. *The Second Bill of Rights: FDR's Unfinished Revolution and Why We Need It More Than Ever*. Basic: New York, 2004.

Syse, Henrik. *Natural Law, Religion, and Rights: An Exploration of the Relationship between Natural Law and Natural Rights*. South Bend, IN: St. Augustine's Press, 2007.

Taylor, Robert J., et al. *Papers of John Adams*. Vol. 1. Cambridge, MA: The Belknap Press of Harvard University, 1977.

Tierney, Brian. *The Idea of Natural Rights: Studies on Natural Rights, Natural Law, and Church Law 1150–1625*. Grand Rapids, MI: William B. Eerdmans, 1997.

Tindal, Matthew. *Christianity as Old as Creation*. London, 1730.

Trible, Phyllis. *God and the Rhetoric of Sexuality*. Philadelphia: Fortress, 1983.

Tuck, Richard. *Hobbes: A Very Short Introduction*. Oxford: Oxford University, 1989.

———. *Natural Rights Theories: Their Origin and Development*. Cambridge: Cambridge University Press, 1979.

———. "Introduction." In *The Rights of War and Peace* [De Iure Belli ac Pacis]. Edition by Jean Barbeyrac. Liberty Fund: Indianapolis, 2005. http://oll.libertyfund.org/title/1425.

———. *Philosophy and Government*, 1572–1651. Cambridge: Cambridge University, 1993.

———. *The Rights of War and Peace. Political Thought and the International Order from Grotius to Kant*. Oxford: Oxford University Press, 1999.

Tully, James. *A Discourse on Property: John Locke and His Adversaries*. Cambridge: Cambridge University, 2006.

Vattel, Emer de. *The Law of Nations or the Principles of Natural Law Applied to the Conduct and to the Affairs of Nations and of Sovereigns*. London: C. G. and J. Robinson, 1797 [1758].

Velasquez, Manuel G. *Business Ethics: Concepts and Cases*. 5th ed. Upper Saddle River, NJ: Prentice Hall, 2002.

Viguerie, Richard A., and David Franke. *America's Right Turn: How Conservatives Used New and Alternative Media to Take Power*. Chicago: Bonus Books, 2004.

von Leyden, W. "Introduction." *Essays on the Law of Nature*, by John Locke. Oxford: Clarendon, 1954.

Waldron, Jeremy. *The Right to Private Property*. New York: Clarendon University, 2002.

White, Eugene N. "The Stock Market Boom and Crash of 1929 Revisited." *Journal of Economic Perspectives* 4:2 (Spring 1990), 67–83.

Williams, Bernard. "The Idea of Equality." In *Problems of the Self*, 230–250. Cambridge: Cambridge University Press, 1973.

Williams, Robert A., Jr. *The American Indian in Western Legal Thought: The Discourses of Conquest*. New York: Oxford University, 1990.

Wills, Gary. *Inventing America. Jefferson's Declaration of Independence*. Garden City, NJ: Doubleday, 1978.

Wilson, Bryan R., ed. *Rationality*. Oxford: Basil Blackwell, 1970.

Wilson, James. *Considerations on the Nature and Extent of the Legislative Authority of the British Parliament*. In *Collected Works of James Wilson*, edited by Kermit L. Hall and Mark David Hall. Indianapolis: Liberty Fund, 2007 [1770].

Wolterstorff, Nicolas, "Locke's Philosophy of Religion." *The Cambridge Companion to Locke*, edited by Vere Chappell, 172–198.

Wootton, David. *The Essential Federalist and Anti-Federalist Papers*. Indianapolis: Hackett Publishing, 2003.

Wrigley, E. A., and R. S. Schofield. *The Population History of England: 1541–1871*. Cambridge: Cambridge University Press, 1989.

van Velthuysen, Lambert. *Epistolica dissertatio de principiis justi et decori, continens apologiam pro tractatu clarissimi Hobbaeit De Cive*. Amsterdam: L. Elzevit, 1651.

Yolton, John, ed. *John Locke: Problems and Perspectives*. Cambridge: Cambridge University Press, 1969.

Zuckert, Michael P. *Natural Rights and the New Republicanism*. Princeton: Princeton University Press, 1994.

Index

www.ingramcontent.com/pod-product-compliance
Lightning Source LLC
Chambersburg PA
CBHW061956280526
45787CB00005B/1892